T3-AOR-283

THE DUCK-HUNTINGEST GENTLEMEN

The author and a friend (photo by R. Dugald Pearson).

THE DUCK-HUNTINGEST GENTLEMEN

*A Collection of
Waterfowling Stories*

Keith C. Russell
and
Friends

*Illustrated by
Jonathan Newdick*

WINCHESTER PRESS

Published by arrangement with The Dairypail Press.
This book was originally published in a limited edition of
one thousand serially numbered, autographed copies by
The Dairypail Press, Pepper Pike, Ohio

Copyright © 1980 by Keith C. Russell
All rights reserved

Library of Congress Cataloging in Publication Data
Main entry under title:

The Duck-huntingest gentlemen.

Pepper Pike, Ohio.
1. Waterfowl shooting.   2. Duck shooting.
I. Russell, Keith C., 1920-
(SK331.D82 1980)   799.2'4841   80-17607
ISBN 0-87691-328-1

Printed in the United States of America
1 2 3 4 5   84 83 82 81 80

WINCHESTER PRESS
1421 South Sheridan
Tulsa, Oklahoma 74112

GOD to Noah and his sons:

> The fear of you and the dread of you shall be upon every beast of the earth, and upon every bird of the air, upon everything that creeps on the ground and all the fish of the sea; into your hand they are delivered.

> Every moving thing that lives shall be food for you; and as I gave you the green plants, I give you everything.

—GENESIS 9:2-3

No matter how many duck-blind dawns have embraced a waterfowler, he welcomes each one as he would a lover.

Indeed, all such dawns are like women of spirit emerging from sleep—soft or stormy, tremulous or cold—but always fascinating.

—NELSON BRYANT

One man who understands part of the mystery of hunting is James Beard, the gourmet. He once remarked when discussing the preparation of cooking wild ducks, "You should treat them with golden tongs!"

This book is dedicated to
Margie,
this particular duck hunter's wife, who, in common (my guess) with most
duck hunters' wives, is more loved for her sometimes begrudging tolerance
of my love affair with waterfowl than she realizes,
and to
Jacquie,
this particular duck hunter's daughter, whose always consistent admonition
to her father as he departs on another hunting trip is "Please, Dad, miss
the first one for me," which request has been involuntarily complied with
on all too many occasions. It nonetheless pleases me greatly to know
that indeed she too shares my love for wildlife.

CONTENTS

CONTENTS

CONTENTS

[xi]

CONTENTS

CONTENTS

An Introduction
to the Author
and This Book

Dear Reader:

You are about to delve into a book that deals entirely with hunting of waterfowl. It is a collection of stories about memorable duck and goose hunts, and very little else.

It is composed of many chapters written and contributed by many authors. However, unlike the writers of most introductions, I cannot say that these contributors are "the acknowledged, foremost authorities on the art and sport of waterfowling." There is no way this book is going to give you a shooting tip that will enable you to properly lead and consistently hit a shot-at, but missed, mallard who is leaving the scene by way of a towering, going-away angle. Neither will this book teach you how better to set out a spread of decoys or train a retriever. Indeed, it will not impart to you any particularly useful information. I would hope, however, that it will provide many hours of armchair enjoyment for you, the dedicated wildfowler, during that period of time when you cannot actively pursue your favorite sport—and, perhaps, prick your memory and recall for you some of your own more memorable days in the marsh.

The Duck-Huntingest Gentlemen is the brainchild of my very old and very dear friend and hunting partner, Keith Russell. Prior to the time the title was selected, it was always referred to simply as "the book." As long as I have known him, he has had a favorite expression, used at the end of a particularly satisfying day afield. While reliving the day and savoring his after-the-hunt-drink, he'd invariably drawl, "Well, Señor, today was another chapter for the book," and from this expression of his appreciation for a good and happy day of hunting or fishing came the idea for "the book."

Unlike having a real baby, the birth pains really started after the idea was born. Keith set about contacting his many friends in the duck-hunting fraternity, asking each to write a chapter, however long or short, or even an anecdote, about a day or an incident that still lived on in his memory as something special to him that he could share with Keith and his other friends. Indeed, most all of the contributors to this book are close friends and hunting companions.

The problem was that Keith's friends, the contributors, are pretty much business and professional people and, as such, lead busy lives filled with responsibilities that make substantial demands on their available free time. Besides which, I have always noticed that duck hunters generally tend to be pretty good procrastinators. In any event, he then spent the next couple of years pleading with, cajoling, threatening, and generally bugging a substantial number of friends to take pen in hand and produce a contribution to *The Duck-Huntingest Gentlemen.*

At the risk of his tipping me out of the punt boat into the muck this coming fall, I would like to tell you a little something about my friend.

Keith is an astute businessman who has rendered much to his community here in Cleveland, Ohio, and his efforts, fortunately and deservedly, have brought him a fair share of worldly goods. This has enabled him not only to become the most avid hunter I have ever known, but to devote himself—his time and his resources—unselfishly to the cause of conservation. Offhand I can think of some twenty conservation organizations in which he is interested, not just as a "joiner" who pays his dues, but as an officer, trustee, or other active participant in the affairs of these organizations.

Most important, however, Keith presently serves as a Vice President and a National Trustee of Ducks Unlimited, Inc., which many knowledgeable people consider to be the premier conservation organization in the world today.

He created and still supervises the Ducks Unlimited Commemorative Shotgun Program, which has raised millions of dollars and which will, in the future, raise additional millions for the ducks. He also has been a valued member, since its inception, of the committee that supervises the Ducks Unlimited Artist-of-the-Year Program, which has raised hundreds of thousands of dollars in the cause of waterfowl conservation.

He is also a director of Ducks Unlimited (Canada), in which capacity he travels to Canada several times each year to attend meetings.

In 1976, Keith founded a new nonprofit organization known as The Canvasback Society, the first tax-deductible national conservation organization ever formed for the express benefit of one particular species of sporting waterfowl. Indeed, The Canvasback Society is in the process of establishing a Technical Committee composed of leading waterfowl biologists in the United States and Canada who have extensive experience with and intense interest in canvasbacks. This committee of professionals will be the cornerstone of the society's operations. They will meet or otherwise communicate from time to time to assess the total canvasback situation and what the society can best do about it. Their recommendations will be submitted to the Board of Trustees of the society for their consideration and approval of projects for the benefit of the species.

There is an old phrase used in conservation circles: "Put Some Back." You can see from the foregoing that Keith has put more back than he could ever take out of the waterfowl resource. I think, more than anything else, that it was the fact that each of us who has contributed something to this book was aware of how much Keith has put back and how great his contribution has been to the perpetuation of our sport that finally got all of us to put a few words on paper—that and the fact that we wanted to share with each other and with you those happiest of all days in the life of a duck hunter, those days spent hunting ducks.

WILLIAM E. DAVIS
Cleveland, Ohio
April 1977

Preface

The question may well be asked, Why this book?

Why indeed. Must there be a reason for everything? The truth is that like seeing the other side of the mountain, I just wanted to do it. Fortunately, after four years and with a little "stimulation" along the way, my friends have made it possible by recording their most memorable waterfowling experiences. While all of them are dyed-in-the-feather duck hunters, their stories came as a pleasurable surprise and I congratulate them. For all of their interest and time and effort in support of *The Duck-Huntingest Gentlemen,* I also thank them.

There is one more person to whom I would like to express my deepest gratitude and appreciation: my wonderful Irish secretary, Gerry Payne, who patiently typed most of the manuscript for this book and who helped in so many other ways as well.

For your information, these stories aren't in any particular order. You will note that my own are in two groups, at the beginning and at the end. The contributions of my friends—the real "meat in the sandwich"—have been shuffled around in various ways. Perhaps you'll read them in the order I finally settled on. Perhaps you won't. It really doesn't matter, because all waterfowling is fun. And so are the people who enjoy waterfowling. This is their book. I like to think it is a slice of waterfowlers everywhere and their experiences while pursuing the sport they love. I hope you will enjoy it.

KEITH C. RUSSELL
Pepper Pike, Ohio
June 1977

THE DUCK-HUNTINGEST GENTLEMEN

PART I

Why I Hunt Waterfowl

K. C. R.

"The thing that a man hunts when he hunts is himself!"
Whoever came up with the foregoing probably explained waterfowling more truly than anyone. Of course, there are a great many quite evident pleasures. The beauty of dawn (or sunset) on a duck marsh; the thrill of whistling wings; the challenge of identification and of shooting ability; the shared enjoyment of companionship in the blind; the satisfaction of good dog work or a good decoy layout; the oneness with nature; the quiet relief from daily urban activity; the sights, smells, and sounds; the mysteries of migration; the beauty of the birds themselves. All contribute to the appeal of waterfowl and waterfowling —and yet they can't completely explain it; there remains a mystique that is, I think, unique. I know of no other sport or outdoor activity to which this term might be more properly attributed.

Webster defines "mystique" as "an attitude of mystical veneration conferring upon the subject an awesome and mystical status; qualities that set something apart and beyond the understanding of an outsider."

So we get back to the hunter hunting himself, and invariably finding himself, in the process of "waterfowling." The size of the bag counts not, or the weather, or really anything else; what really is important, what really counts, is the process itself; the experience.

This then is why I hunt waterfowl: the sum total is a bathing of the soul, compounded of many things, but the net result is a cleansing, a renewing, a rebirth. My soul isn't perfect. It needs help now and then. What helps it most is a day in the marsh.

Little Siberia

K. C. R.

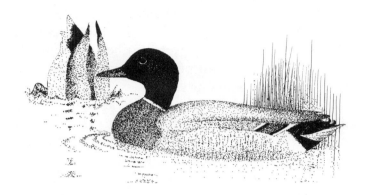

I know now why it's called Little Siberia! The name fits—a vast, bleak, uninviting area, hard to get into, even harder to get out of, and uncomfortable while you're there. In other words, not at all an attractive place to visit voluntarily—that is, unless you happen to be a duck or a duck hunter. Then it's a little bit of heaven.

It all started when I decided to do something about my duck calling. For years I had gotten by with a very mediocre hail call, come-back, and feeding chuckle. You know how it is. My knowledgeable duck-hunting friends weren't laughing at me, but I knew what kind of results I'd been getting. The number of ducks in the decoys relative to the number of what I considered "possibles" left a lot to be desired.

So I took the bull by the horns! (Obviously only an A.A.— amateur author—would use such a metaphor in a duck-hunting story.)

I was reading one of the "big three" outdoor magazines one summer evening and came upon an account of Chick Major of Stuttgart, Arkansas, a man whom I later became fortunate enough to call friend. At the time, however, his was a new name to me. He was described as not only one of the outstanding duck callers in the United States and a former World Champion, but also as the maker of the famous "Dixie Mallard Call." In addition, along with two of his daughters, Pat and Dixie, both of whom were also World Champion callers, he had cut duck-calling instruction records and was wont to give personal lessons, particularly to the small fry in and around Stuttgart.

Now every duck hunter worthy of the name knows that Stuttgart, in the center of the Grand Prairie region of central Arkansas, is the Duck-Hunting Capital of America. Those legendary pin-oak flats are world-renowned. It is a pilgrimage to Mecca that every duck hunter must make at least once in his lifetime.

It therefore all became crystal-clear. Opportunity was knocking. Hell, it was banging down the door. Personal duck-calling lessons from a man who was a living legend—it would be like taking golf lessons from Jack Nicklaus. Nothing like going right to the top. Plus a visit to the DHCOA (Duck-Hunting Capital of America). What better combination? Like two greenheads with one shell!

First thing next morning, pick up telephone. Dial information. Get Chick Major's number in Stuttgart. Place call to Chick. Talk to Chick. Tell him what I have in mind. Chick says, "Great. Come on down." Demonstrates call over phone. A first for me. My secretary later won't believe it. Make a date (with Chick, not secretary).

Next stop, the biggest name on the Mississippi flyway, home area to the largest population of ducks in the United States, where babies cut their teeth on duck calls, where duck hunters are born, not made, where you're disappointed if you don't find some shot in your meat.

Fly to Little Rock. Rental car to Stuttgart, 123 Meadow Lane. I expect house to look like huge duck call. Meet Chick and wife, Sophie, also a champion caller. In five minutes I feel as if I've known them all my life. What wonderful people they are. And what a wonderful family they have. Three beautiful married daughters, every one a champion caller along with one World Champion Duck Caller son-in-law. I can't understand what happened to the two other no-account sons-in-law with no calling titles to their name.

After two days of intensive instruction, I decided I would never be a champion. (Actually, I knew *that* before I started.) It was, however, almost as much fun as hunting ducks, and you know that's saying an awful lot. I finally did learn to grunt, which was a giant step for this particular mankind. Most important, I met some of the nicest people God ever made, people who I know will be friends for life. Yes, my Stuttgart trip was more than worthwhile, but Little Siberia was yet to come.

That same fall, for some strange and unknown reason, I was asked to judge the World Duck Calling Championship, which is held each year in—guess where—Stuttgart. Naturally, now that I am a graduate (some come loudly) of Chick Major's Quacker College, I quickly accepted before the event's sponsors could learn of their mistake.

The contest is conducted at the time of the opening of the Arkansas duck season—when else? This affords a contest judge the opportunity to relax a little from his weighty responsibilities by getting in a little chance at the webfeet.

Of course, the next move was automatic. Get the Señor to go with me! The Señor is my best friend and hunting partner of long standing. And the lawyer who tries to keep me out of trouble with the IRS. And the one who got me involved with Ducks Unlimited—for which I may never forgive him, or maybe always thank him. Anyway, his name is Bill Davis and he said he'd go, in a hurry.

Stuttgart, at contest time and duck-season opening, is out of sight. The town's permanent population is multiplied several times by visitors from coast to coast, and about nine out of every ten people have one or more duck calls hanging around their necks, members of the liberated sex included. Hail calls, comeback calls, feeding chuckles, and miscellaneous other assorted calls can be heard from one end of the blocked-off main street to the other. A duck hunter's Shangri-la.

The Señor and I—which is to say the two Señors, since Bill thinks I am the Señor—are into this scene like a mallard goes to corn. We've even been told there is a lady restaurant owner in town who owns a full-length coat made out of mallard feathers. We're keeping an eye out for her.

We arrive Thursday night and hit the sack after checking on our Friday-morning hunting plans with Wilbur Stephens, son-in-law of Chick Major. We don't know where we're goin', but we're goin', no doubt to the Grand Prairie's famous pin-oak flats. And even though Steve cautions that the area water conditions are not too good, there being an unnecessary and undesired surplus of that substance, nothing can affect the usual unrestrained optimism rampant at such a time.

Friday morning arrives. We stoke down a hunter's breakfast, which could easily pass undetected for either Thanksgiving or Christmas dinner.

We're hunting today with Chick Major. How about that, having a World Champion callin' 'em in for you!

Well, we didn't hunt in pin-oak flats. Rather we were in a conventional blind in a conventional marsh, quite similar to those we regularly frequent in northwestern Ohio. At least we felt at home. And Chick put on a terrific calling demonstration—but sadly, to small avail. Apparently, we were told, a combination of warm weather to the north, resulting in fewer than normal ducks down the flyway, along with the high-water conditions conspired to limit our first day's toll to a grand total of three birds among us. Certainly this was less than fair. Nevertheless, tomorrow would be another day and a different story. So we thought.

Friday afternoon we spent moseying around Stuttgart with various members of the Major family and calling on some of the better known of the local citizenry. Garner Allen, editor and publisher of the *Daily Leader*, Stuttgart's largest (and only) newspaper, wanted a story on us with pictures, for reasons unknown. We met a local druggist, Eddie Buerkle, who has what might be called a floating cocktail party in the back of his store all during the duck-calling contests. He invited us to attend, for which we were most appreciative. You know what dry work all that listening and watching can be.

Of course, we paid a visit to Mayor John Bueker, who welcomed us officially to the festivities and said he would see us at the Sportsmen's Banquet that night and naturally in the back of the drugstore Saturday afternoon.

The highlight of our afternoon, and really our entire safari, was running into Rex Hancock, a Stuttgart dentist and well-known sportsman whom I had first met on my earlier trip to Arkansas in search of duck-calling prowess. Rex is one of the great ones! The following year he would be named *Outdoor Life* magazine's Conservationist of the Year. Rex was to be our man of destiny who thirty-six hours later would fearlessly lead our expedition into the wild unknown of Little Siberia. For the moment, we renewed acquaintances. You should see the collection of North American big game at Rex's home, which he has taken with bow and arrow. *Un hombre muy macho!*

The annual Sportsmen's Banquet that night was a nice affair, if a little slow. You see, Stuttgart, I forgot to mention, is a "dry" town. Sack time again was early, with those usual big expectations for the morrow.

At last we finally made the pin-oak flats. The Señor and I are up to our whatchee in water, each leanin' in against a big old oak, just restin' easy waitin' for shootin' time (notice that Arkansas accent), confident we'll be back at the motel with our limits within the hour.

We never fired a shot all day. Skunked is what we were, plainly speaking. It was a wrong-way miracle. A second coming in reverse. The impossible happened. And to us. In the world-famous pin-oak flats of Arkansas.

Naturally there was only one thing to do. Head for the drugstore. Which we did.

Saturday afternoon is contest time. Unfortunately for me, I have to go to work. The Señor gets to spend the afternoon in the drugstore.

Pal that he is, he not only looks after himself but also does his best to drink my share too. Actually, he did quite a good job of it. And I appreciated his effort in my behalf, *in absentia* as it were.

Well, later, after I have completed my chore of helping to select a new World Champion Duck Caller, and after all the bodies and debris have been cleared away from the drugstore party, the excitement of the contest has subsided, and the adrenalin level has returned to near normal, the Señor and I realize that we do indeed have a problem. It is now Saturday night. We have one half-day more of duck hunting tomorrow, and that's it. Board the big bird and head for the barn. It's then or never, and if the last two days are any indication, as the medics say, the prognosis is poor. So what to do?

The unvarnished truth is we didn't do anything. It was done for us. For the past two days we had been needling our local friends about the quality of shooting here in the Duck Capital of the World. This semi-pro acupuncture apparently paid off, because at the award dinner that night, Rex Hancock came over to say that everything was all set for the next day's duck hunting. "Don't worry—we'll have to fight 'em off tomorrow," he said. "Be sure to bring plenty of shells because we're going to Little Siberia and you'll sure need them."

"Yeah, sure, Rex," we replied. "Seeing is believing."

Well, we went, we saw, and I'm not sure that we conquered, but brother, do we believe!

Next morning, Sunday, Rex showed up in company with Eddie Holt. Eddie is a banker, another son-in-law of Chick and Sophie Major and, most important, another World Champion Duck Caller. We were glad to see Eddie and expressed the hope that there would be ducks for him to call.

It turned out that Little Siberia was not in eastern Russia after all but rather only a few miles from Stuttgart. It was, however, a very "different" sort of place.

We parked our car in a farmer's drive, pulled on chest-high waders, grabbed our guns and ammo, and headed off across a very large field toward some trees off in the distance. I mean, way off, but that was only the beginning. When I asked Rex why no decoys, his only answer was, "You'll see!"

After we reached the trees, we were treated to another half-mile stroll through woods, brush, deadfalls, and all. And then we reached our first water. It wasn't much, but it soon got deeper. We were still in trees and the number of deadfalls seemed to increase in geometric proportion, only now they were mostly under water. You knew they were there when you tripped or stumbled or otherwise found them inadvertently, or they found you. If it wasn't a deadfall, it was a hole. And the brush continued heavy as well.

It is a real fun walk—or rather, wade. It is also long, and the Señor, whose varicose-veined legs prevent his appreciation of any hike longer than a hundred yards, has been complaining since we were five minutes away from the car.

Somewhere along the line, he has acquired a long wading stick, which, with his stocky stature, gives him a Falstaffian appearance.

We are continuing our aquatic struggle when a bitter oath escapes the Señor's lips, which indeed is most unlike him. Indeed! I quickly turn to learn that he has somehow managed to drop his trusty 1100 in the drink. Now this does present a problem. The water is muddy, so, of course, the gun can't be seen. It is lying in about three and a half feet of water, which is also something of a challenge, since it is deeper than our arms are long. Well, the Señor does locate it with his wading staff, than does a swan dive, and finally makes the retrieve, to the applause of all present.

After pouring the water out of the barrel and looking down it to make sure that it's not stopped up with mud, he gets off a couple of test shots. So, with firepower restored and a silent prayer of thanks to Remington for designing and manufacturing a gun that can take it, we resume our mission.

After what seems like an eternity, including innumerable bouts with those damn unseen underwater slashings, we arrive at Little Siberia. We know, because our leader Rex tells us so. Our group of four, which started the trek in close formation, is now strung out over maybe a quarter-mile, with the Señor playing red light. We have been busy enough struggling to put one foot ahead of the other in waist-high water, without pulling a Mark Spitz, to pay much attention to where we are. With the announcement of our arrival, we regroup and take stock of Little Siberia. The name fits.

Actually, Little Siberia is a water reservoir created by cutting down thousands of trees and then flooding the area. It is surrounded by thousands more trees left standing and is studded throughout with dead bushes and trees, which somehow escaped the saw and the bulldozer. It is like a lunar landscape and altogether a real pretty sight—not because of what is on the ground, however, but because of what is in the air. Ducks! Dozens! Hundreds! Thousands! Almost all mallards and spoonbills. We had finally found where the Grand Prairie webfeet were coming to water!

Well, we made the most of it, and in a hurry. Now we knew why decoys were unnecessary. Sexy Rexy Hancock had found them for us; World Champion Duck Caller Eddie Holt proceeded to coax them in to where we could almost swat 'em with our gun barrels. We each just took stands alongside dead tree trunks and let fly. That day the Señor and I found a little bit of duck hunters' heaven.

We all four rapidly limited out. Too soon. Too soon. Then we just stood there and watched all those ducks work. What a show, and from front-row seats. The price of the tickets was a little high—that safari in and out. Another year older and we'd never have made it. And I think that when we did get back out, we were another year older. But happy. Very happy!

Well, so long, Little Siberia. We may never get back, but we'll never forget. And we'll never forget our great, good Stuttgart friends.

Russell Pond

K. C. R.

To say that there is any resemblance between Russell Pond and Walden Pond would be stretching the truth more than a little bit. And I'm no Thoreau. Russell Pond is, however, my pond, which does give me certain rights, if not qualifications. These rights I am now about to exercise.

What I mainly want to say is that ponds are fun. Everybody ought to have one. They are bigger than a breadbox and smaller than a lake. Russell Pond is therefore classic.

Located as it is in close proximity to our house, everything it has to offer is very handy to the eye and to the ear. This is important. You really miss a lot of action if you have to travel any distance to visit your pond.

Probably most people have a particular reason for wanting a pond. I am no exception. As an avid duck hunter, I just plain like to look at ducks and geese—the more the better, and the more frequently the better. As an avid Labrador retriever man, I like to have water close by in which to work dogs. The perfect answer: Russell Pond! Half an acre of great satisfaction, and utility too.

Would you believe a couple hundred mallards and blacks and maybe a hundred Canadas all on such a little body of water at the same time? This occurs with regularity during the peak of the fall migration.

What a sight to watch them skim in over the treetops with wings set and landing gear down. On the water or in the air, to me they are a never-ending source of fascination. It seems that I am constantly learning things I never knew before about waterfowl, and a lot of other birds and animals as well.

Have you ever seen a duck drop a good hundred feet absolutely vertically, sideslipping all the way, to land quite casually—apparently right where he wanted? I never knew they could do that.

The courting displays of both geese and ducks, and mating itself. The constant preening; the stretching and wing flapping; the chasing, quacking, and chuckling. The swimming in long, single file. The taking off and landing; the circling; the diving; the waddling on land looking for food; the skidding on the ice when they land in winter. The woodies in the trees; the geese honking. The occasional visitors (once four red-head drakes, once a male bluebill, and even a blue heron). The fighting. The alertness of the geese; the spookiness of the ducks. The beauty of plumage; the tremendous appetites for corn. The cuteness of ducklings, their dartings here and there, following mother about.

And the wondering where they came from and where they go when they leave. How did they happen upon this particular postage-stamp-size bit of water? How is the word spread that there is corn to be found alongside Russell Pond? Do any of them come back another year? What percentage are migratory and how many stay here year round? Why do they seem to have no fear of dogs? What kind of weather do they really like best? What food is the tastiest? What do they fear most? How do they navigate? How do they know when it's time to migrate? Are blacks a color phase of mallards? What effect does the moon have on their lives? What about predation? Why don't we get any teal, widgeon, gadwall, or pintails on our pond? Is the sentinel goose selected or a volunteer? Why don't the woodies use our nesting boxes?

The sound of wings as they pass low overhead; the identification game.

All these things, and yet there is so much more. Hundreds of small-mouth bass, largemouth bass to five pounds, jumbo bluegills and perch call our pond home. What a joy they are on a light fly rod! No worms allowed here, and dry flies preferred. These restrictions are frequently lifted in the case of small boys.

Sometimes I think that we live in the middle of a bird sanctuary. The pond can't help but contribute to their welfare. And we enjoy them all, even the blackbirds and the grackles. Our special favorites are the cardinals, the blue jays, and the mourning doves, all of which we have in abundance. What a dreary place the world would be if there were no birds! Their beauty and song lift the spirit, which seems to need lifting more than ever today.

We go to sleep nightly to a bullfrog chorus and the waterfall sound of water from an aerator fountain. That's my kind of sleeping.

My Labs, Bibi and Squidance, like our pond. They retrieve thrown dummies from it. They love to swim in it, especially to cool off on a hot day. All the waterfowl activity intrigues them mightily, and they follow all the aquatic and airborne action with the greatest interest. All retrievers worth their salt love the water. Russell Pond is just the ticket to keep mine happy and healthy and in good form for the next duck season.

In winter, the snow-covered pond is just plain beautiful, mostly frozen over, but there is always open water around the aerator fountain. How those webfeet all crowd in! And how they enjoy it. They seem to take special delight at this time of year sporting about, dipping their heads and bringing water up to run down their necks and onto their wriggling backs.

Even though we're pretty far north, we have a substantial number of birds, geese, and ducks that winter over with us. If food and open water are available, that's all they need. I sometimes wonder just how far north they would and could winter, given those two requirements.

The numbers of waterfowl using the pond are always swollen during migration time in the spring and fall. Summer is the quiet season. I don't feed during the summer months. The birds don't need it. The pond is also fished fairly heavily then, which tends to discourage the birds. We also have a sailing dinghy on this "sweetwater sea," which races with waterbugs in weekly regattas.

A pond is different things to different people. I guess you make of it what you want it to be. Russell Pond is, to me, a waterfowl refuge, and everything else is secondary to that purpose. It is work, and it costs a little money, but the investment has been repaid a thousand times in the sheer pleasure and enjoyment it has given us and our friends. Live entertainment at its best, and educational, too. How can you beat that?

"Where have all the mallards gone?"

They're all on Russell Pond!

Opening Day Eve

K. C. R.

The Opening Day of duck season ranks in importance for certain people right alongside Christmas. It is a day long planned for and much anticipated, what with getting one's equipment in shape—guns, decoys, calls, boats, motors, clothing, waders, et cetera ad infinitum. Licenses must be obtained, duck stamp and ammo purchased, flask of heart starter replenished, dogs conditioned, and most important, the place where you will hunt determined. With duck hunting, it's just like the travel posters say—getting there is half the fun.

All of this preseason effort builds up to a crescendo of excitement on the night before the season opens—Opening Day Eve. Let me tell you about a memorable one. No names, please!

It was back in the middle to late sixties in northwestern Ohio where a select group of dedicated greater Cleveland duck hunters were wont to gather annually in observance of those very special and secret rites relative to Opening Day. As usual, the brethren were gathered in the back room of an area oasis known colloquially as the Cabin, discussing important matters. For the next several hours of Opening Day Eve, only "duck" will be spoken: tales of past glories and future expectations, weather, dogs and dog work, guns, gauges, chokes, shells, shot size, powder charges, manufacturers, duck "factory" production, water levels, marsh conditions, wind, phase of the moon, punters, decoys and decoy placement, Ducks Unlimited, geese, game wardens, point system, duck calling, bag limits, shooting hours, and a lot of other duck talk, mostly concentrating on how quickly each blind will limit out on the morrow.

Once covered, it is all gone over again compared with the year before and then again compared with the year before that. Favorite old chestnuts are retold as they are every year to an audience as receptive now as to the original telling. Duck calls are limbered up and the Labrador retrievers present get caught up in the contagious atmosphere. "Ducking fever" is running rampant!

We must now go back to a scene which took place a few days previous to Opening Day Eve. One of the good ole boys of the group was in between wives at the time. He was, however, currently courting the girl he was to marry. It also seems he was a might concerned about his beloved's reaction to his spending Opening Day Eve as usual, with the other good ole boys. And so, facing right up to the situation, he announced his intention not to participate in this year's festivities. Being also equal to the occasion and rising to it, his paramour at once stoutly denied any design on our hero's annual fun and insisted he carry on his custom as usual. This he finally agreed to do, with much protestation and display of reluctance. In addition, in the fullness of his cup running over, he promised to call home during the evening to report his safe arrival and any other news of interest. The stage was now set.

It's just under two hours' driving time from home to the Cabin, where wait those heavenly deep-fried fresh Lake Erie perch, those out-of-this-world home-fried egg-and-onion potatoes, and those delicious, nutritious, and pleasing-to-the-palate silver bullets. O.H. (our hero) prefers them made with House of Lords. Not to forget, of course, the true companionship of kindred souls; the kind of oneship which can be achieved only by people of like mind—in this case, dyed-in-the-marsh duck hunters all.

O.H. arrives at the Cabin in good time and on schedule. Calls wife-to-be immediately to report this good news. W.T.B. happy to hear good news and happy for O.H. O.H., thirsty after long drive, orders S.B., looks about for other good ole boys; finds some; starts talking duck; orders second S.B.

More good ole boys arrive. Duck talk now under way in earnest. Third S.B. on way. Oh yes, must call W.T.B. Hi, honey. Just want you to know everything is going great. I'm having a lot of fun and sure appreciate your wanting me to be here. See you tomorrow. Love yuh! Bye.

Back to the good ole boys. Time for another S.B. Duck talk in full swing. Remember that day last year? Wind is right, looks good for tomorrow. Betcha ten we're first out of the blind. I feel good. Any bird within fifty yards will be an automatic. Hey, Tillie. How about *uno mas?* Might as well call Mother while I'm empty and let her know what a super time we're having. Hello, dear. You sure were nice to let me come. Everybody's here and they all send their best. You know I miss you but it really looks good for tomorrow. See yuh then. Tillie, where's my drink? While you're at it, better bring two.

Nothing like being with the old gang again. What a great bunch of guys. And to think that I almost didn't get to make it this year because of W.T.B. That stinker. I'm really going to tell her off. Where's the phone? John, where'd you hide the telephone? Oh yeah, there it is. Thanks, John. You sure are a good guy. One of us. That's more than I can say about so and so. She's tryin' to break up our friendship. Doesn't like ducks either, to shoot 'em or eat 'em. I'm goin' to really give her a piece of my mind.

Hello, W.T.B. Just what do you think you're tryin' to do? You don't want me to go duck hunting or come up here any more, do yuh? My friends aren't good enough for yuh, are they? It's a good thing I found you out before it was too late. Well, you know what you can do. Go find yourself a golfer. We're through. Finis. Kaput.

We now mercifully ring down the curtain on this little charade and with trepidation await the last act.

The scene shifts to the next day—Opening Day! A telephone rings back in Cleveland.

Hello, sweetheart! Wow, what an opening. We limited out in forty-five minutes. Ducks all over the marsh. We're going to have some lunch and then head for home. Oh, by the way, hon, I'm sure sorry I forgot to call you last night and let you know everything was okay. I just got busy yakkin' with all the boys, you know how it is. See ya soon. Love yuh, honey. Bye.

One more Opening Day Eve and Opening Day have come and gone.

Duck-Marsh Dawn

K. C. R.

Half full or half empty? Optimist or pessimist? According to Webster, a marsh is a swamp and a swamp is a marsh. To people who appreciate and understand it, it's a marsh. To those who don't—who think it is unattractive and uninviting—it's a swamp.

Getting right down to cases, who ever heard of a duck swamp? It must be that duck hunters are optimists. Positive thinkers. "Right" thinkers to whom a marsh is a beautiful place to be—anytime. A duck marsh at dawn, however, is something special. The world is reborn every twenty-four hours at daybreak. How wonderful these fresh starts, these new beginnings! And the closer we are to nature, the more receptive we are, the more impressive, the more awe-inspiring such a time becomes. Just to watch the world of nature wake up.

Yes, the duck hunter drinking in a duck-marsh dawn well knows the truth contained in the musical line "and the dawn comes up like thunder." He also knows that sometimes it just steals in like a thief in the night. Before you realize it, it's there.

Then there are all those in-between dawns. They're all different. They're all good. To each his own, I suppose, like most everything else in life. We all have our favorites. Mine is what Homer quite aptly described as a "rosy-fingered dawn." I don't think further elaboration is necessary. At least all duck hunters know what I mean.

Of course, there are a lot of other things that go with duck-marsh dawns. Such things as alarm clocks or loud raps on the door, heavy wool socks sometimes still wet, hip boots or waders, hot coffee usually not very good, greasy eggs, dogs to walk, guns, shells, decoys, duck calls, dog whistle, Thermos, brandy flask (for use only in extreme emergencies), hat, gloves, camera, film—and that's just for starters. Other lists may be twice that long, but I like to go light.

It's still black dark and you're off for the marsh. Want to be settled in the blind with decoys out about half an hour before shooting time.

It's that thirty minutes which sometimes is the best of all. Packed solid with anticipation. Alert to every sight and sound. The clock moves slowly now. You hear wings overhead, but can't make them out. Your dog is all aquiver. Load your gun and place the shell box handy. Check to make sure the safety's on. Look at your watch again. Look toward the east. Is that faint light? It is, and more, and more. Here we are again. Where many of us would rather be than almost anyplace on earth. We're witness to another duck-marsh dawn.

The World Champion Duck Caller

K. C. R.

Probably ninety percent of all the duck hunters in the state of Ohio, even if they have never shot there, have heard of Nielsen's Marsh. Located on the southern shore of Lake Erie in northwestern Ohio between Sandusky on the east and Port Clinton on the west, Nielsen's offers the best duck shooting in the state except for the private clubs and private leases in the same general area.

The Nielsen family business is commercial fishing, which, in recent years, has been a sometime thing. The duck marsh was a sideline. I say "was" because following the death of Charlie Nielsen, the head of the clan, the marsh was sold. Two Nielsens, sons of old Charlie, still carry on, however. Cy, the eldest, and Mickey fish in the spring, summer, and early fall. Then during duck season, as they have for most all their lives, Cy and Mickey hunt ducks—that is, they act as guides for the sports who shoot Nielsen's Marsh. It is Mickey who, among the regulars, is known as the World Champion Duck Caller. His technique is somewhat unusual. His results are admittedly indifferent; nevertheless, his call, and he uses only one, never fails to impress those nimrods fortunate enough to share a blind with him, especially for the first time.

When a flock is sighted, this famous, near legendary call, given in a low, hoarse, awed whisper, is heard floating out over the marsh and into all eternity: "Look at all them ducks!"

Results? Who cares? To know him is to love him!

Butterfly Day

K. C. R.

I have never gone duck hunting and been skunked in my life. Sure, there have been some days when I never pulled the trigger. That happens to every duck hunter once in a while, but I've never been skunked. You know what I mean. There are a lot of guys whose day is ruined if they don't get any ducks. I feel sorry for them. They don't know what it's all about.

Now, I'm human. I enjoy going duck hunting and shooting ducks. Naturally, when I venture forth, I'd like to have the opportunity to swing on at least a few. If I limit, that's even better. And I like to eat 'em, too.

My point is, when it comes to duck hunting, it's all good. Some is just better. Take a "butterfly day," for instance. It seems that when duck-hunting success has been substantially less than maximum, the most common reason given is, "It was a butterfly day." A butterfly day ranks at the top of the list, way ahead of "I couldn't hit the water if I fell out of the boat," or the wind was wrong, or there was no wind at all, or the wind was too strong, or the blind was located wrong, or I brought the wrong gun, or the wrong shells, or I'm not used to my new glasses, or there were a bunch of damn sky busters next to us, or I think I must have bent my barrel, or the guide put out the decoys wrong, or the duck shooting's always lousy during a full moon, or I never can shoot with a hangover, or so-and-so's (never your own) dog flared all the ducks out of range, or the lousy blind spooked all the ducks, or it was just bad cess all day, or the flyway patterns must be changing, or D.U. sure needs to do more than they're doing, or my horoscope was bad, or why does it always have to be me, or it was too foggy, too cold, too rainy, too snowy, too icy, too wet, too too too you name it. And I'm certain you can.

Well, okay. Let's start over. You didn't get any ducks. Why not? Of course, because it was a butterfly day! Everyone is supposed to know what that means. I really don't. So I looked it up in Webster's latest. It isn't there. How about an educated guess? A butterfly day most likely is one with plenty of sunshine, no wind, and warm temperature; a day calculated to be most suitable for delicate butterflies to sport about; a day during which most ducks will just drowse on the water and rarely take wing. A day to try the soul and patience of duck hunters. But not this duck hunter. No, sir!

This duck hunter not only enjoys just being outdoors. I especially and particularly like to be outdoors in duck blinds, any kind of duck blinds, even standing alongside a tree or squatting in brush. It's just being *there* that counts, and everything else is a plus. A bonus. Look at it this way. It's a matter of alternatives. If you're not duck hunting, where would you be? In the office working? In bed sleeping? At home working? Come on. Where would any normal duck hunter really want to be? Why, duck hunting, naturally, butterfly day or no. As a matter of fact, when you really come to think of it, when you really get dead serious about it, butterfly days aren't so bad after all. Are they?

Picking a Partner

K. C. R.

Next to picking a wife, the selection of a shooting partner is perhaps the single most important decision a waterfowler ever
has to make. And made right, both are for life, too. Therefore,
there are many things to think about and to be taken into prayerful
consideration.

At this point it should be understood that the following comments
are not ranked in order of their importance. But high on my list of
requirements for the ideal hunting partner, for example, is the kind of
a guy who always remembers to bring on a hunting trip all those things
which you always forget.

That a prospective partner should be a good shot, of course, goes
without saying. Good, yes, but not quite as good as you are. It helps too
if he owns a good retriever. Good, yes, but not quite as good as yours.

I also rate a good cook very high. One who can whip up a tasty
meal, regardless of the adequacy of cooking utensils or groceries. And
even more important, one who enjoys preparing delicious game dinners
for you and your respective spouses using his ducks, thereby saving
yours for another occasion.

Naturally your partner should be capable of intelligent and lengthy
discourse on any subject—especially dogs, guns, and women—always
giving you the last word. Oh yes, and he must never tell one of your
jokes as his own.

Another most important quality is his readiness to go hunting at
any time, regardless of work, weather, or wife.

And speaking of wives, it is highly desirable that your hunting partner's mate be a nonshooter. Otherwise there are times when she will insist on accompanying her hubby—your partner—on ducking safaris. Since three hunters in one blind is definitely a crowd, you know who is thus left out of the blind, in the cold, and from the trip. Also, she should be compatible with your own mate so that they can commiserate with each other during your frequent "business" trips throughout the duck season.

The right attitude is another factor to be carefully investigated before placing a final stamp of approval upon your prospective partner. For example, suppose you're both in the blind and suddenly out of nowhere a couple of ducks arrive within shooting distance. You jump to your feet assisted by one hand hard on your partner's shoulder, at the same time crying, "Let's take 'em!" You down a double while he is still struggling to get to his feet, having "accidentally" been impeded in his efforts by your own. He then says to you, "Great shooting, pal, you're really on today." Sign that man up as your regular hunting buddy quick. He's got the right attitude.

To sum up, I'm glad the Señor picked me!

Who is the Señor? The Señor is, well, the Señor: duck hunter, deer hunter, fly fisherman, dove hunter, skeet shooter, Labrador-retriever enthusiast, gun collector, wildlife-art collector, martini fancier, bill-fisherman, coyote hunter, quail hunter, gourmet chef, pheasant hunter, gourmand, bon vivant, raconteur, beer lover, goose hunter, plant grower, conservationist, Mexican aficionado, bear hunter, snorkler, Ping-Pong player, football buff, girl watcher, shuffleboard player, photographer, decoy carver, public speaker, and lawyer, which last enables him to be and do all the other things. So now, at this point, you should know him pretty well. He is also my best friend and hunting partner, and I have shared a fair-sized slice of life with him. And I hope there are a lot more slices to come. God willing.

Not long ago, the Señor suddenly and unexpectedly had to undergo a serious operation. At the time, I told him that he couldn't die because I was too old to break in a new hunting partner. Thank God the Señor cooperated, perhaps with a little help from on high. Currently he has a new kick—gardening indoors, all manner and sizes of plants. Things are at the point now where it is necessary to get a malaria shot before going into his house.

Well, enough of all this. I digress. To get back on the track, the Señor and I, over the years, have spent a lot of time in duck blinds together.

Obviously, we haven't yet done it all, but we're working at it. The Señor wipes my eye occasionally and once in a while I get back at him. Most important, we get along. A lot of people are not so fortunate. A good hunting partner, as I've said, makes all the difference. He makes a poor day a better day and a good day a great one.

Anyway, we're looking forward to a lot more duck hunting in the future in a lot of other places on this here planet. I understand there's this hot spot in India where the ducks are as thick as black flies in Canada at the peak of the black-fly season. . . .

Ducks Unlimited

K. C. R.

The Señor, as noted elsewhere, first introduced me to Ducks Unlimited. Since then, he has claimed that this act was his major contribution to what many believe to be the world's finest conservation organization. This exaggeration may be excused on the basis of the fact that he is my closest friend and hunting partner. That D.U. is the leader in its field *can* be pretty well documented.

The fact is, while others talk, D.U. does the job! Approximately 80 percent of all contributions received is actually put to work benefiting wildlife (waterfowl first, of course, but also including over three hundred other species of birds, animals and fish). Since D.U.'s founding in 1937, over $40,000,000 has been invested in habitat. This organization of approximately 250,000 members has the smallest professional staff and the largest staff of unpaid volunteers of any major conservation group. Currently D.U. has over 2,500,000 acres of prime waterfowl habitat under lease. This includes almost ten thousand miles of shoreline. Since 1937, D.U. has completed over 1,350 projects ranging in size from ten to half a million acres. Looking to the future, a Greenwing Program was begun in 1973 for boys and girls under the age of sixteen. Current membership is about fifteen thousand.

Yes, Ducks Unlimited does the job!

It might also be of interest that every contributor to this book is a D.U. member. Somehow that fact seems important and tells a story all by itself.

The real story, however, lies in results—the results for which Ducks

Unlimited is almost solely responsible. It has been said by many recognized, knowledgeable waterfowl experts that D.U.'s Canadian nesting-habitat program is the reason we have ducks to enjoy today, for viewing and for sport. Sure, they wouldn't have become extinct, and some do nest in the United States. But hunting seasons? Very possibly there would be none. And even just viewing? Who knows?

D.U.'s record of accomplishment is evident for all to see and to enjoy. Ducks and geese are still coming down every year in respectable numbers. This fact, however, is only the half of it. So much more remains to be done—needs to be done—and we have so little time in which to do it. The next five years are crucial. If we don't do the job by then, it will probably be too late. "Civilization" will have taken over. Instead of the vital nesting habitat required to maintain a healthy waterfowl population, in its place will be found residential developments, shopping centers, agricultural lands, and the like.

D.U. has an ambitious program for this period. It is planned to acquire an additional 4,500,000 acres in Canada before they succumb to "progress." More new members and more money are needed to ensure waterfowl for generations to come, for our children and our children's children. And their children, too.

Can we accomplish this goal? Consider the following: only about 10 percent of all Federal Duck Stamp buyers belong to Ducks Unlimited. We've got all the rest to go. Obviously, the potential is there to reach our goal. It boils down to this: The choice is still ours, but the hour is late. Therefore, all you nonmember duck hunters, bird watchers, and conservationists, will you help too?

Put Some Back; Support Ducks Unlimited!

Games Duck Hunters Play

K. C. R.

Try this one at your duck club next season.

Vic Bracher, retired Remington Arms representative and exhibition shooter, superb decoy carver, and most of all gentleman, whom I am proud to call friend, used to participate in a really super ducking game in the old days. You remember the old days—when a dollar bought five gallons and more of gasoline and five dollars paid for dinner for two and a night on the town.

Back then, Vic and a few of his duck-hunting cronies played it this way. Each target duck had to be correctly identified out loud, by whichever hunter whose turn it was to shoot, prior to his making the shot. If the duck was missed, or if it was killed but found to be improperly identified, five dollars was owed to each of the others sharing the blind. Each downed bird was carefully tagged with the name of the hunter responsible. At the conclusion of the shoot, the ducks were drawn and picked and searched carefully for shot holes and shot. For every shot found, our hero must pay one dollar to each of his companions.

Well, that's it. Neat, eh? Oh yes, don't forget when you play the game, the money might be increased to five and twenty dollars to allow for inflation.

One thing more. Vic says to be a winner it is not only necessary to know your ducks and to be good at on-the-wing identification, but it is also highly desirable to be sufficiently adept with a shotgun to be able to head-shoot all your ducks!

Any takers?

The "Rem-Win-Ith" Shotgun: The Story of the Ducks Unlimited Commemorative Shotgun Program

K. C. R.

It was early 1970. I had been a member of Ducks Unlimited for several years and active in the Cleveland, Ohio, Committee more recently. My best friend and hunting partner, Bill Davis, the Señor, was responsible for my initial involvement in D.U. Over lunch one late winter day, I told him of my idea. We both were well aware of D.U.'s need for funds. This outstanding international conservation organization, founded in 1937 to improve the nesting habitat and, as a result, the numbers and status of North American waterfowl, had really taken off under the inspired leadership of Executive Vice President and waterfowl pro Dale Whitesell, of Ohio. However, something was lacking. Funds were being raised and new members signed up at dinners held annually by individual D.U. chapters throughout the country. We were growing at better than a 20 percent compounded rate, but if we were to get the job done before it was too late, something new was needed. A spark. I thought I had it. As it turned out, I did.

The idea was simple: a Ducks Unlimited Commemorative Shotgun. Although a number of commemorative rifles had been produced in the previous few years to raise funds for several worthwhile groups, with varying degrees of success, there had never been a commemorative shotgun created for a private organization.

The Señor bought the idea and agreed to present it to the Ducks Unlimited Board of Trustees, meeting a couple of months hence. He did. They were receptive.

I decided to go for experience. That same year, my first contact was with Winchester, and for what I thought was a very good reason. They had produced more commemorative guns (rifles) than any other arms manufacturer. Jim Rikhoff and Rock Rohlfing lent first sympathetic, and then enthusiastic ears. I was elated. It looked as though we were off the ground and on our way.

Then we crashed and burned. Although Winchester wanted very much to work with us, it was decided, after several months of considera- tion, that their production schedules just couldn't permit them to go ahead at that time. Later, probably, but not right then. It was now 1971.

Remington Arms, however, could, would, and did. They pioneered with us. Working closely with Pete Morgan, Herb Albaugh, Ted McCawley, and Phil Burdette, we determined to go first with the inter- nationally famous Remington Model 1100, America's best-selling shotgun.

We couldn't have made a better choice. The gun was produced in two models: first, a series of 10,000 "retail" commemoratives, serial numbers DU 04000 to DU 14000, to be sold by Remington dealers across the country over the counter; second, a series of 500 special "auction" commemoratives, serial numbers DU 001 to DU 500, to be sold only at auction and a selected few special raffles at our fund-raising dinners throughout the United States during the period July 1, 1973, to June 30, 1974. In addition to all the features that have made the Model 1100 autoloader a famous waterfowl gun, plus the special serial numbers in gold, the D.U. auction Commemorative Model 1100 offered "B" grade American-walnut stock and fore-end, gold-plated trigger, special scrollwork in gold on the left side of the receiver, and the official D.U. crest in the form of a four-color medallion. It came with a hard gun case and was accompanied by an embossed card containing copy relative to the gun, D.U., and Remington. All guns were 12-gauge, with a 30-inch full-choke, ventilated-rib barrel.

On the retail guns, Ducks Unlimited received fifteen dollars per gun, which was built into the selling price. This money was then credited to our account by Remington toward the purchase price of the auction guns. In total, our Model 1100 program raised an amount nicely into six figures for D.U. Not too shabby, one might say, for starters.

Flushed with success, discussions were then held with Remington regarding what to do for an encore. We soon settled on the Model 870 "Wingmaster" pump-action shotgun, of which over two million are owned by sportsmen throughout the world, making it the most popular pump gun ever made, a universal favorite among waterfowlers throughout the country.

For our second go, we stuck pretty much to the same now-proven format. We again went for two models: a series of 10,000 "retail" commemoratives, serial numbers 04000 DU to 14000 DU, and a series of 600 "auction" commemoratives, serial numbers 001 DU to 600 DU. These guns were marketed from July 1, 1974, to June 30, 1975. Apart from the change in the special serial numbers, the other "cosmetics" were similar to those described earlier for the Model 1100. This time, however, D.U. received eighteen dollars per retail gun, which, along with the sale of the auction guns, resulted in an even larger sum for the ducks. Our program was now contributing a significant percentage of our total funds raised. Quite obviously, we had something very good going.

The issuance of these commemorative shotguns combined both support and recognition by Remington of the valuable work Ducks Unlimited had carried out since 1937 in restoring, maintaining, and creating waterfowl habitat in North America. Purchasers of these guns have not only a handsome, very limited-edition shotgun, but one that provides visible evidence of their support of D.U. wherever the gun is displayed or used.

Simultaneously, these commemoratives salute the American sportsmen whose contributions to D.U. over the years have enabled it to carry on its essential work.

A couple of important things should be mentioned at this point. In developing our marketing strategy for our first commemorative shotgun program—the 1100, which number incidentally tied in beautifully at the time with the completion of D.U.'s 1100th project in Canada—it was decided to hold back auction guns DU 001 to DU 030, and make them available at the end of the year to those persons paying the twenty-five highest prices for the guns at our fund-raising dinners across the country—the highest bidder in the United States thus being able to exchange the actual gun he bought, regardless of serial number, for serial number DU 001, and so on down the line.

Secondly, a strong effort was made during the second commemorative program to send the same serial number auction Model 870s, particularly those with lower numbers, to the bigger fund-raising dinners as the particular chapter had a year earlier of the Model 1100. This created the possibility for the continuity of serial numbers of commemorative shotguns which would enhance value and, we hoped, result in higher auction prices.

After two highly successful years of working with Remington, the time then seemed propitious to reapproach Winchester. Which we did. The Winchester Model 12, the slide-action shotgun that became a legend, the classic gun of the waterfowler, was our quarry, and we bagged it. We were able to contract for only 800 auction guns, mind you. No retail guns at all. But we were very pleased. From mid-1912, when the Model 12 was first introduced, to December 1963, when production ceased, nearly two million shooters became proud owners of this gun. Public demand brought it back in 1972, but all too soon, inflationary pressures forced a cutback. In 1975, it was decided to produce the 12 only in a trap model. Production of the field-model gun was halted once more, an unusual case of making something too well, to the point of economic impracticality. There was just one exception to this decision: 800 Ducks Unlimited Commemorative Model 12 Shotguns, our "rarest ever" commemorative. This gun again was 12-gauge, with 30-inch full-choke ventilated-rib barrel and the following special features: special etched engraving on both sides of the receiver, the left side featuring a highly polished bronze medallion depicting a canvasback duck by noted D.U. Artist of the Year Larry Toschik, the right side spotlighting a jumping duck; special highly polished bronze pistol-grip insert of the official D.U. crest; stock and fore-end crafted of select American walnut with special deep-cut checkering; gold-plated trigger; special serial numbers 12 DU 001 to 12 DU 800. All of this, of course, in addition to the hallmark qualities on which the Model 12 built its renowned reputation, proven design, and solid dependability in a gun crafted from machined-chrome molybdenum steel.

Collectors guns indeed!

This series set new highs for bidding on these special commemorative shotguns at our fund-raising banquets. The total net revenue to D.U. from this, our third program, also reached a new all-time high. How about that, sports fans? The Model 12 provided a very tough act to follow.

So onward to number four in the series. With our two-year stint with Remington to guide us, in addition to the very happy experience with the Model 12, we again joined with Winchester, this time in the development of the Ducks Unlimited Super-X Model 1 Commemorative. The "One" was only brought out in 1974 and already was hailed as the automatic version of the Model 12 in looks, feel, and reliability. What more could we ask?

This fourth series of 950 auction guns, serial numbers 1 DU 001 to 1 DU 950, again with no "trade" guns, continued our now well-established pattern. Once more, as usual, the specifications called for a 12-gauge with a 30-inch full-choke ventilated-rib barrel; special etched receiver engraving, right side with flighted ducks in an oval, with embellishments, left side with a highly polished bronze mallard medallion by Larry Toschik and embellishment; a bronze official D.U. crest, pistol-grip insert; "Semi-Fancy" grade American-walnut stock and configuration fore-end, both with high-gloss finish; "Skeet Grade" checkering on stock and fore-end; gold-plated trigger; white spacers on butt plate and pistol grip; packaged in fitted Styrofoam, plus a "Certificate of Ownership" suitable for framing.

Following right along in the shot path of our three preceding D.U. commemorative shotgun programs, the super Super-X Model 1 produced another new high in net income for the ducks. Additionally, and importantly, the four guns in the program to date—two Remingtons and two Winchesters—had genuinely become collectors' guns of high magnitude.

1977 was a very big year for Ducks Unlimited, which celebrated its fortieth birthday. The well and very favorably known Ithaca Model 37 pump gun was selected for the honor of becoming our 40th Anniversary commemorative, and it is indeed a super-special program in every way. Just listen to these features: gold-plated trigger and slide release; Pachmayr presentation-grade recoil pad; jeweled slide; Bradley-type front sight with middle bead; serial numbers 40 DU 0001 to 40 DU 1075; hand-checkered, fancy-grade American-walnut stock and fore-end; highly detailed brass grip cap with special "40 with duck" logo; left side of receiver specially etched with Ducks Unlimited 40th Anniversary logo; right side of receiver specially etched with the inscription "Ducks Unlimited 1937–1977 Four Decades of Conservation Pioneering." The D.U. crest is also incorporated into the right-side etching. The gun, of course, is 12-gauge with 30-inch full-choke ventilated-rib barrel. The Model 37 is packaged in a luggage-type hard gun case with information and printed material suitable to the occasion inside.

And, in addition to all of the foregoing, with each gun and case and with the same serial numbers as the gun it is shipped with stamped on the back, there is a beautiful pewter-finished brass belt buckle displaying the D.U. 40th Anniversary logo.

And that's just the auction-model program. Ithaca is also producing several thousand special "trade" Model 37 commemoratives whose cosmetics are only slightly less spectacular than the auction guns, and which come without the hard case and belt buckle. For each one of these guns retailed, Ithaca will contribute eighteen dollars to D.U.

This tremendous combination of D.U.'s 40th Anniversary, the very special and beautiful Ithaca Model 37 pump gun, and the belt buckle will, without doubt, set a new high for dollars for ducks raised by our extremely successful commemorative program—a program which we expect to continue for some years to come and a program which is creating collectors' guns for waterfowlers throughout the country to enjoy now and in the future, along with all the millions of ducks they have helped to pay for.

PART II

They're in the Bottoms

JOHN M. COGAN

About once every three or four years the calls are made. Dimes are popped into pay telephones in such unfamiliar places as Ripley, Hornbeak, Newbern, Troy, and Forked Deer, all remote and thinly populated communities in western Tennessee. Pay phones are used because few of the callers have ever experienced the luxury of a telephone in their modest cabins. Furthermore, telephone service is simply not available in areas where they choose to live.

These collect calls go to a broad spectrum of Americans: a priest in St. Louis; a stockbroker in Cincinnati; a professor in Iowa City; a furniture salesman in Cleveland; a banker in Chicago; and a Tennessee Congressman in Washington, D.C. There is no socio-economic denominator present within this group. They accept the calls because of their faith in the River People, secure in the knowledge that duck hunting at its best lies ahead.

The conversation is abrupt, no greeting or exchange of social amenities—definitely not a profitable call for Mother Bell. With a few variations, the brief exchange is something like this: "Hello, this is Virgil. They're here, in the bottoms. Moved in here last night on the full moon. Must be twenty thousand of 'em. Mostly greenhead and widgeon. A trace of teal. No blacks, they'll come later. Plenty of water, backed all the way to the green timber. Lotta food—they oughta stay here a week or ten days. You comin' down? Good, I'll meet you at the truck stop Tuesday mornin', say about three-thirty."

Within minutes plane reservations are made—return portion open —and cars reserved at airports in Nashville or Memphis. Business dates and social functions are canceled. Wives are mollified with promises of furs, jewelry, or a trip to the Caribbean. The hunt is on. To where? The Obion River bottoms!

Reelfoot Lake, some fifteen miles east of the Mississippi in the northwest corner of Tennessee, was, so the geologists say, formed by earthquake movements in 1811. From top to bottom it is perhaps twenty miles long and no more than five miles across at its widest point. What at one time was priceless timberland, abounding in cypress, is now a shallow, flooded forest dotted with rotting tree stumps. During the day an eerie quiet prevails. At night the place is just plain spooky. Year after year it produces record catches of bass and crappie. And every year thousands of migratory waterfowl, wending their way southward along the Mississippi flyway, make the scheduled stopover at Reelfoot.

This most unusual North American body of water is rich in legend, some fact, and some fiction embellished with the passage of time. Two of these Reelfoot "legends" were real people. I saw them, witnessed some of their feats, and, on occasion, drank hard cider with them.

"Slingshot Charley" was the most memorable to me as a youth, and then as a younger man. Before the drought and resultant diminished duck population of the thirties, the daily duck limit was twenty birds. The guide fee at Reelfoot was five dollars per day, which included cleaning and dressing the kill. That meant a hunter and his partner could take sixty ducks a day, including the guide's limit. This parcel of information has to make today's modern waterfowler drool. The automatic shotgun, while on the retailer's shelf, was not a popular weapon, and considered much too expensive. The thirty-two-inch side-by-side, the old shoulder bruiser, was the gun of distinction. But not for Slingshot Charley. This illiterate, and probably illegitimate, product of the bottomland killed his limit almost every day with his slingshot, using marbles, ball bearings, or carefully selected stones. I personally never saw Charley kill a duck with his slingshot, since his fee was ten dollars, an exorbitant sum in those days and one my father could not afford. However, my father's more affluent friends who engaged the services of Slingshot swore over drinks that Charley could kill a duck "clean" at thirty-five yards with a round rock. What I can remember, and vividly, is Charley's regular evening appearance at camp, always with twenty ducks—no more, no less—for sale to those hunters who had failed to bag their limit or, in some cases, failed to hunt at all because of a bout with some Tennessee Dew the preceding night. It never occurred to me at that impressionable time in life to examine the birds for evidence of shot.

After the sale Charley would always offer to give an exhibition by lantern light with his trusty slingshot, and invariably won his guide fee several times over. First, a plate sailed in the air for fifty cents. The next step was a tin cup for a buck. After a few bourbons had sufficiently loosened the hunters (nobody drank Scotch in those days), the silver-dollar exhibition—three out of five for ten dollars, a princely sum in Depression days. I never saw Charley lose this wager; sometimes he hit all five coins. I also remember that for this bet he used no marbles or stones, always ball bearings. While the side bets were being settled, Charley never failed to retrieve the silver dollars—those he hit and those he missed.

Cirrhosis finally claimed Charley shortly before Pearl Harbor. Perhaps his passing at this time did much to preserve Charley's reputation, since ball bearings were in short supply with the beginning of hostilities.

The other legend of my youth was the complete antithesis of Charley, a tall, genteel, imposing man by the name of Earl Mallard Dennison. Earl was indeed an atypical personage in western Tennessee, the owner of a skillfully cultivated British accent that he used after a few nips on the bottle. No one has been successful in tracing the ancestry of Earl. He just happened to appear one day with his whittling knife. Earl was prematurely gray, and since hair dyes had not been created and haircuts cost fifteen cents, some credit must go to him for anticipating the longhair styles of today. His long silver locks touching the velvet collar of his Chesterfield stamped Earl as Newbern's most distinguished citizen. But Earl did not rely on appearance alone—not this showman. Earl trained a pinioned female mallard to sit on his left shoulder and quack at a given signal. Then Earl would return the call with one of his hand-carved calls. Back and forth went the dialogue. Which was the duck and which was Earl. No one could recognize a difference, and this was the reason Earl could charge such a high premium for his hand-carved cypress calls. The duck's name was Suzy, which I am sure accounts for female mallards being identified in this way along the lower Mississippi flyway. I have never heard the female called a suzy in other duck-hunting areas. "Buy one of my Stradivariuses and call ducks into your oven" was Earl's sales pitch.

I don't know how many calls Earl made, nor do I have any

supporting evidence that all of his calls were hand-carved. Some folks claim he kept woodworking tools buried in his back yard. I only know of nine such calls in existence today, and two of the owners have refused bids of four figures. Legend? Maybe yes, maybe no. But who can forget this six-foot-plus man walking the streets of Newbern, his long white mane draped over his frayed Chesterfield, with Suzy's droppings on his left shoulder, selling duck calls to Yankees, cash before delivery? Delivery? "When I find the right wood and have time to whittle one to fit your lungs."

Earl Mallard Dennison is gone. Slingshot Charley is gone. True, Reelfoot remains, but it bears little resemblance to the Reelfoot of the past. Too much civilization, and not necessarily the right kind, prevails. The lake is surrounded by motels, neon-lighted taverns, and the always-present trailer parks. Too much litter and too few places to dispose of it have created an aura of shabbiness, with beer cans lining the shore of the lake. Nonetheless, the hunters still come every fall, as do the ducks, some 250,000 of them during the peak of the migration southward. But the hunters are different. They arrive with their cameras, their Purdys and Parkers, and their over-and-under twenty-six-inch barrels, almost walking advertisements for Abercrombie and Fitch. For the purists only one old-style hunting haven remains in the area.

Flowing into the Mississippi not too distant from Reelfoot is a small river called the Obion. It circumvents its way through rough native timberland, the soil on either side of its banks virtually untillable. The proud people who reside here for the most part pay taxes, reject welfare, and eke out a living from fishing, trapping, and odd jobs in the nearby "cities." As for the Indians along the shores of James Bay, waterfowl from a dietary point of view is a necessity. Broad-minded and understanding conservation officers seldom visit this remote region during the hunting season. Those that do are usually transferred, because these folks, as mentioned earlier, never forget to pay taxes and vote. On occasion Mother Nature sends a bonus quantity of ducks their way. Excessive and unpredictable rainfall extends the banks of the Obion several miles on each side. The water backs up into the green timber, expanding feeding grounds by a significant margin. What hungry migratory duck can turn down a tasty meal of pin-oak pods? That is when the phone calls are made, when the water reaches the green timber.

Breakfast at the truck stop, while ample in quantity, is, in all candor, lacking in quality. It is not recommended for those with weak stomachs or ulcer histories; however, it is part of the package and calls for compliments to the cook, who offers to fix some sandwiches for lunch. Those who have been there before politely decline.

From the truck stop, various routes, some through fields, are taken to the banks of the river. Boats are launched all along the Obion. The distinctive and indestructible Reelfoot boats, their propellers rotating from the protection of a hollowed-out bottom, can carry a party of four over logs and snags, maintaining the same speed in eight inches of water as they do in eight feet.

It's first come, first served in the bottoms. The early arrivals head for the tree blinds, some two-by-fours and scrap plywood wedged in the fork of a tree fifteen to twenty feet above the water. The tree blinds offer two advantages. One quite obviously is the height and increased visibility they offer the hunters as the ducks circle the flooded timber. The other is their rapid convertibility to a kitchen. Along about mid or late morning, after the early flights have settled down, the guide will shinny down to the boat and return with a gas can, some charcoal, and wieners. The briquets are stacked and doused and bingo—a five-foot flame leaps in the air and you begin to wonder how much of this the old wooden blind can take. In a matter of minutes, the wieners are devoured (the second gourmet meal of the day) and the burning briquets kicked into the water below. All that remains is the blackened, partially burned plywood floor, still capable of supporting some one hundred and seventy-five pounders, but posing the question of what the fate might be of some real heavyweights. From a hunting standpoint, a charred floor blind is a good omen, since it is indicative of regular and productive use. The less fortunate, the late arrivals, are destined to stand all day long in cold, hip-deep water, content to munch on candy bars and soggy sandwiches.

Dogs, those wonderful and loyal retrievers, while not taboo in the bottoms, are not received enthusiastically by the locals. Many a fine retriever has had his spirit broken trying to cope with this unfamiliar and demanding environment. Once hoisted into the tree blind by his master, he faces the twenty-foot plunge to retrieve the kill. You can't blame a dog, even the best, for displaying some reluctance over this new challenge. Those who make the dive then have to be hoisted once again into the tree blind after each successful shot, a time-consuming if not exhausting exercise. The guides, to show their disdain, seldom offer to lend a hand.

Decoys are used but sparingly in the timber. The thick cover obscures the view of interested ducks, greatly reducing the decoy function. Then too, decoy lines have a way of becoming hopelessly entangled in this country that was dry land only a few hours earlier. Besides, say the guides, "We don't have no room in the boat for them things that don't make no noise."

The duck call is indispensable in Obion country. The sounds emitted from the guides defy description. It's a mixture of crow, loon, and hound dog, a sound certain to chase away marsh or open-water ducks. But it works in the bottoms, echoing off the trees in sharp, piercing staccato tones. Why remains a mystery to me and others fortunate enough to have hunted the bottoms of the Obion for a number of years. We know this type of calling won't work in other parts of the country. Perhaps more than any other single factor, I think it is this calling mystique that lures most of us back to the timber when the little Obion departs its banks.

When the ducks find the flooded bottomland, they usually work all day long, enjoying their newfound source of food after the long flight from the North. As a result, the action in the bottoms, with occasional lulls, is reasonably active from sunup to sundown unless limits are taken early. Normally, one or more blinds are calling at any given time. The better guest callers can contribute, but "your" guide is the payoff. He can seduce the birds better and more frequently than his competitive brethren from the bottoms. Just who is the best enticer is a moot question, and the subject of many a heated debate. It really isn't important, since all hunters get their ducks when the birds hit the green timber.

The hunting pattern, while exciting, is to a degree repetitive. First, get their attention. Then follows three wide circles of the blind, each circle becoming tighter with each pass. The feed-call "chuckle" is mixed in with the welcome call. If the ducks show signs of leaving, a quick tune change to the pleading "highball." Finally, the ducks decide to pitch in, sideslipping through the trees, looking for a place to sit down. The better gunners pick their ducks at treetop levels, since fields of fire and gun mobility are limited at the horizontal or below in the tree blinds. Clean kills are a must. Misses are simply not tolerated. It is duck hunting in its most challenging form.

At sundown the always reliable Reelfoot taxis pick their routes out of the flooded forest. Depending on wind shifts, the average party will be in two or more blinds per day, so the journey homeward is, to say the least, an experience. No compass or celestial navigation, an unknown art; just faith in your guide to get you back to where it all started. I know they get lost, but admit it—never. Somehow, some way, after right turns, left turns, circling, and backtracking, you arrive at a familiar landmark.

The ducks are picked by a hastily prepared fire, entrails tossed into the river. This is not considered pollutive. The rationale is that the turtles and catfish, a source of good food in the Obion country, have to eat.

The hunt is over. Farewells are brief but sincere. Addresses are taken, ostensibly for the purpose of exchanging Christmas cards, but probably more to share the pleasure of the hunt, and relive a warm hunting escape. Now it is time to say goodbye to your guide, the guy who put ten cents in the phone and called you collect. How do you say goodbye to this character who calls ducks out of the sky with a screech that wouldn't earn 157th place in the annual Duck Calling contest held in Stuttgart, Arkansas—a rare kind of American who says, "Hunker down, buddy, them are my ducks," and in a matter of minutes turns a flock from a blind a half-mile distant and brings them into range? He's the salt of the earth, with a rusty old shotgun (double-barrel, of course) that shouldn't fire, but does, and backs you up every time you miss.

Fortunately, you don't have to. He says it for you. "Buddy, we got 'em today. Sorry you can't stay over. They'll be around for a spell. I'll call you next year if they get to the bottoms." Somehow his old truck starts and he disappears into the darkness. You walk to your rented car, change clothes in the chilling darkness, and begin the pensive drive to the airport. Tomorrow you will be home, back to the grind, almost forty-eight hours with no sleep. Your wife, your friends, and your children, on your arrival, shake their heads in a manner that implies some degree of insanity. Only you, who have been to the Obion bottoms, know they are wrong.

It's All Been Good

RUSSELL BENGEL

I just couldn't pick out my most memorable or enjoyable waterfowl hunting trip. Really every one of my hundreds of them is most memorable because on just about every one I was in heaven or as near as I could be.

I started duck hunting in 1912 when I was fourteen years old. With those old liberal bag limits, long seasons of September 15 to December 31, very small numbers of duck hunters and large numbers of ducks, it was really a wonderful time to get started, and I seemed to have the greatest opportunities possible. I lived on the edge of a small town in Michigan. Within easy walking distance of my home were several good duck marshes and one good duck and goose lake. Almost directly in back of our home lived one of the best of duck hunters. He hunted for the sport of hunting and also for the market. In a couple of years I became his regular partner any time that I could go. He hunted some time during the day almost every day during the season. So you can see what a tremendous start I had at duck hunting. We had three duck boats and three sets of about fifty decoys always at different locations. During a few weeks in the summer we were busy carving new decoys and repainting and refinishing the old ones. Later on in the mid-twenties I started going to lakes in northern Michigan, then on to Saskatchewan, Manitoba, northern Ontario, and Lake St. Clair and Lake Erie.

So, when I look back over the many, many days when we picked only drake canvasback, redheads, bluebills, and greenheads, and had great hunting companions and most liberal bag limits, you can see what a difficult job it is to pick one as against another. I recall sitting in a marsh in Jackson County, Michigan, one late evening waiting for my last greenhead and during those last ten or fifteen minutes having two hundred to three hundred prairie chickens flying over to roost, all in small flocks and all within fifty yards of me.

Almost every year while I'm in a hunting camp with a group of hunting companions, each of them tells of one special hunt that stands out among all others. My most successful ones I don't like to talk about. Since 1925 or 1926 I have shot ninety-one banded ducks and five Canada geese banded by Jack Miner. Most of the ducks were banded by the Fish and Wildlife Service, about a dozen by private banders, including two by Gar Wood.

Now if I just had to pick my best and most memorable duck hunt, it would have to be a hunt back in 1924 when I think I got two bluebills, but indirectly out of that trip a few months later I had the opportunity to meet the greatest girl in the world, Ruth Ingram, who has been since 1926 Mrs. Russell Bengel.

Jason

GAYLORD DONNELLEY

One of my most memorable waterfowling experiences centers on a magnificent golden retriever, Little Hill Jason. Jason was imported from England by our friends Bobby and Betty Pirie of Chicago about 1940. They placed him for training with the dean of American trainers, Martin Hogan. An Irishman with extensive game-keeping experience in England, he was brought in the twenties to Barrington, Illinois, by Thomas Howell to manage his kennel of retrievers.

My wife Dorothy and I judged Jason in a number of retriever trials and observed him in others, all with Martin Hogan as handler. Martin was such a superb marker and handler that we never did know whether Jason had a nose or any natural hunting ability. We kept these doubts confidential in our judges' notebooks and private conversations, because of our warm and close friendship with Martin and the Piries.

In the summer of 1941, Bobby Pirie was transferred to New York by his company, Carson Pirie Scott and Company, and the Piries decided that Jason was not for New York City. Imagine our surprise and discomfort when they offered him as a gift because we were the only people whom they felt happy about having their treasure!

Our worst fears were realized on a duck and upland-bird hunt in Saskatchewan in the fall of 1941. Jason even stepped on a crippled duck, which squawked, and didn't smell him. He was useless on a moonlit shoot around a pothole. Martin Hogan was incredulous, and believing the dog was ill, urged us to take him to two elderly brother veterinarians near my office who were known for their thorough checkups. After three days and many tests, a four-page, single-spaced report indicated that Jason indeed had a stomach condition that could impair his scenting ability. After the indicated medication, he went on later that fall to turn in a superb performance on the duck marsh and in the pheasant field. He was a fine pet, of which we had several at the time, and a favorite of old and young.

The scene shifts in the fall of 1942 to Norfolk, Virginia, where Air Group Nine was based at the Naval Air Station for training and to await the commissioning and battle readiness of our carrier *U.S.S. Essex*. Back Bay and Currituck Sound were well known for their excellent water-fowling, and we hastened to make arrangements for each and every Wednesday of the season, that being our day off. Unfortunately, some shoots had to be canceled because bad weather grounded the squadron on other days of the week, and no flying time could be lost.

One Wednesday, I went with a squadron mate of mine, Francis B. Wadelton, Jr., to a venerable duck club on Currituck Sound. Before dawn we were left in a blind with lunch, Jason, and decoys (no boat), to be picked up at some undetermined time in the afternoon. The weather was pleasant, and the duck hunting fair, but about noon half a gale sprung up, fortunately to our rear. Not too long after, four Canadas beat their way to our decoys. Wad and I knocked down three. The first retrieve was an easy one. The wind had blown the second one about a hundred yards beyond the blocks. Jason had marked the falls well, and required no urging to go for the third. By the time he reached it, it had floated some three hundred yards or more downwind, almost out of sight to us high in the blind. When he turned toward the blind with his goose, the waves were breaking over his head, but he never wavered. That was a picture I will never forget. And to think of our early doubts!

His keen hunting desire was never in question. The next summer he was driven almost wild by the sea ducks skimming the surf along Virginia Beach. Unable to stand it longer, one afternoon he took out to sea on his own. The Coast Guard, who had come to know him well, conducted a search to no avail. Anxiety gave way in hours to gloom. After dark Jason appeared at the house—wet, bedraggled, worn out, but with a dead fish in his mouth!

Sad to relate, many breedings to various bitches failed to develop an offspring at all comparable to the sire, and Dorothy and I gave up on goldens, with Jason a wonderful memory.

A Day for Ducking

A. H. (ROCK) ROHLFING

I grew up in Missouri, near the Mississippi River, during the Depression, when the better stores would break a box and sell you five shotgun shells in a brown paper bag. The idea was to see how many ducks you could get for your five shells. The idea of using ducks per box as a yardstick of shooting ability never occurred to us. We never had a whole box of shells.

My steady hunting companion in those days was a schoolmate named Blaine Ulmer. He was, and is, one of the finest wing and all-around shots I've ever known. We grew up together in those simple days hunting ducks from Mississippi sandbars and quail in the rolling blue hills of the Ozarks, where our leader was a native ridgerunner named Roy Adams, an uncanny shot on quail with an ancient Winchester Model 11.

We were a pretty unsophisticated lot in those days, making our own blinds from driftwood and using any decoys we could beg, borrow, or steal for duck hunting and shooting quail over a succession of highly suspect dogs, including one collie, who actually performed quite well.

But many years ago the pursuit of an elusive fame and fortune brought me to New England and left Blaine in Missouri, where he did, indeed, prosper. But old habits endure, and I transferred my attention to ducks that move down the salt bays of Connecticut and to the magnificent thunderer of the Northeast, the ruffed grouse. And I tried, Lord, how I tried, to make Blaine understand that no matter how good his shooting was, mine was even better.

Finally, business did bring him to New York during duck season, and I was able to get him to sample my newfound delight in shooting ducks in the time-honored New England manner.

In some ways it resembles our boyhood approach, except that we now buy shells by the case, not the bag, and that offshore rocks a mile in the salt water take the place of sandbars. Fortunately for both of us, our first trip out was a howling success. Our guide, Frank Dolan of Guilford, Connecticut, put us on the lee side of a tidal rock about a mile from shore, spread about 120 decoys in front of us, and retired to a distance of about half a mile in his properly named boat, the *Wild Duck*.

We cleaned up. On the way in, after helping pick up decoys and with the sun not much more than an hour old, Blaine said that he wanted to come again next year. How often have we all heard that? But, of course, I urged him to come again and lied to an old friend when I told him that the shooting was always that good, only sometimes better.

He was as good as his word, however, and a year later found the two of us sorting our gear in my study in preparation for another day on the rocks. Filled with the spirit of the occasion, I called Dolan at home to reaffirm a meeting time and place, only to learn that we were to meet at his home instead of the dock. Most unusual, but with good reason.

Below his house lies a large tidal marsh cut by drainage canals and natural creeks, and on that particular evening Dolan had noticed large bunches of black duck and widgeon pitching into the marsh. This, coupled with a freshening wind that was making the open water start to turn over, had changed his plans. We would go inside and shoot a blind he had in the marsh. Okay.

The next morning the three of us stood in the halflight of a coldly breaking day. Two things stand out in my mind. It was the sixth of December and the thermometer stood at six below zero. Cold, you might say. We stood on the bank of the main drainage canal for the marsh right where the rushing water was running out to join a falling tide. At our feet was a tiny plastic boat that was supposed to take us the two hundred yards or so upstream to the blind.

Somewhat tentatively, Blaine climbed into the bow, put his shotgun alongside, and attempted to steady the boat. I was next, and I stepped into the middle of the boat, put my shotgun to my left, and tried to help Blaine stop the rocking of our little craft.

This left only Dolan, and he stepped into the stern as the first two of us sat trying to keep the boat upright. I didn't like the whole thing one darn bit, but before any serious second thoughts could cross my mind, it happened. Dolan hit the boat squarely, but the nasty little beast simply wasn't up to holding all of us. With a swift, silent twist, the boat turned upside down, dumping the three of us into twenty feet of icy, rushing water.

It's peculiar how your mind reacts at such a time. I saw the boat was going to roll, and I pitched my shotgun over my head onto the bank. When I hit the water, my first thought was, "It's warm." Of course it was. The air temperature was minus six degrees Fahrenheit, which made the water a lot warmer. There was no struggle, however, as the boat rolled toward the shore and dumped the three of us on an underwater ledge about five feet below the surface and well above the maximum channel depth.

With no regret, I saw the outgoing tide and current carry that mean little craft out to sea as the three of us climbed out of the water and stood on the bank. I retrieved my shotgun, admired the new dents in the stock, and felt my clothes starting to stiffen up.

Right at this point, sensible people would have called it a day, but we weren't sensible people, we were duck hunters. Dolan disappeared for about twenty-five minutes and re-emerged, forcing a pounding boat of respectable size through some mighty rough water but aimed at our landing. He had long oyster tongs aboard and found his shotgun and Blaine's in about fifteen minutes. These he checked out by the simple expedient of pouring the water from the barrel and firing a shot through each. It worked for him, but I don't recommend it.

You guessed it. Blaine, Frank, and I went duck hunting. We got a limit of blacks and widgeon by ten o'clock and, by that time, our clothes had frozen solid. We were pretty well frozen solid as well, and I came away from the adventure with five frostbitten fingers that still remind me, on nippy mornings, of our near miss.

But times change. That was nearly a quarter of a century ago. Blaine and I are grown gray and thin on top. Frank is now a most successful restaurateur; and although he talks of going "ducking" again, he never does. He does send a free drink to my table when my wife and I dine at his place.

But although more than forty years separate us from that sandbar in the Mississippi, Blaine and I still span the miles to shoot together. This year, we're going to meet at Dick Shorts' place south of Dover, Delaware, and have a go at the geese. We'll get 'em, too, because they're there; but we've eliminated one problem. We won't get dumped in the water. It's awfully hard to turn a concrete field pit upside down.

Alaska '69

JOHN A. RUTHVEN

I have been on a lot of duck and goose hunts in my life, but the one that stands out as the most unusual is my trip to Hooper Bay, Alaska, in the spring of 1969. This was different because it was spring, and, of course, spring shooting has not been permitted for some fifty years. This was a scientific trip, being carried out under the auspices of the University of Cincinnati. Another wildlife artist and I were sent to procure a specimen of a male and female of each of the eider ducks that occur in Alaska.

We flew from Cincinnati to Hooper Bay via Chicago, Anchorage, and Bethel, Alaska. Since there are no accommodations in this area we were prepared to camp out as well as fix our own meals, consisting of dried food and anything that we could get off the land. This trip was to last two weeks; we were prepared to stay in this area that long because of the tremendous flocks of waterfowl, and the plane wouldn't return for that period.

We arrived early in the morning, landing on the gravel beach near the town of Hooper Bay, which consisted of some two hundred Eskimos. All of our gear was unloaded—tents, guns, ammo, food supplies, and cameras. Unbeknown to us, we had a welcoming committee. It seems that one of the biggest social events in Hooper Bay is watching the biweekly plane come in. We were asked if we needed a ride to town by one of the leading citizens, Mr. Francis Bell. The only trouble was that he had room in his car for our baggage and nothing else. It seems that the arrival of a plane is such a social event that nearly the whole town turns out to get a look at any new arrivals. Consequently, Mr. Bell had his whole family along, making it mandatory for Bill, my artist friend, and me to ride outside on the bumper.

During the course of our ride, we couldn't help noticing the myriads of waterfowl that were flying overhead—ducks and geese by the hundreds and of almost every description. Our excitement grew by the minute as we contemplated the search for the eiders the next morning.

Our unexpected host not only gave us the ride into town but offered us accommodations in an extra house that he owned. This was a happy surprise, until we realized that the house was really a large shack that he used to store seal meat. It was unheated, of course, and most of the windows were gone. But the worst thing was the smell! Believe me, there are few things that smell worse than old seal meat. We couldn't refuse his offer, so we spent the next two weeks using the house as our head-quarters. We didn't realize at the time that the smell of old seal is almost impossible to extract from clothing. Consequently on our flight back to the lower 48 everyone gave us a wide berth.

Early the next morning we were off on our scientific hunt. Our newfound friend and host, Francis Bell, insisted upon acting as our guide without pay. As we proceeded out across Hooper Bay in a home-made boat, I couldn't help thinking how it must have been in the early days of duck hunting when spring shooting was the order of the day. With every splash of a wave, we were kicking up flock after flock of scoters—all three species, surf, common, and white-winged. Overhead, brant and white-fronted geese were heading for their feeding ground. My mind again turned to the past, thinking how easy it must have been to obtain waterfowl because of the multitudes.

Upon reaching the opposite shore we noticed large feeding flocks of old-squaws in full spring plumage, the males sporting their long plumelike tails. After nosing into the mud we all disembarked—I say "all" because our guide had brought his family along to collect bird eggs for their larder! First his wife and three kids (the youngest was four), then Bill and myself.

We immediately set up our blind while the family went off egging. Francis Bell was an excellent caller. Since we were only interested in eiders, we didn't shoot at everything that came along, but Francis did. Eskimos, as you know, still hunt in the spring and shoot whatever they want. Francis told us, though, that he would not shoot a swan because they were protected.

Just before lunch we were able to get our first spectacled eider, a beautiful male. I immediately made color notes and took closeup photos of the flesh parts for a future painting. When the rest of the Bell family returned from their egg hunt we all sat around a small fire and had lunch. Bill and I had beef jerky while our hosts had boiled eggs and dried seal meat. If they were lucky they found an embryo in the egg and considered it a delicacy. Francis said that the eggs "had people in them."

During the course of the next two weeks, we were able to collect almost all of the ducks that we sought plus getting a chance to take closeup color photos of the ones that Francis shot. One afternoon, while in a blind along a small creek, we called in a beautiful specklebelly. While Bill and I were admiring the bird, our friend quickly cut off one of the feet and started to chew on it! Eskimos relish the feet of ducks and geese. Also the fresh fat of duck is eaten like butter.

On our last day, while heading home across the bay, Bill spotted the only eider that we didn't have, a Steller's. After much planning we were able to call it into shooting range and filled out our list of birds.

Before beaching our leaking boat, a large flock of whistling swans flew overhead, signaling a final note to a trip that involved more water-fowl than I have ever seen in my life.

Mas Cartuchos, Por Favor

WILLIAM E. DAVIS

When Keith Russell, the old Señor, asked me to write a chapter for "the book," it occurred to me how many times—after one of our days together on the water after billfish or on a trout stream or shooting doves out among the cactus and mesquite—over the end-of-the-day martinis he'd give me an often weary but always happy grin and drawl, "Hell, Señor, we've just lived another chapter for the book." As I've explained in the introduction Señor Russell asked me to write for this book—a most flattering request—it was really from that expression that his determination to publish "the book" was born.

"Write a chapter on your most memorable waterfowl shooting experience!" The "most memorable" part is a bit tough, since Señor Russell and I have shot waterfowl together all over the U.S.A. east of the Mississippi, in Canada, and in most of the better spots in Mexico, and that's a helluva lot of places. Remember, Señor, when you were invited to judge the World Duck Calling Championships at Stuttgart, and I told you that I doubted you could tell a highball, comeback, or feeding chuckle from a flatulating mallard? It was a great trip, though, even though the ducks were still up in the flooded fields of southern Illinois and didn't arrive in Arkansas until a week after we'd left for home.

Or how about the day down at Cabo San Lucas, Baja, Mexico, when we simultaneously hooked striped marlin and those two magnificent fish greyhounded for a couple hundred yards across the water behind the boat, side by side, for about twenty jumps? Man, that was one for the book!

Or how about all the whitewing doves we've shot together on the Baja, out of Puerto Vallarta and Culiacán and so many, many places in that happy and romantic land of Mexico. Or, speaking of Culiacán, how about the thousands upon thousands of pintail we saw on the Pichiguila Marshes just outside that city and the awe and thrill a couple old Midwestern boys felt when, for the first time, we held those beautiful red cinnamon teal in our hands?

Or how about that drive before dawn over the mountains out of Puerto Vallarta when our guide thought he was Barney Oldfield and for the two hours it took to make the trip ignored the brakes on the Volkswagen Safari and negotiated every damned hairpin turn with the accelerator jammed hard against the floorboard? But once over the mountain and back on flat ground, we really had a day for the book. Remember how first we had a great shoot on both whitewing and mourning doves—and then we went into a grove of really tall coconut palms and took the blue rock pigeons as they burned across us over the tree tops, fantastically fast, tough pass shooting at about maximum range even for the loads of high-brass seven-and-a-halfs. I'm a little sorry we shot that big iguana on the hike back to the car, but it was about the only chance we'd ever have to inspect one up close. I'll never forget that godawful, butt-bustin' drive back to Puerto Vallarta after the shooting, where, upon arriving, Manuel took us to his home and proceeded to pour out straight shots of tequila with the pinch of salt and slice of lime. Our good wives never did figure out how we managed to get so clobbered so fast.

Or, closer to home, how about some of those great mallard shoots we've had on Walpole Island on Lake St. Clair with our buddies who've helped write "the book"?

But enough of reminiscing, as pleasant as it is to turn over again all the old and warm memories. It's time to make good on my promise to you to scribble out my recollections of the trip among them all that, on reflection, I'd say was the most memorable and satisfying.

To me, Club de Patos "had it all"—and I mean all of everything! You already know this because you were there, but for your readers, Club de Patos is located at the little village of Sisal on the Yucatán Peninsula of Mexico, at which club our wives, by comparison to some of the really grim places we've hauled them on our hunting and fishing trips, thought they'd died and gone to heaven. While we were out shooting ducks in the mornings, they lazed around the swimming pool on padded chaises soaking up the sun with waiters shagging margaritas to them and, now and again, a banana daiquiri. The club has, as I recall, twelve double rooms, clean, comfortable, and looking for all the world like the typical Holiday Inn. The club was the realized dream of Bob Crawford and other friends of his from Atlanta, Georgia, who operated it along with Mexican partners.

Upon our arrival, we were ushered to the main clubhouse, an attractive adobe building somewhat larger than need be—with the surplus space dedicated to the bar and cocktail lounge. Beyond the bar is the light and airy dining room, and off the bar is the equipment room with its guns, shells, boots, and other hunting gear. Down in a field in front of the clubhouse is a regulation skeet field, about which I plan further and extensive discourse.

Immediately upon arrival, and while the staff was depositing the luggage in our rooms and seeing to the care and feeding of our shotguns, we were ushered to the lounge and served the usual and appropriate drinks "on the house." No sooner were we seated and enjoying a tall cold one than a voice boomed out, "Davis, you old S.O.B., what the hell are you doing here? And I hope that's your wife with you, 'cause you're caught!" There stood Bill Custer, eminent junk dealer, Ducks Unlimited supporter, and old high school classmate, who, when run out of Cleveland, made it as far as Toledo in search of fame and fortune. Bill had come down to the Yucatán with several other Toledo couples to shoot ducks and quail.

So much for the physical attractions of Club de Patos. They leave little to be desired and certainly qualified as far as my statement that the club "has it all." The next "all" has to be the food, a subject close to the hearts of both of us. In order to ensure a top-notch table, meat and fresh produce are flown in from Miami every day or two. The result is an excellent and varied menu featuring native fish and good old U.S. cornfed prime steaks and roast beef. Ducks are served once a week, and the chef is a master with the orange sauce. I know you will recall dinner the night Custer and the Toledo group opted for quail rather than duck. They returned to the club early in the afternoon with a full basket of quail. The chef performed his magic, and that night all guests dined in gourmet style.

It came as quite a surprise to learn that the native quail of this area in Yucatán is the same good old bobwhite we have up here in the States. Due to relatively few predators, excellent cover, plenty of food, and little hunting pressure, their populations far exceed anything to be found in the States—or anywhere else in the world as far as I know.

By way of illustration, the Toledo group were driven about an hour from the club to the area chosen for the day's hunt. The club keeps two competent pointers for use of its quail-hunting guests. In any event, in a two- or three-hour hunt, Custer and gang put up some forty coveys. There just was no point in hunting down the singles as each covey was broken up. Even if it were not for the great duck hunting, the quail shooting alone would make the trip to Club de Patos worthwhile.

However, ducks were what we came for, and ducks are what I'll tell you about now.

The game laws in Yucatán are unique, the duck limit being ten birds on weekdays and twenty birds on Saturday and Sunday. Naturally, Señor, we shot Friday, Saturday, and Sunday.

The typical day at the club starts at two A.M. with the head guide whistling reveille at your window and then pounding on your door, just to be sure you got the message. Then to the dining room where you can pretty much have whatever your heart desires for breakfast—bacon and eggs, pancakes, melon, just about anything short of bagels and lox! As you know, Señor, we usually opted for orange juice (lightly laced with tequila), bacon, eggs, toast, jam, and the best coffee in the world— hot, strong, and black.

After the breakfast fertility ritual, the guests pile into jeep station wagons for the trip to their respective shooting areas.

Now, most of us are accustomed to questing for ducks in a marsh. In no way do the shooting spots of Club de Patos resemble a marsh. You put out your decoys in what might best be described as a mangrove lagoon. The shooting area is about fifty miles long and maybe four to five miles wide. It is separated from the Gulf of Mexico by a strip of higher land that averages not more than fifty yards wide. When a good blow comes off the Gulf, it is flooded by seawater, hence, the lagoon water is brackish. The water in the lagoon, I'd say, averages about a foot deep, the bottom being firm white sand. Apparently the attraction to the birds is a very tough seaweed that densely roots in the sand. On the surface floats a water plant that closely resembles duck wort. As far as the ducks are concerned, it must be meat and potatoes.

The jeeps with their loads of hunters proceed in the dark along the strip of sand separating the lagoon from the Gulf, dropping off from the caravan one by one as they reach the place along the lagoon edge where their guides are awaiting them. As you will recall, Señor, said jeep ride is not among the many virtues of Club de Patos. The jeep track along the sandy strip is forty-five miles of ruts, potholes, and other problems of geography, all designed to destroy the human spine. You will further recall that first morning we were assigned to shoot at the far end—the full forty-five-mile treatment, naturally.

Finally, we arrived at the end of the strip and were dropped off along the edge of the mangroves in that absolute darkness that just precedes the dawn. At this point, out of the underbrush emerged our two Indian guides. We never did figure out how in hell the guides managed to get all the way down there at that hour of the morning.

These Indians are the descendants of the Mayans who at one time flourished in Yucatán and down through Central America, as the absolute rulers of this vast piece of real estate. They developed an advanced culture, as anyone who has ever visited the ruins of their great cities at Uxmal and Chichén Itzá can testify.

Our Indians did not speak a word of English, but we always managed to be understood with our limited Spanish and plenty of sign language.

An aluminum flat-bottomed square-ended boat was pulled up on shore, with a canoe fashioned from a hollowed-out log lying beside it. The Indian who turned out to be the chief guide loaded us in the john boat and proceeded to punt us out through the mangrove clumps in the dark. The other Indian, standing in his hollowed log, disappeared into the night. From time to time the water would become too shallow, and we would climb out and wade a bit. This was no problem, since the water was barely ankle deep and the bottom was good firm white sand.

After perhaps a half-hour of poling and wading, we came to a large lagoon surrounded on all sides by mangroves growing up fifty to sixty feet above the water on their stiltlike roots. Just as dawn was breaking, we lashed the flat-bottomed boat securely to a network of mangrove roots to make a perfectly stable shooting platform, several dozen inflatable rubber decoys were set out, and brush was cut and pinned down in the sand to complete our blind. We were set to sample some of the fastest wingshooting the world can offer, the thousands upon thousands of blue-winged teal that winter in these Yucatán lagoons. We had heard the stories of burning hands on hot gun barrels, of constantly being caught by the next flight of birds with an empty gun in your hand. Here we were in teal heaven, set up in the first light of dawn and ready.

For the first hour we stayed ready, since there were no teal in that particular corner of teal heaven. Anticipation had given way to panic when our Indian friend in the dugout canoe, whom we had not seen since we shoved off in the dark, came poking around the corner.

After a bit of Mayan-type conversation, the boat was untied, decoys were picked up, and off we went through the mangroves again. For perhaps twenty minutes our guide poled us down narrow waterways walled in by the tropic greenery until at last we came out upon another lagoon much like the first one, an open circular area about thirty-five yards across. The big difference was that edges of this lagoon were rimmed with floating feathers—literally the whole circumference was delineated by a border of feathers. We could only conjecture how many ducks must have filled this bit of water, preening throughout the night, to account for this unbelievable amount of down and feathers. We also then realized that the job of the second Indian in his dugout was to move around the area scouting out the lagoons the teal were using.

In short order, the boat was lashed tightly into the mangrove roots, blind material was built up around the front of the boat, decoys were set—and all hell broke loose!

We had no sooner loaded our guns when, as though someone had turned on a spigot, teal were coming into the lagoon before us, singles, doubles, bunches, diving and twisting from all directions and in all directions. There was no sitting down between shots. You stood, gun at the ready, as if you were about to call for a target in a skeet field.

Within minutes, we were yelling at the guide, "*Mas cartuchos, por favor—mas cartuchos!*" We'd hold open the pocket on our camouflage jackets, and he'd dump in the shells. We quickly learned to shout "*Muerto*" when a duck hit the water dead and "*No muerto!*" when a cripple needed another shot on the water. I remember shooting a glance at you when you yelped upon having grabbed the barrels on your Browning to break it for loading and burned your hand. The limit that day was twenty apiece, and we had our forty teal dead on the water in about an hour and a half. I still can't believe the number of ducks in that kamikaze flight of teal or the intensity of the shooting. Shoot, load, "*Mas cartuchos*," shoot a cripple, and load again. It simply never let up.

At this point, I feel a word or two is in order as to the conservation aspects of duck shooting in Mexico. Obviously, if there were as many duck shooters in Mexico as we have in the States, the resource could not take this sort of pressure. However, the average Mexican cannot afford the cost of shells to shoot birds, ducks, doves, or quail. A Mexican will buy four or five shells, and these will not be shot up for a few mouthfuls of meat. His game is the small deer that abounds throughout

Mexico and that will provide a week's supply of meat for his family at the cost of one shell. You'll recall that we stopped short of a limit the third and last day—just because we felt we'd killed enough and, perhaps, our consciences were beginning to hurt a bit.

Another thing I like about shooting in Mexico is that no game goes to waste. Excess birds are distributed to and gratefully received by the poor people in surrounding villages, and Club de Patos regularly sends birds into Merida, where they are dropped off at orphanages and like institutions. Remember, too, that in many parts of Mexico doves and blue rock pigeons are regarded as vermin, since they are so numerous and do tremendous damage in the grain fields.

The next two days of shooting never quite attained the fever pitch of that first wild morning, but by any standards they were two damned fine mornings of duck shooting.

Shortly after noon each day we would be back at the club for a martini or two before lunch, sipped while lying on a chaise around the pool after a refreshing swim to cool off and get the dust out of our hair. Like all meals at the club, lunch was always more than adequate.

I'm sure you recall, Señor, that it was after martinis and lunch one day that we conceived that great and immortal sporting event, the Club de Patos Annual International Invitational Skeet and Margarita Tournament.

We first convinced the various guests at the club as well as Bob Crawford that just because they'd been up and about since two A.M. was no reason for a siesta. Whereupon about fifteen of us walked down to the skeet field for a hundred-bird event. Due to the heat of the day and the natural thirst induced thereby, Señor Crawford had one of the bartenders shagging half-gallon pitchers of ice-cold margaritas from the club lounge.

The first few rounds of skeet proceeded along pretty much in regulation style. However, as additional pitchers of margaritas arrived, the ground rules took on twists never thought of by the governing body of the National Skeet Shooting Association—for example, the last round was shot while seated flat on the ground.

In any event, it was a great, if somewhat hairy, afternoon. In memory of which, if this contribution of mine to "the book" should induce any reader to sample the delights of Club de Patos, hanging on the wall above the bar he will find the engraved plaque that you and I, Señor, had made upon our return home and shipped to the club, the name of each year's champion to be inscribed thereon. The first champion, naturally, being Guillermo Ernesto Davis.

So, Señor, all in all, I still feel the Club de Patos caper was the best so far. But who knows the delights yet to be tasted in that sunny land we both so love.

Vaya con Dios, muchos patos, y mas cartuchos!

Five-Minute Shoot in Canada

D. C. GROFF

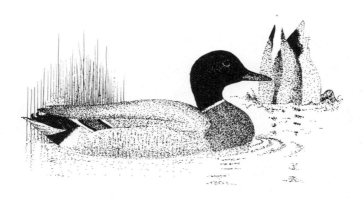

Have you ever been within range of five thousand greenheads at one time? Well, I was in 1975, and let me tell you, it was really exciting.

Four of us were out for the day near Ste. Rose du Lac, Manitoba, some 150 miles northwest of Winnipeg.

Usually all the birds have gone south by this time of year, and the ice on the lakes and marshes was two inches thick, but there were drowned fields of swathed barley in the area, and the drake mallards had it so good they were reluctant to leave.

Anyway, it was a beautifully warm day and there were tens of thousands of them shuttling back and forth between the fields and open water in the middle of a small lake (kept open by their body heat), but they were flying high, and we weren't doing too well.

Along about four-thirty, an hour before sunset at this time of year, I decided to inspect a marshy area surrounded by round-stem bullrushes I had seen a few birds settle into.

After walking a quarter-mile through frozen marsh growth and over ice, lo and behold, there was a hole fifty by ninety yards that was wall-to-wall ducks.

A few strays came over that were much too tempting, then all hell broke loose as they took to the air in every direction—certainly five thousand within range at one time, but not for long. Needless to say, I managed to fill out the bag limit for our party in those exciting five minutes.

Shoot the S.O.B.

WILLIAM H. EDMISTON

This tale is about a very close friend of mine, "J," an avid duck hunter with whom I have hunted for many years, and his beloved yellow Labrador retriever, "G." It involves an area at the western end of Lake Erie, namely a famous marsh by the name of Nielsen's. The story also concerns the camaraderie among a group of people that usually begins with drinks and dinner at the Island House Hotel in Port Clinton, Ohio. Port Clinton is not known as the climate capital of the world nor as America's playground; however, during duck season, it becomes quite a popular place.

The action ordinarily begins at approximately five o'clock in the evening. We go down to the bar, usually pre-dressed for tomorrow's hunt. Depending on how fast you can shut off your alarm clock, you might show up for cocktails in a pair of waders or a pair of hip boots, and, most certainly, with your great friend and companion, your Labrador retriever. Sometimes you can get away with having martinis and dinner in the dining room without being thrown out, but then again, when the owner decides to take a head count, he will politely ask that you return the dog to the room, which was the case this particular evening. After dinner, the conversation usually turns to how many ducks you killed the day before, how many flight ducks were down, whether the big freeze will end the season next week, and where you are going to shoot the next morning.

After numerous scotches and three or four Grand Marniers, the favorite line of the subject of this story—who, as I said, is my great and good friend— is, "We'll kill a hundred by eight A.M." The group then generally proceeds to the Avalon Night Club, where more drinks and camaraderie are enjoyed with some of the local inhabitants. Then most of us return back to the Island House for a restful night's sleep prior to the next day's hunt.

We would normally leave a wakeup call for sometime around four o'clock, when we assemble our equipment and our dogs and go down to the local restaurant—known as Grundy's or the Greasy Spoon—and have breakfast.

This particular morning we gathered, gulped our O.J. and eggs, and headed out to Number 1 blind on the north side of Nielsen's Marsh. It was black dark. We put the punt boat in the water, the dogs got into the boat, and we rowed out to the blind to set up our decoys. After all of these early-morning chores were completed, we got into the blind, lit the stove, and pulled down the lid, anticipating a great hunt.

At this point we suddenly realized that one of our buddies was absent. After approximately twenty minutes of discussion of what could possibly have happened, the birds flew and we got into a few of them and suddenly we lost interest in the fate of our missing companion.

Then, at about ten A.M., we heard the cry of a man who was desperately in trouble. It sounded like "Help me! Help me! I'm drowning!" Well, realizing full well that there was nobody else in the marsh but the two of us, we could not figure this out until suddenly it dawned on us that it possibly could be our friend who might be taking a short cut into the marsh. We placed the noise and, crossing over two canals, we spotted our third companion. He had apparently realized he was late in showing up, parked his car on the highway, got his dog, G, who, in my opinion and that of many others, was one of the best marsh dogs who ever lived, and thought he could wade a very deep canal. Air was trapped in his waders, which became buoyant, and his feet were floating and he was splashing desperately to keep his head above water. The dog, in the meantime, was swimming around him, barking, and not trying to help him in any way. The only thing we could do was to go back and get a punt boat, because of the depth of the water, and paddle out to get him, which we did.

However, as we approached his dog, who presumably is man's best friend, he began to attack us and would not let us get near his master. Apparently the dog had decided that he was going to let his master drown. We could only surmise later that J either (1) didn't feed him, (2) was mean to him and beat him, or (3) couldn't shoot ducks.

Well, anyway, after we had made several unsuccessful rescue

attempts and had been driven back each time by the protective efforts of J's pride and joy, J, who by now thought he might be going down for the count, in desperation and reaction to Nature's oldest law, that of self-survival, in great anguish yelled for all he was worth, "For God's sake, shoot the son of a bitch and get me out of here!"

Fortunately, it wasn't necessary, and we finally got him out of the water. The really funny part of it is that when we asked him why he was late, which he had never been before in his life, he said he had left a call for five A.M. at the Island House and apparently arrived back in his room after the wakeup call had already been made.

After having retrieved our friend and got him in the blind, with his dog—who finally realized that we were not hostile and whom we tied to the back end of the blind—all of us settled down, looking forward to a good afternoon's shoot. Before long, however, due to a rapid breakfast and a lot of coffee, J found it necessary to get out of the blind to take care of certain personal duties.

Well, from time immemorial boys have been boys, and it was time to have a little fun with him. It was a great opportunity to add insult to injury. So we—and this is an old trick which I wouldn't recommend to too many people—stripped his gun of his three shells, took a knife, cut the shot portion, and reloaded the gun. Then he got back into the blind in great anticipation of killing some ducks and we said, "J, the next flight that comes over, you take 'em."

So we sat down to wait, and sure enough, here came some nice flight mallards. They worked the pond while we talked to them. We kept the lid down in great anticipation, and J was sitting there shivering with excitement. Suddenly we popped the lid, he stood up and put three shots out to a duck that was coming head into the wind right over our blocks, and the duck flew off.

We said, "Shoot the son of a bitch."

And he said, "Goddamit, I did, but he flew away."

EDMISTON'S EPICUREAN EPIC
SLICED DUCK BREASTS

Slice duck breasts horizontally. It should be possible to obtain three slices from a mallard or a black. Heat butter, finely chopped onion, and a small amount of red wine, or sherry, to a depth of about one-quarter inch in a frying pan. Do not bring to boil. Sauté breasts for one minute (or more to taste) on each side. Pour melted-butter mixture over breasts and serve separately from the following sauce: equal parts melted currant jelly, ketchup (yes, ketchup), and red wine or sherry.

[68   ]

A Bad Day in a Blind

JOHN B. PUTNAM, JR.

I sat dreamin' over a cigarette, all doubled up to keep warm,
The decoys out front a-bobbin', and jumpin' 'round before the storm.
My old choke-bored fowler was leanin', 'gainst t'other side of the blind,
And with teal, geese, or mallard, of better days on my mind.
Then sudden, that old growl of wings, come driftin' down from up there,
And my how I jumped and caught inside, you'da thought I'd heard a
    bear.
With a lung fulla smoke, I froze stiff, way outa reach o' my gun,
And watched 'em through my eyebrows; go a-shootin' by, one by one.
Like three green bats outa hell, they went out to the east,
Full-breasted young mallards, damn it! I shoulda had one at least.

Half-hearted I thought, "They'll circle," but they'd been low and looked
    good at my stool,
Off into the east they kept goin'; that head drake warn't nobody's fool!
I stood up and watched 'em again, and cussin' myself back and forth,
When I caught somethin' outa the corner of my eye, a stray swingin'
    outa the north.
He spotted my blocks and then careful like, circled around kinda high.
He kept right on circlin' though. This is one that ain't a-goin' by.
I guess they looked all right to him, 'cause on his second trip 'round,
He set his wings 'n' fanned out his tail and pitched on down at the sound.

I come up, my cheek on cold steel, and he flared with a twist of his wing,
M'old left barrel jumped back, he got his harp and went to a sing.
It was a long, cold day in that old blind, and no more ducks came by,
I know some folk who woulda said, next time I ain't goin' to try.
But for those three I saw, and for that stray a-lyin' in my lap,
I woulda set right there an' froze to death. Happy as hell at that.

Captain Putnam was a fighter pilot in World War II. He wrote this poem in the fall of 1943 while on a duck-hunting trip and was killed in combat in Europe in 1944.

Guns and Games

DALE E. WHITESELL

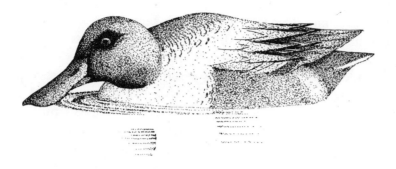

T his has to do with the problem I have had recently in keeping the firearms I use in my waterfowl hunting.

The first instance of the loss of my gun was in connection with a major dinner here in the Midwest, when one of the Ducks Unlimited officers in the area stuck ten raffle tickets in my pocket and although we normally don't accept gifts or prizes if we win them, as staff members, I thought, well, there's no risk of winning anything as there were well over seventy-five hundred tickets sold that night. But I won three prizes. The first one I gave away to one of the punters of the man who gave me the ticket; the next prize, decoys, I gave to another punter at the club where some of the members attending the dinner belonged. But the third one I wanted to keep, and also it was more or less demanded that I keep it once we saw what it was: a Model 870 20-gauge, which was a perfect match for the gun that had been given to me by the game protectors and fish and game biologists for the state of Ohio when I left there as chief, just before coming to Ducks Unlimited.

I took the gun and left that particular community that night, and the next morning headed down the road to another D.U. fund-raising dinner before returning to Chicago. To that dinner I was taking along a gun from the state committee where I had been the night before that this particular local committee could auction off, a Model 1100. So I knew they had no other gun.

The event began on schedule about seven o'clock. I was sitting between one of D.U.'s top officers, a man who was later to become president of D.U., and the director of the state Department of Natural Resources at what appeared to them, as I found out later, to be an opportune time. They asked to be able to use a key to my room as the local public restroom facilities were closed. Being rather large in stature and, in this instance, equally dumb, I let them have the key to my room; twenty minutes hadn't passed when they started the auction off with an interesting item. I listened to the auction for perhaps several minutes before it dawned on me that they were auctioning off an 870 and not the 1100. I wondered, "Where did they get it?" Well, then I recognized the gun case that was being auctioned off too. Both the gun and case were brand new, but I recognized the case as one that I had purchased that very afternoon down the street from the hotel so that I could properly carry my new gun back to Chicago. So, before I could even utter a word of protest, the gun was auctioned off and sold. That is the story of gun and case number one.

Naturally, as I entered into that fall's hunting season, I was minus a gun; I had looked forward to using the 20-gauge.

Interestingly enough, the officer of D.U. who had been sitting at the table next to me at the dinner, whom I thought had masterminded this bit of deception, showed up in my office, bearing a gift—and, of course, it was a 20-gauge shotgun, much like the one which had been auctioned off. I was appreciative of the gesture and realized they had had an entertaining time with my gun.

This gun episode was a favorite discussion around dinner tables and lodges across the country for the next couple of years. And then the time came for D.U. to have a third special gun-of-the-year program, and as everyone knows, this new gun was the Winchester Model 12, which was a highly desired gun.

It turned out that I was able to obtain one of these guns for "field testing" and was quite proud of it as I had fired a Model 12 years earlier, and had found that gun much to my liking. So I was taking very good care of it and everything was going well. I took it with me on several trips and was quite successful with it.

Then I was invited to a particularly nice camp owned and operated as a very fine waterfowl hunting camp along the Gulf Coast. In fact, the individuals present were also people who were high up in D.U. circles and so I had no real concern when I was there for my personal safety or the condition or safety of my property; all were highly regarded businessmen and so forth. However, upon my arrival at the local airport something rather mysterious happened that I could not immediately explain, but I accepted it because the arrangements were being made by others and, of course, I went along with them. Later, looking back, I realized how I had been set up. These were all very honorable, high-positioned people in the U.S. corporate business world and also in D.U., and very fine gentlemen; and several years had gone by since the other escapade with my gun. I was off guard, to say the least. So the possible loss of another gun, especially this one with which I had been so successful, never crossed my mind.

My baggage was taken from me and flown down on an earlier aircraft and I was flown in on a later flight. This seemed a little strange, because normally the type of aircraft used, twin-engine, provided adequate room for our baggage and ourselves. Additionally, when I got to the camp I was taken on a grand tour of the facilities, which seemed to be a little bit out of place because normally I'd be left to my own devices to knock around to find out how things operated. But I received the grand tour by the owner himself, whom I formerly referred to as one of my close friends. (I still do, except that this episode caused me to refer to him otherwise for a period of time—laughingly, that is.)

Everything went well the rest of that afternoon, and in the evening we looked around the marshes and the club facilities and had a very fine dinner; afterward, we had some pleasant conversation and I went to bed. Normally at this camp, getting up to get ready to go out into the marsh is not a big rushed thing; everything is scheduled just right and you get up, have coffee, juice, whatever will sustain you until you can get back, because you never hunt these marshes after nine o'clock in the morning to give the birds a chance to settle down for the rest of the day until the next morning. But this particular morning I was really rushed; you might even say I was impolitely rushed. "Come on, Dale, come on, Dale, let's go, let's go . . . everybody else is out here, come on, let's go . . ." Then I finally realized that I had not been awakened until a little after some of the others.

My favorite gun, which was in a special hard case, and locked, as the airlines required when it is shipped in baggage, was on the front porch of this screened-in area of the camp with all the other guns. We all had our little bit of breakfast and were ready to go into the blinds, and everybody got onto the front porch, chattering away like a band of monkeys—till I walked out; then most of the chatter seemed to fall off. I wasn't too aware of it at the time, but then I became more aware of it. And then, when I reached down to pick up my gun case, I first checked to see if it was still locked, because now little alarms were starting to sound inside my head and little red flags were flying around. Something seemed to be up. As soon as I touched the case that whole porch got so quiet you could even hear the armadillos rooting around outside. Now, on that porch were the top officers of Ducks Unlimited de Mexico, Ducks Unlimited (Canada), and Ducks Unlimited, Inc. here in the U.S. So, there were a few of us there—maybe ten or fifteen people.

I was very quiet and as I lifted the gun case, still locked, I realized that the case was way too light—way too light for a Model 12. I took out my key and it was as if it weighed ten pounds—just like a lead key. I could hardly get it into the lock. I couldn't imagine what had happened. I opened the case and there, staring up at me, was a hundred-and-fifty or two-hundred-year-old (of course, that's an exaggeration, but it looked to be that old) Ithaca, single barrel, the most beat-up gun—it had to have laid on a saltwater marsh floor under tidewater for months to gain the thickness of crust of rust that it had all over; the stock was split and worn, parts of it broken off and, of course, after several large, loud, extensive groans—no, screams of anguish—I could then make out some small little sneezing sounds, or choking sounds really was what they were, from individuals scurrying to get out the door before breaking up. I thought, well, I'll go along with this thing because these guys are not about to make off with my new Model 12—I'm just field-testing, you see. And so I assembled this magnificent wreck of a pump gun which had been substituted for my fine-shooting Model 12.

I took it out, started for the boat with my punter and the companion with whom I was to hunt (who was the President of D.U. de Mexico), thinking surely that someone would at any time take this thing which was a complete threat to anyone in the marsh out of my hands and reinsert into my outstretched arms my Model 12. But it didn't happen. I went to the blind; we were properly situated when the first birds came over. I'll say this, that old Ithaca was one of the finest-shooting old guns I had ever had my hands on, but it was not my Model 12. Needless to say, I didn't do as well as I would have with my Model 12—and that's my best excuse for my poor showing that day. I made several very terrible shots with this gun, which didn't fit my shoulder. The muzzle blast could be seen for miles. The conversation, when there was a lull in the flight of birds, got around to a discussion between the punter and me as to what happened to my gun. He could hardly get his breath, and ended up holding his sides from laughing so hard—yet he wouldn't break a bit; wouldn't say who was in on the gun-napping and didn't know where my gun was or if I would ever see it again.

About this time I started thinking about my host, who I was sure was mightily involved in, let's say, the removal from my possession of this fine firearm and the substitution of this "other," because he owned the aircraft on which it was transported away from me and he owned the camp, and the employees who were chortling over the entire episode were all his employees. I noticed that he had also been able to provide in front of this and the other blinds a fine raft of new, special plastic imported decoys. So I told the punter I was going to pattern the gun, and I thought the best thing I might pattern it on would be some of the decoys. Well, after he got up off his knees from pleading that I not do it because not only his job but perhaps his very life would be at stake if anything happened to those decoys, I finally relented and decided not to pattern the decoys.

Well, the hunt was concluded and we came back to camp. Hardly anyone would say anything to me—wouldn't even speak to me. I mean, it was as if *I* was the thief—and, you know, that is exactly the way they tried to portray it, that I had come down there with this old beat-up gun and tried to perpetrate a theft by substitution and perhaps, having claimed that I had brought a better gun, was then going to hold out for something like this from this group of fine gentlemen.

That evening, it became the subject of discussion at the dinner table. All of us were sitting around this huge table, with the host sitting at the far end. Finally, completely off the subject being discussed, my host looked at me and, very graciously, with a constant smile on his face (he's a very cheerful man even when he's taking your gun away from you!), he said: "Dale, what kind of pattern did that new gun of yours throw today?" A few chuckles went around the table. I responded, "Well, I'll tell you just what kind of pattern it throws. You know how far that spread of new decoys of your reaches out there, how wide is it? Well, now, that pattern stretched from the left side clear to the right."

Well, the whole group just broke up; they could just see me there, disappointed in having had my good gun taken from me, with this substituted old gun in hand, and maliciously pumping shot after shot into his new decoys. That broke the thing up for a while because he wasn't too sure until he checked with his punter whether or not I had shot the decoys. So at least that was some retribution—just the fact that his entire countenance changed; the smile disappeared from his face. He just wasn't too sure for a while whether or not I had deep-sixed his decoys as retribution for the theft of my gun.

The interesting part of this is that it has been a year now since this episode. I have no idea yet where my gun is. His pilots and some of his punters have made some mistakes in their ensuing conversations with me. I finally got it down to the fact, though, that this gentleman had more than a little to do with the disappearance of my fine Model 12.

An interesting side note is that some individual, who I know was in on the conspiracy to remove the first gun, the 20-gauge 870, from me several years earlier, was also in attendance at this camp at this time, and much of the very definite detailed snooping that I have been able to work out since then indicates that these two gentlemen were involved. I would guess that the last report I could make on this particular story is something that is rather fearful . . . fearsome . . . scary. I might relate it this way.

Only a couple months ago, many of these same gentlemen were gathered at a rather large and important waterfowl symposium held in the U.S. I received a phone call shortly after that meeting and was told that the individual calling me had overheard a discussion between several people, and hands were shaken on it . . . that I would not be permitted to ever again own a nice gun. Now, you know to a man in my profession and business, with my background and interest in wildlife conservation, that is a frightening concept, especially when I had to stop and consider that they had just definitely removed from my possession the two guns I had held in high regard. This in itself is enough to be very disconcerting. The worst thing is that I have one gun left, and this particular gun has a special plaque on it, and is the gun that was presented to me when I left the Ohio Division of Wildlife before coming with Ducks Unlimited. It was given to me by all the employees. I am very proud of that gun and hold it in very high regard. I can't hit much with it, but, then, these friends of mine tell me I couldn't hit much with whatever I fired anyway. But this is the frightening thing, with this one gun remaining. I have heard innuendos dropped in at least three different instances within the past several weeks that "they" have a special present in mind this year for the gentleman who owns this fine camp where we go together to hunt, as we normally get him something nice after the season for all his fine hospitality. This present for him this year, which already has been selected but not yet obtained, is said to be something he probably would treasure above all else. I have the very frightening feeling that it could be the only gun I still own—but then, only time will tell.

Bomb Away

FREDERICK B. DeCAMP

In October of 1975, Jack Longstreth, my longtime hunting companion, and my oldest son, Jim, age twenty-five at the time, decided to believe all that we had been reading about the goose shooting at Lake St. Mary's, Ohio, and arranged for a blind at Pay & Farm on the south shore of the lake.

Three in the blind was a little crowded, but we settled in. In a matter of half an hour, some geese began to appear, and it seemed that they flew over every blind but ours, and it stayed that way until minutes before closing time. I spotted a small V headed our way, but they must have spotted us, too, because they began to climb as they got closer. They must have been seventy-five yards up and moving.

We decided it was the last chance of the day and we might as well dirty our barrels. We let fly, and sure enough, the big leader was head-shot and started to fall. We all looked up and watched, and it became apparent that that goose was going to land in the blind on top of us. We must have looked like the Marx Brothers going through a revolving door, trying to get out of the way. It was like being caught in the bottom of an elevator shaft with the elevator coming down.

He finally landed about two feet outside of the blind, weighed fourteen pounds, and ate well.

Smokin' 'Em

OAKLEY V. ANDREWS

It was beginning to get dark as Bill and I left Cleveland. Thanksgiving was only a few days away and we were already beginning to feel the first cold weather of the season. As we reached the turnpike entrance it began to rain and we turned on the car radio to get the weather report. "Rain—turning to snow flurries later this evening—temperatures in the lower thirties—strong northeast wind," the report told us.

"Rotten weather for ducks," said Bill.

I agreed. "Maybe it will clear up by tomorrow morning," I suggested.

"Doesn't look like it," said Bill, "but let's hope so."

There was surprisingly little traffic on the turnpike for a Friday night, and so we rolled along uneventfully until, all of a sudden, a huge traffic jam appeared ahead. "What's this all about?" asked Bill.

"Don't know," said I. But as we finally approached the place where most of the cars were stopped, we could see what was causing the problem. The drive-in movie adjacent to the turnpike was showing an X-rated film and it was just too much for the turnpike drivers.

"Son of a bitch," said Bill. "Did you ever see anything like that?"

"Not on the turnpike," I replied.

Well, it took quite a while for that traffic jam to unstick, as you might imagine, but we finally got on our way about the time the cartoon came on.

Half an hour later, we had left the turnpike and were on Route 250 headed toward the Holiday Inn. "Did you make reservations for us?" I asked.

"Of course I did," replied Bill. "Called just this afternoon and reserved one of the 'down and out' rooms."

"Are you sure?"

"Don't worry, I talked to the desk clerk myself."

A few minutes later we pulled into the Holiday Inn and Bill and I went in to pick up our room keys and register. "Got our reservation?" Bill asked the desk clerk.

The desk clerk looked for it for at least ten minutes. "No—no reservation here for you," he finally informed us.

"What the hell," said Bill, looking hard at the clerk. "I called this afternoon."

"Well, I can't find any record of it."

"Can you give us a downstairs outside room?" Bill asked, observing that most of the room keys were still on their hooks.

"I don't know, I'll have to see."

Finally, after a lot of looking, the clerk came up with a key for Room 107 and reminded Bill that next time, he ought to make a reservation. I got Bill out of there before he hit the clerk, and we unloaded our gear into the room a few minutes later.

"Why don't you get some ice," Bill said, "and we'll have a quick one here and then go over to the Log Cabin for dinner."

"Fine," I replied, picking up the plastic ice bucket. The room with the ice machine is located next to the laundry, and you have to walk all the way around the end of the building to get to it. I left the room and walked along the side of the building, noticing that none of the other "down-and-out" rooms were occupied, turned the corner, and started to open the door to the ice room. Just then I noticed that there seemed to be an awful lot of water on the floor outside. As I opened the door to the ice room, the source of all the water was immediately visible. Something had gone wrong in the laundry and the whole ice room was three feet deep in soapsuds.

When I returned to the room with an empty ice bucket, Bill asked, "Where's the ice?" I told him about the situation in the ice room. "You've got to be kidding," he said, shaking his head.

"Don't worry," I told him, as I unpacked a bottle of Scotch. "You won't miss the ice. The booze got cold in the trunk of the car on the way up."

So we had a drink, changed our clothes, and left for the Log Cabin to have dinner. As we walked into the Log Cabin, we were greeted by John's familiar voice from behind the bar. "Oh, Jesus, look who's here." Bill and I allowed as how they were damn lucky that we were there, since we were a couple of their very few paying customers. "Screw you guys," replied John, laughing, and proceeded to make up a couple of drinks.

The Log Cabin is owned and operated by John Maschari and his wife, Bertie. Besides serving the best food in the area, John and Bertie are great people and good friends of all of us who hunt the area. It just isn't a duck hunt unless it includes some time spent sitting at the bar of the Log Cabin enjoying the camaraderie.

After a while, Bill Hawgood and Doc Bell came in, followed by the Morton brothers, Charlie and Jim Kehres, and Dug Pearson. Keith Russell came over from Ottawa and we all sat down to dinner about nine-thirty. Dinner was a great affair that night, with a continuous stream of some of the best jokes and biggest lies I've ever heard. As usual, the perch was great and the glue potatoes did their job. John's wife, Bertie, makes the best home fries you've ever tasted, with eggs and onions. One good-sized helping stops you up for at least three days, sticks to your insides like concrete, and soaks up anything that happens to be in your stomach. The only trouble with the glue potatoes is that when you finally can go, you've got to watch out or you may break the bowl or crack the bathroom mirror.

By the time dinner was over, everyone was pretty smooth and the stories were getting better and better. Dug regaled us with his great tale about baiting the pitcher's mound at Cleveland Stadium and shooting pigeons from the dugout. Bill Hawgood related the story about his hunt two days earlier, where he and Doc Bell didn't shoot any birds, but managed to burn down the blind with their charcoal stove. Keith explained the proper protocol for shooting grouse in Scotland in kilts in a high wind. Then Chris Morton went into one of his Canadian meat-hunt stories and everyone made their usual remarks about the noble Indian guides who always manage to break the boat motors, lose the decoys, or get drunk and forget to ever show up. John finally closed up shop about ten-thirty and we went back to the Holiday Inn for a nightcap.

The Holiday Inn at Sandusky is not exactly like the 21 Club, but there was a local band in the bar, blowing its brains out, and you could get a drink if you were patient enough. The South American hostess finally brought us a round of drinks and Keith proceeded to amaze us with his commanding mastery of the Spanish language, as he kept her spellbound for at least a whole minute with a rambling discourse on the beauties of Puerto Vallarta. His Spanish must have been better than we thought, because he ordered a Scotch and wound up with two Seven & Sevens.

By the time we turned in, the snowing had stopped. The weather had cleared a bit and a few stars were out.

"Maybe that snow will hold off tomorrow morning," mused Bill.

"Good luck," said I.

When you are duck hunting, five in the morning rolls around much sooner than you'd expect, particularly when you went to bed only a few hours earlier. Somehow, as always, we managed to get ourselves out of bed and struggle into our hunting clothes.

Now Bill is a hell of a hunter and a very bright guy, but he has a terrible habit of forgetting things. One time we got out in the blind and he said, "Okay, now give me my gun."

"What gun?" said I.

"You mean you don't have my gun?" he said.

"Hell, no, why would I have your gun?" I replied.

"Well, Christ," he said, "it must be back on the top of the car."

With that, the punter handed him the oars for the boat and, an hour later, Bill was back in the blind with his gun. By then, the punter and I had shot one bird short of our limit, so we sat back with some amusement as a beautiful flight of six greenheads came right in on the decoys and Bill could take only one of them.

This morning, Bill had forgotten only his hunting shoes, his waders, his gloves, and an extra pair of socks.

"Did you manage to bring any shells?" I asked him.

"Of course, of course," he said. "Just look in my kit bag."

There I found two boxes of 12-gauge number fours and a box of 20-gauge skeet loads. "What are the skeet loads for?" I asked with a smile, knowing that he had brought his 12-gauge 1100.

"They're cripple killers," he replied.

"What are you going to do with them, throw 'em at 'em?" I asked, showing him the box of 20's.

"Oh, Christ, I thought those were 12's," he said. "But don't worry—we won't need them anyway because today it's going to be nothing but face shots, right?" I agreed.

We finally got our clothes on and most of our gear together and stumbled out into the dark to find our car and load it up for the trip to the marsh. The wind was blowing hard again, and the snow was beginning to come down faster than the night before, but mixed with a little rain.

"It's going to be hell getting 'em to fly today," I said.

"You're not kidding," replied Bill. "They'll just sit on that rest pond all day long if this keeps up."

It was five-fifteen and we weren't due to meet Cy at the clubhouse until six-thirty, so we drove up to Bay View to have breakfast at the Baybell diner. The Baybell doesn't open officially until six, but they unlock the door around five-thirty so you can get coffee and sit there with the lights off until six, when they will put together some breakfast for you. By the time we got there, most of the other members of our gang had arrived. We ate breakfast amid a fair amount of gloom and doom, owing partly to the weather and partly to a few hangovers from the previous night's activity.

As we left the diner, I noticed they had a special on cigars, two for eight cents. Bill is a great cigar smoker and likes nothing better than a good cigar, so thinking I'd do him a favor, I bought a whole handful of these fine cigars. Getting back into the car, we noticed that the wind was blowing harder than ever and the rain, mixed with snow, was flying so hard the windshield wipers could hardly handle it. As we turned into the clubhouse drive, we could see Cy standing by his battered old red Ford, waiting for us.

No one knows how old Cy is. My guess is he's moving into his middle sixties, but he has been punting and shooting ducks about as long as anyone can remember. Cy is strictly a decoy man—that is, he relies almost exclusively on his spread of decoys to attract the birds and does little or no calling. Volumes and volumes have been written about different decoy layouts and spreads. I doubt whether Cy has ever read any of those books, but when it comes to setting out decoys, he is a true artist and I'd be willing to bet that very few so-called experts can set decoys any better than Cy. Cy never uses a duck or goose call as such. I don't think he even owns one. He does use a voice call to turn the birds, or at least to attract their attention, and I must say, it seems to work very well, although I can't imagine why, because it sounds more like a cross between a crow and a donkey. In any event, the ducks seem to like it.

We parked the car, said hello to Cy, and got the rest of our gear out. Bill had managed to turn up a pair of hip boots and I struggled to get into chest waders. It was still pitch dark and the wind made it a really foul morning. Cy was anxious to get out to the blind and get set up.

"What's the hurry?" said Bill. "It's not even six-thirty, we're not legal until well after seven, and it's only a ten-minute row out to Number 16."

"Can't row out there this morning," replied Cy. "It's too damn windy. We'll have to walk, and I'm going to have a hell of a time getting my blocks out with it blowing like this."

So we started out to walk to Number 16. It's really not a long walk, but in the dark, with the wind, snow, and rain blowing in your face, half freezing and carrying all your hunting gear, it seems like about ten miles.

Cy set off in front of us to lead the way. He had a flashlight; we had forgotten ours. I never cease to be amazed at how fast that old bird can move, and that morning was no exception. He set off at a good clip, with Bill and me struggling like hell to keep up with him.

We came to the drain ditch about fifty yards from the clubhouse, which you have to cross on a half-rotten 2x8. Cy crossed it without even breaking stride and stopped on the other side to hold the light for us. "Watch the board," he said. "It's icing up."

As I gingerly worked my way across, I discovered damn fast that the freezing rain had encrusted the plank with a coating of thick ice when I almost slipped off into the water. I finally got across and Bill worked his way across behind me. On we trudged, through the cornfield behind the marsh, and as we walked, it seemed that the wind was picking up at every step. Perhaps this was because we were getting closer to the open side of the marsh and out of the protection of the wooded cover that runs along its side.

Finally we reached the clearing at the end of the path and Cy's flashlight picked out the white rag he had tied to a tree to mark the way to the boardwalk across the marsh. Cy climbed up the bank and disappeared over the other side onto the boardwalk, while we followed about twenty feet behind. As we reached the top of the bank, we were hit full force by the wind, which was blowing harder than ever, unchecked, across the open marsh and was churning that ordinarily placid and shallow body of water into a veritable sea of waves.

The boardwalk across the marsh consists of odd planks, none wider than eight inches, set in a kind of zigzag pattern on pilings driven into the muddy bottom. The first part of the boardwalk crosses a channel which is usually only two and a half to three feet deep, but because of the high water, it was now almost five feet deep, to the level of the boardwalk. The water was washing across the boardwalk its full length, and the surface was completely frozen. The situation was becoming worse every minute as the wind picked up and the snow, mixed with rain, reduced the visibility to nearly zero.

It was still dark, but I could see Cy in the dim reflection of his flashlight, walking quickly but carefully along the boardwalk about fifteen feet ahead. "You all right, Cy?" I called out.

"Yep," came back the answer. "Watch the ice."

I started across the first part of the boardwalk and found that the slightest wrong move was certainly going to put me in the water. The wind and blinding snow didn't help at all, but I gradually crept across the boards, hoping to God I could cover the fifty-foot length of walkway without falling in.

Bill was right behind me, and I yelled back, "Watch the ice, Bill, this thing's damn slippery."

"Okay," he replied.

I went on a couple of more steps. "You okay, Bill?"

"Yeh, sure. . . . Oooooooh s——"—followed by a giant splash.

Just as Bill had reached the end of the walk across the channel, his gun case had slid off his shoulder and he lost his balance and slipped to the left. Rather than fall close by the boardwalk where he might hit one of the pilings, he shoved off with all his might and propelled himself well into the channel.

Luckily he hadn't gone into the deepest part and was able to stand up quickly with the water coming only to his waist. If he had been wearing waders, he probably would have remained fairly dry. However, his hip boots immediately filled to the top with water and he was soaked from the waist down.

Cy came back with his flashlight after hearing all the commotion and, seeing Bill in the water, said, "Jesus, Bill, I wish you'd quit screwing around so we could get into the blind."

Bill didn't say anything, just gritted his teeth and sloshed his way back over to the boardwalk where, with quite an effort, Cy and I managed to get him back on the boards. He poured water out of every pocket, and water flooded out of his boots when he rolled them down below his knees.

We crept across the remaining forty feet of the boardwalk and finally made it to the blind. Cy went out to set his decoys. We got into the blind, pulling the top down tight. Bill pulled off his boots, raised the top, and dumped out the rest of the water over the side of the blind. He pulled off his socks and wrung them out and took off his pants and wrung them out too.

There Bill was, sitting in that steel blind in his wet underwear, and all he could do is look at me, shake his head and slowly mutter, "Son of a bitch."

Well, I lit the kerosene heater and turned it up as high as it would go. By this time, Bill's teeth had started to chatter, and so I moved the stove right over next to him. He did everything but sit on it, and before long his shorts were steaming and the teeth-chattering abated somewhat.

I found I had an extra pair of socks in my kit, which he was very happy to put on, and by laying his pants next to the heater, we managed to get them dry enough so he could put them back on. He was sure damn miserable at that point.

"Maybe we should get you back in," I said.

"And walk over that goddam boardwalk again? No way," he replied. "I'd rather sit out here and freeze than try to make it back across that boardwalk."

I had remembered to bring a Thermos so we got that out and had some hot coffee. But Bill's teeth were still chattering intermittently and the heater wasn't throwing off enough heat to keep the blind really warm.

Cy returned to the blind, having put his blocks out, but the snow and rain were still coming down so hard you could barely see the string of decoys.

"How do you feel, Bill?" said Cy, with sort of a chuckle. "Get a little wet back there?"

"You're damn right I did, you little bastard, and it's all your fault," said Bill.

"How's that?" asked Cy, smiling. "You fell off the boardwalk, not me."

"Yeh, but if you'd been there to catch me like you should have," said Bill, "I wouldn't be all wet right now."

"Well, just try not to let your teeth chatter too hard, 'cause it spooks the ducks," said Cy.

"What ducks?" I asked, looking out at the rain and snow. "Nothing's going to fly on a morning like this."

"Don't worry" said Bill, the eternal optimist. "We'll get our birds. You've just got to be patient."

By seven-forty-five it began to get a little bit light, and by eight, the rain had stopped and the wind had died down, but the snow was still falling. Nothing was moving. By ten we hadn't seen a thing, but the snow finally stopped.

Bill was still pretty cold and we'd just about finished the coffee, so we broke out some other warmer-upper I had brought along in case of emergency. After a little of that, Bill allowed as how he was feeling much better and proceeded to blow a few notes on his duck call. Unfortunately, his teeth were still chattering, so the call sounded like a duck with hiccups and gave Cy quite a laugh.

"What are you laughing about?" said Bill. "I've heard that nyah-nyah-nyah of yours and you couldn't get a duck into a cornpile with that call."

Well, so it went. The morning dragged on and we didn't see a solitary bird. All our warmer-upper was gone and we were all feeling pretty dismal.

"Looks kind of slow today," Bill finally said.

"I know," I replied. "Well, there's always one way of getting them in."

"How's that?" he asked.

"Smoke 'em," I replied.

"What do you mean, smoke 'em?" said Bill.

"Don't you know that ducks are really attracted to the smell of a cheap cigar?"

"Oh bull," said Bill. "The fact is the smoke will scare them off."

"Have you ever tried it?" I asked.

"Of course not. Who'd be stupid enough to try that trick?"

"Well then, how the hell do you know that it doesn't work?"

"I just know," said he. "Any fool would know."

"Well," said I, pulling out one of the cigars I had bought at the diner, "you try it out and see what happens."

Bill lit up that cigar, puffed it, and oh God, was it a bad one. Bill kind of winced at the first puff, and Cy and I winced when we had to smell the damn thing. Bill sat back and puffed on the cigar for about fifteen minutes.

Well, nothing had happened and he was about halfway through that cigar and he kept telling Cy and me that nothing was going to happen, when a flight of five of the prettiest black ducks you ever saw came right in on us and sat in the decoys. It was still kind of foggy out and they seemed to come out of nowhere. We didn't see them until they hit the water.

"What did I tell you, you fat bastard?" I said, prodding Bill. "There were probably eight in that flight and you only smoked it hard enough to get five in."

We got ready, popped the top on the blind, and managed to get three birds out of the lot.

"Nice shooting, partner," said Bill.

"You too," said I.

And Cy went up and picked up our birds. Well, that was great. At least we weren't going to get skunked, and we started scanning the horizon in earnest for the next bunch of ducks. We searched and searched the skies the next hour or so and nothing was flying.

"Can't go home with just three birds," said Bill. "Give me another one of those cigars."

"What happened to the first one?" I asked.

"Oh, nothing," said Bill.

It turned out that in the excitement, Bill had bitten through the end of the cigar and had lost it in the bottom of the blind.

"Now I know this won't do any good and this is a bunch of crap," he said, as he lit up the cigar, "but these are great cigars and I really enjoy smoking them."

Cy and I got a laugh out of that, because they had to be the worst cigars anybody ever saw in the world, and Bill couldn't lie worth a damn anyway.

Well, he puffed and puffed and blew smoke all over. He even lifted the top of the blind and blew smoke around, and, by God, in about ten minutes, a flight of mallards went over and made a turn and came back over again. They looked kind of spooky, so we just sat there and watched them. Pretty soon, they set their wings and started to come into our blocks. About the time the first big greenhead hit the water, Bill said, "Let's take 'em!" and we pulled four birds out of that string.

By now, Bill's wet clothes were completely forgotten and he was as happy as a dog on a meat truck, chomping away on that cigar. By noon, we had our limit and they were still coming in. It was a real air show and we sat back and watched them land, flight after flight, for about forty-five minutes. Cy went out to pick up his decoys and we sat back congratulating ourselves on what great shots we were and generally enjoying the hell out of recounting the morning's exploits.

The ice had gone off the boardwalk, so we didn't have any trouble going back, even carrying a pile of ducks. When we got back to the car, some of the other shooters were pulling in, and we compared notes, or lies, over drinks. Somebody pulled out a bottle of Crown Royal and poured us each a healthy drink and passed the bottle to Cy, who took a long draw on it, wiping his mouth on the back of his hand.

"How's that, Cy? Bet you don't get fine Canadian like Crown Royal every day," we said.

"Well, I still like that Corby's" said Cy, "but that stuff ain't too bad."

In fact, Cy tolerated it enough to finish the bottle. Cy had to leave, and so I walked over to his car with him to pay him.

About then we heard Bill tell Dug, "Say, did you know that ducks love the smell of a cheap cigar?"

Filled Out and Drowned Out

THOMAS F. COAKLEY

First, it should be said that everyone knows I am the epitome of legality and truthfulness. Second, of course, it is equally well known that events in pursuit of waterfowl are full of ifs, maybes, buts, and might-have-beens. With those qualifications, here goes.

The place was Currituck, North Carolina. The time was in early December. These were the days before our government, in its infinite wisdom, had declared sink boxes illegal. We left the dock in the dark, about four A.M. A crew of original Carolina outlaws had us in their power, and we were two anxious hunters. My partner on this particular day is now long gone: a dear friend, one of God's great people and a magnificent shot. One peculiarity he had, which I admired, was that he put V.O. on his cornflakes.

The boat was putting us in the middle of Albemarle Sound; we were breaking skim ice, which was obviously cutting our boat in half at the waterline. Skim ice acts like a razor blade on wooden boats. Finally we stopped and one big man shoved the sink box over the side and said, "We're here, I'll put out the decoys." Sonny and I jumped in with our guns, lunch, and ammunition. The big man put out more than a hundred decoys and left.

We were alone—waves chopping at the flaps—stiff breeze and sunrise was coming—decoys looked great. But water was rising in our box. The question in my mind was, are we sinking? Suddenly ducks started moving: you name them—mallards, gadwalls, pintails, butter-balls, redheads, and cans.

We were shooting fast and taking our share, but obviously our blind was sinking and there was no sign of our mother boat. Maybe it had sunk! If we ever needed life jackets, it was now. Where was the goddam boat?

We were filled out on ducks. Water now hip deep. Don't panic! we thought. Let's make a plan. It's broad daylight and they're bound to find us— or some wreckage.

We had a sandwich and coffee. Now the water was waist deep; lots of cold water in the box. We were sitting on the edge of the box, our limit of ducks clustered on a bank a mile away.

Sonny said, "Have to go." He promised not to tip the blind. Water now over the flaps—dangerous. Sonny finally finished. No paper.

"Mark! Mark!" I called. "Eleven o'clock."

Sonny was facing five o'clock. Pants down, but with the skill of one of the few great hunters, he does a 180°, facing five big Canadas, and drops two; I drop two. Never saw shooting like that before. He, with pants down around his ankles, had turned and taken another.

Five out of five—with one cheek hanging over a sinking blind and the other ass (me) trying to make change for a twenty. (He finally used the wax paper from my sandwich.)

Just then our boat pulled into sight and positively saved our lives. The blind sank, but we managed to escape with guns and ammo, plus collecting all the ducks and geese.

Waterfowlers are surely a breed apart. God bless us all.

Fish and Fowl

C. VICTOR BRACHER

"I've lived in Northwest Territories all my life and this is the first time I've ever seen anything like this!" So says Lawrence Yanik, Indian Forestry Supervisor, now stationed at Fort Chipewyan, on the west end of Lake Athabasca in northern Alberta.

What we had witnessed was a jackfish (northern pike) jumping clear of the water onto a small three-inch plastic "Cree-Duck" lure, manufactured in Oregon, Ohio.

On my very first cast into the rum-colored water, we could see shadows of big fish and occasionally white bellies of these hungry "jacks" as they chased my fast retrieve. Lawrence looked at me as I prepared for my second cast and said, "They sure are in there." This time my cast was to the opposite side of the canal, or muskeg drainage ditch. As I started a slow retrieve a fifteen-pound jack leaped from the water four feet from the duckling lure and with his mouth open wide came down on the plastic lure like a bolt of lightning, only to find himself thoroughly hooked in the gills.

An ardent fisherman or a sportsman interested in conservation naturally asks, "Where is this place?"

It all started when my friend Amos Burg and I planned a canoe voyage down the Athabasca River from the village of that name into the waterways leading into the Great Slave Lake in Northwest Territories. We started our voyage on May 23, 1968. The Athabasca River was in flood stage because of the spring runoff from headwaters in Jasper National Park and the east-slope drainage of the Rockies. For the next six weeks we would cover seven hundred miles of the Athabasca, Peace, and Slave rivers, into Northwest Territories and the Great Slave Lake, where I would leave Amos, who would continue a voyage he originally made in 1929, and he described in *National Geographic* magazine, August 1931.

Only a few weeks earlier the river was clearing itself of ice, and we were told when we embarked that the Great Slave Lake was still ice covered.

Soon after our departure we knew we were headed for wilderness country, for hardly a day passed without our seeing deer, bear, and moose. Overhead were V's of Canada geese, all heading north. We talked about the migratory waterfowl that we would see when we reached the delta of the Athabasca, where the river empties into the west end of Lake Athabasca.

Early in the voyage we encountered our first rapids, which are part of any wild-river navigation. On the fifth day, near Pelican Portage, we came upon a goldeneye hen with four downy youngsters on her back; obviously she was protecting her brood from the vicious jackfish. (If you are interested in fishing and reducing the number of predatory jackfish, plan a trip to Fort Chipewyan, known as Fort Chip, and hire an Indian guide to take you to any of the vast marsh lands at the west end of Lake Athabasca. The only way you can reach Fort Chip is by canoe, boat, or float plane. About fifteen hundred Indians live in the village, completely cut off from the rest of the world. They are happy in their homeland, as any of the missionaries will tell you.)

Lake Athabasca claims to have the largest lake trout in Canada. At Fort McMurry, Walter Hill, druggist, produced a picture of a 102-pound lake trout caught by commercial fishermen in nets. The reason for such large fish, he says, is an abundant food supply and the fact that Lake Athabasca opens up earlier in the spring and is free of ice longer in the fall than the lakes farther north.

We planned to spend several days at Fort Chip to make pictures of native life, and it proved interesting. Migratory waterfowl were always in sight, and off the Forestry docks diving ducks skimmed the water. On the third day of our stay in Fort Chip, Chief Forester Lawrence Yanik invited me to see some good moose country, northwest of the village. With his fourteen-foot fiberglass boat and a forty-horsepower outboard motor, we literally flew down the "Catfish" channel and into the southern end of Wood Bison National Park, which overlaps Alberta and Northwest Territories. It's the largest national park in the world and the nesting area for whooping cranes and other migratory waterfowl.

Just before leaving the main channel, Lawrence pointed to a mallard hen and four youngsters all huddled close together, frightened by our speedy approach. Soon we were in a narrow channel with banks covered with grass and occasionally a wild rose bush. There are no trees in this boggy flat muskeg country.

When Lawrence cut the motor, it was quiet, extremely quiet on this balmy calm day. I immediately snapped on a two-inch red-and-white Dardevle spinner. We could hear the distant yell of a loon. Lawrence tossed a broken twig into the water a few feet ahead of the boat, and instantly there was a swirl and the flash of two white bellies. "Those jacks chase anything that moves," Lawrence said, as I made my first cast. We estimated the first jack weighed fifteen pounds. Four consecutive casts netted four big hungry jacks that literally fought for the spinner. The third one had a fresh cut on its belly, where another fish had slashed it, fighting for the lure. Disgorging the treble hooks took more time than to cast, hook, and land the lunkers, with my stiff rod and fifteen-pound-test Stren filament line.

Now we had eleven jacks in the well, back of the rear seat, when I showed Lawrence the "Cree-Duck" lure. He said, "That will work!" So it did.

No sooner had the duckling lure hit the water than the surface looked like feeding time at the Bonneville trout hatchery. Mad hungry jacks were fighting for the lure. We could have filled the boat. It was a treat to see twenty-four-inch jacks jump clear of the water to gobble up my plastic duckling. We now had over twenty fish, and Lawrence pointed to some ugly dark clouds fast approaching from the west. Lawrence said we'd take the fish home and feed them to the dog; some we'd eat ourselves.

On the way back to Fort Chip we flushed many ducks, and a lot of them were females. I wondered where their brood was. No question in my mind, that jackfish take untold numbers of ducklings each year. Now that the Indians and Eskimos are turning to snowmobiles and deserting their dog teams, the jacks will continue to multiply and feed on the spring duck hatch.

In Kip Farrington's book *The Ducks Came Back*, he lists considerable data on losses of waterfowl on the Canadian breeding grounds. It was estimated that jackfish destroyed 8,700,000 ducks in the 1940 nesting season. He says, "Jackfish alone get as many ducks as do the sportsmen and don't even buy a Duck Stamp."

Those Wonderful Waterfowling Twenties

CARL M. BORGH

The week of Thanksgiving 1925, I returned to my native Boston area after being in Florida on a three-month business trip. A few days after my return, the girl to whom I was paying serious attention told me that as a surprise and a welcome-home gift, she had arranged for me to spend a couple of days duck hunting with some of her Cape Cod relatives.

This was truly a very welcome gift because, by my absence, I had missed out on all my usual fall hunting, and also because although I had hunted extensively in all of the upper New England states, I had never hunted on or been on the justly famous Cape Cod. The Cape at this time still was considered one of the premier duck and goose spots on the Atlantic coast, and for me a trip there had to be considered a wonderful opportunity.

Consequently, it was with excitement and great anticipation that several days later I boarded the New Haven train for the trip to the Cape.

As I rode along in the slow, dusty, and sometimes smoky train, I had plenty of time to reflect on the briefing I had been given on the people I was visiting and what I might expect. I would find that the family consisted of widowed mother, single daughter of about fifty, and bachelor son of about forty-five, living on their old farm that was no longer cultivated.

The son—commonly called Junior—was something of what is now called a "free spirit." He had never had any regular employment and his great and only interest was duck hunting.

I had been instructed not to burden myself with rubber boots or excess clothing—which puzzled me, as in my duck hunting experience I would about as soon leave my gun at home as go without rubber boots.

On arrival at Brewster, Junior and I had no difficulty in recognizing each other, as I was the only alighting passenger and he was the only person waiting on the platform.

Greetings over, he led me to an old Model T Ford touring car that showed much rough wear and nothing in the way of cosmetic treatment. The fabric top was down—later to my distress, I learned that it couldn't be put up—and sitting on the front seat was a large brindle-colored dog weighing about seventy pounds. He showed evidence of being a mixture of several large breeds, and later I found that he had gained all of the good and smart qualities of each of them.

Junior motioned me to get in front, and with some pushing, the dog grudgingly made way for me, and off we rode with the dog sitting proudly between us.

I learned that the dog was called Tige, and I knew without being told that he was named after the dog that appeared in the famous cartoon strip of many years back—"Buster Brown and His Dog, Tige."

Several miles farther on, we turned into a sandy lane that led to an old farmhouse and outbuildings. This was the family homestead, and here Junior and his sister had been born. The buildings were beginning to show some neglect, and the surrounding fields, once cultivated, now had a sparse growth of uncut hay.

The greetings from mother and sister were warm, and after some small conversation, I was shown to an upstairs bedroom and told I might rest before supper.

I had been told by Junior that they were also expecting an old friend who was driving down from Boston, so I was not surprised when I heard the sound of an approaching automobile. Looking down from my window, I saw a large Packard touring car stop below me. A large man dressed in a rumpled and well-worn ankle-length raccoon coat and leather cap got out of the car and was happily greeted by Junior. At supper, I learned that my partner-to-be was a stove manufacturer named Burns, which I recall I thought was an appropriate name for his occupation.

Later, Burns came into my bedroom with a stout nightcap, which he assured me was the "real stuff." At this period, good liquor was a rarity, as Prohibition had been in effect for about seven years.

The drink was an icebreaker, and I learned that Burns was the last of a group that had previously leased the duck shooting for many years from Junior's father. The last few years, the stand had been leased by a different group, but a dispute had come up the middle of this season and the group had defaulted on the arrangements. Consequently, for several weeks no organized shooting had been done at the stand, and this, of course, was the reason that I was able to be invited.

Burns also bore out what I had previously been told about Junior's life style. Junior ate and slept ducks and geese the year round and made them his vocation as well as avocation. At that time he probably had about forty ducks and fifteen geese which he used as decoys. In the spring, he would raise several hundred ducklings and about fifty goslings. Keeping only the selected ones for his own purposes, he found a ready market for the others from hunters who wanted live decoys. During the summer he would start training the birds—first by getting them well acquainted with him and the dog, Tige, and at the same time teaching them to come when he rattled shelled corn in a tin pail. They would become so tame that he had no difficulty in picking any of them up at any time. Later in the summer he would take them to the lake so that they would be accustomed to the blind area and to gun reports.

Before daylight next morning, we all were packed in the Model T and on a rutted sandy trail which for three-quarters of a mile led through the back field and low-growing oak and pine to the clubhouse. This was a low, flat-roofed structure, nestled among oaks and pines so that it was effectively screened from the lake. I sensed that we were close to water and could hear nearby the low muttering and rustling of penned ducks.

A side door was opened, kerosene lamps were lit, and I saw that we were in a large room with two smaller rooms on one side. The far corner served as a kitchen area, with a large cooking range, dining table, and cupboards and pots and pans on the wall. A second large heating stove stood between the two doors leading to the small bedrooms. The rest of the room was filled with well-worn upholstered chairs and sofas, and everything gave much evidence of being used and enjoyed by hunting men.

Junior had left to round up some decoys and we had settled ourselves when I noticed a large battery-powered doorbell on the wall. Burns explained that its purpose was to alert anyone inside that their presence was wanted in the blind. He went on to say that we were only about fifty yards from the blind and it was common practice for the hunters to loll about inside if things were slow, or they were in to warm up, while someone kept guard outside. I could readily imagine what a comfortable arrangement this was for duck hunting.

Burns now felt it was time to go and led me through a second door. I found that I was in a tunnel-like path with covered sides and top, similar to a grape arbor. The arbor was heavily camouflaged with native vines and cut pine branches so that one could go from clubhouse to blind unobserved from any direction.

As I emerged from the tunnel, I found myself directly in the blind and was surprised to see what in my experience, at first glance, didn't look like a duck blind at all. It looked exactly like the back side of a five-foot fence, and actually it was constructed in that manner.

It was about forty feet long and had several port holes, about six inches in diameter, near the top to peer through. The ground was hard-packed from many years' use, and about eight feet to the rear were several cages in which decoys that were to be used during the day were kept. The board fence was set back from the water's edge about a dozen feet, and straight in front was a narrow sand spit about thirty feet long. This spit had been made by Junior's grandfather and father when they established the shooting stand about 1890. Wagonloads of sand had been used to make this sand spit, and over the years sand had been continually added. It was on this bank that the decoys would stand and rest.

The lake side of the board-fence blind was concealed by live growing bushes and shrubs, aided by some cut boughs, and inside the blind and at about the middle section was a twenty-five-foot scrub oak tree. All this made for a perfect camouflage, and, viewed from the lake side, everything blended in to make an undisturbed shoreline.

We were now looking over the waters of Long Pond, which is about five miles long and a mile or more wide, and is one of the largest fresh-water lakes on Cape Cod. Junior's stand was located on the extreme west end of the lake and was one of several shooting stands on the lake, but none of the others was in view or closer than a couple of miles.

Junior had put out about ten ducks, which, being accustomed to being fed on or near the spit, were in the proper area and freely swimming about, diving, flapping their wings, and generally having a very good time.

He also staked out two Canada geese in the most visible position, and they too added some animation to the scene. It was now past seven o'clock, and although we had seen in the distance a few small flocks of ducks and had heard some far-off geese, nothing had approached the blind. For the last few days, the weather had been unseasonably mild, and it was obvious that we were going to have a "bluebird" day.

About this time, a pair of black ducks came flying directly toward us, but they landed a hundred yards out. After a long interval, they cautiously swam toward our decoys. After a bit, they were to the side of our ducks—still very suspicious—and Burns, who had inserted his gun barrels through a port hole, took careful aim and his two shots laid the first duck down. As the other jumped, I brought it down and they were quickly retrieved by the dog.

Junior asked that I help him with the flying geese decoys, so, leaving Burns, we went back to the large pens, divided four geese in two bags, and climbed a tree-covered knoll or bank which was about a hundred yards to the left of the blind.

From the lake side, this bank rose sharply from the water's edge, so that standing on top and looking out over the blind, one could readily imagine taking a running jump for a long dive into the water.

On the top of this small but steep hill and near the edge overlooking the lake there was a long narrow platform, and on this were six roughly made boxes, each large enough to hold a pair of geese. Each box had a door faced with chicken wire hinged at the bottom and latched at the top with a battery-powered catch. The box was slanted to the front so that when the catch was released—activated from the blind—gravity would take over and the door would fall open. The startled geese or ducks would jump out and be immediately airborne from this natural flight tower and in seconds be in full flight over the lake.

Sometimes the flying bird would come directly to the sand spit, but most times they seemed to relish their new freedom and would take a wide swing over the lake. Whenever Junior was about to release a flyer, he always gave us warning so that we wouldn't make a mistake and shoot a tame bird, for from all appearances, they looked and flew in like a wild one.

Flyers were released when a wild flock was in the vicinity and perhaps not giving our setup much of a look. Our flyers did not always bring in wild birds, but they always got attention and, on the whole, were extremely effective.

When the geese were paired up in two cages, we sat down for a rest and smoke and I learned more of the operation of the stand. Junior's father had managed and leased out the shooting stand for twenty-five years, and Junior had done the same since his father died. No detailed record had been kept by them of the wildfowl secured here, but Junior estimated that a conservative figure would be that five hundred ducks and more than a hundred and fifty geese were shot each year. This meant that over the thirty-five years the stand had been operating the astounding total of about seventeen thousand ducks and five thousand geese had been taken from this one spot.

Shooting stands similar to Junior's seem to have been peculiar to Cape Cod and perhaps a few places on the Connecticut shore. These stands were not numerous because, aside from the considerable expenses of a manager or guide, plus the cost of feeding and training decoys year-round—baiting, etc.—the sand required a suitable as well as exclusive area on a freshwater pond. Most stands were not as complete or comfortable as Junior's, as they did not have the comfortable and close-by living quarters that his afforded.

Shortly after returning to the blind, another black duck came swimming to the decoys, and again Burns, as he expressed it, "cold-cocked" the bird.

There was another hour of inaction—the sun was quite warm and there was no wind. Most of the duck decoys were now resting quietly in the shallow water or sitting on the sand, so Junior decided that a new set should go out. Rattling some pebbles in a tin pail got the ducks' attention and with the idea it was feeding time, they marched hurriedly into the blind and, with a little urging and help, were put in their cage.

Another group of about ten were then released and shooed to the water, and just like the first group, quacked and splashed with obvious pleasure. However, nothing was moving on the lake, so about the middle of the morning, we moved into the clubhouse for coffee. This operation took some minutes, and while it was going on, Junior would occasionally go out through the doorway and survey the lake, and on one of these trips he pushed the buzzer for us to hurry out.

As we looked over the board fence, we saw and heard two geese about half a mile away coming up the lake. Junior indicated that when they got a bit closer he would release some flyers that were on the hill and that we should be careful of them as they flew in. As we intently watched the wild geese, which apparently were going to pass us by, I was suddenly aware of two more geese out over the lake, wildly calling and flying in a wide arc toward our sand spit. These were the decoys, and without hesitation, they settled down with the two tethered geese. Almost immediately and as if drawn by a string, the wild pair followed them in and were quickly added to our small bag.

Again, there was a long period of inaction—the day was getting brighter and warmer—and Junior and Burns decided that it was practically useless to spend more time hunting this day. They reasoned that because it was late in the season, the big flights of geese and ducks had gone through, and because the blind had not been baited for more than a week, the remaining wildfowl were not accustomed to finding feed at the blind. The weather, too, was just too fine to get the birds off the ocean and salt marshes, so it was decided to go back to the farmhouse. The live decoys were placed in the pens, Junior threw out a bushel of shelled corn for bait, and, with hopes for a better next day, we drove off.

However, the next day was almost a repetition of the first. We drew some encouragement from the small group of ducks that flew from where the corn was placed and from indications of changing weather. But the ducks and geese were still not coming in numbers, and our score was only a bit better than the first day.

Burns was now becoming irritated and edgy at our small success, and I now learned that he had told some of his employees that he would bring them back a quantity of ducks and geese.

As the morning wore on, the weather was definitely changing, and although not uncomfortable, it no longer had the feel of October. About noontime, Junior forecast that tomorrow would be a much better hunting day and suggested that we go back into his house and get a weather report on the radio. By the time this was done and the weather report received of stormy weather coming, it was too late to return to the lake.

My plans had been to take the night train to Boston, but Burns said that if I would stay over, he would drop me off in Boston. So, with the promise of bad weather and a much more convenient return home, the decision was easy. The next morning proved the radio and Junior to be correct, for we now had the beginnings of a type of nasty storm that seems to be characteristic of New England. The strong wind came in fitful gusts, and with it spits of rain. As the day wore on, the storm got stronger, and by nightfall, the rain was coming in sheets.

Daylight had broken by the time we reached the blind—somewhat wet and chilly because of the Ford's nonoperating top—and it was quickly evident that the baiting plus the storm had greatly increased our chances for a good shoot, for around and on the sand spit were fifty or sixty ducks—mostly blacks—and a dozen or so Canada geese. These Junior carefully flushed with the hope of having them return later in small groups.

The decoy ducks and geese were hastily put out, and Junior and I carried up the flying geese. While doing so, we could hear Burns shoot a number of times. When we returned, he gleefully announced that he had three ducks on the beach.

We could now see an intermittent parade of ducks and hear smaller numbers of geese passing down the lake, and we could hear the muffled boom of guns across the water.

There now could be no question about this being a good duck day, for the beginning storm had driven the wildfowl off the ocean and salt marshes. Our decoys were much more active than the previous days, and Junior and I trudged up the hill twice again with more goose flyers, as well as some ducks. As the morning wore on, Junior would toss a duck or two into the air from the blind so that gradually the decoy flock grew to something over twenty.

It seemed that wildfowl were always in view, and as all the activities of the blind were new and interesting to me, I was at a fever pitch. Although it was an old story to Junior, he too was taken up in the excitement. Even the dog could hardly be contained, for he expected every gun report meant a retrieve. Burns was firing at everything that came anywhere near in range, and although his shooting was not very good, his irritation of yesterday was gone.

Sometime after nine o'clock, Junior suggested that we call a halt and count the results. We now had, as I recall, about thirty ducks—mostly blacks—and ten geese. We had four mallards, a few bluebills, and some mergansers (sawbills in New England).

Neither Junior nor I wanted any more ducks, but Burns wanted some more to fill his promises, so after some coffee, we went back to the stand. It was clear that the storm was to continue and probably get worse. This latter thought began to worry Burns about the drive back to Boston, for the rain we were having on the Cape could very well be snow in Boston.

Consequently, about eleven o'clock, he suggested that we call it quits. We now had forty big ducks—sawbills not counted—and twelve geese.

Everything was closed up, and by this time soaking wet, we jounced back to the farm and prepared for our trip to Boston through what now had turned into a classical "northeaster" storm.

As I look back and recall these events of over fifty years ago, I get a feeling of despondency mixed with some resentment that these times are over and can never for anyone happen again.

Events made it necessary to restrict and limit the hunting of water-fowl, and consequently, in 1934, the national law against the use of bait and live decoys was passed, and this sounded the death knell for Junior's gunning stand.

Gone too is Junior's farm—broken up into house lots—and the

lake is surrounded by cottages. Gone too is his Model T Ford and Burns' Packard car, along with the Parker shotgun and the raccoon coat; they are now valued collectors' items. Even the steam train I rode is part of history. But worst of all is the disappearance of the myriads of waterfowl.

The black duck, once said to be so smart that after all the other ducks were gone it would still be plentiful, is still the mainstay of New England duck shooting but is now so reduced in numbers that it is considered endangered. The black duck could cope with the hunter, but it could not overcome pollution and environmental damage.

As I dwell on the past, there is a feeling of sadness that these changes came about—but there also is a feeling of happiness that I was a part of this era and that I was able to see and wonder at the tremendous flights of waterfowl and to enjoy the many happy days spent on water and marsh. Some days were cold and wet, some were bright and warm, many were unproductive. But all, in one word, were wonderful.

Great Job

PETER S. HITCHCOCK

It was a fall day in early October 1973, on Walpole Island, Ontario, Canada. Early morning of the second day of the two-day shoot. It was early in the season, and our guide, John Sony, was a bit hesitant about my dog, Charlie. Charlie is a golden retriever. His experience to date had been rather poor unless the fallen birds were in the open water and visible. But when the birds were down in the rushes and cattails it was a new ball game, and a very tough one! Few of the dogs ever were able to really hunt out the downed birds when in the marsh.

So as I said, Charlie was looked upon rather skeptically by John Sony. He would change his mind before the day was through!

I was shooting with Dr. Ferdinand Hruby, my old classmate of Hawken School and of great hunting experience. The evening shoot, the day before, had been poor—very few birds flying and quite warm. As the evening came on, no improvement in sight. Finally we had to call it a day as visibility was zero. Charlie had had a good time but really wasn't too excited, as he wasn't very active.

Things changed at dawn the next day. Cloudy with some wind but still pretty warm—about sixty degrees. Getting into the blind was a little time-consuming, as it was pitch black and Charlie didn't cooperate completely—he wanted to get in through the front of the blind, through the new fresh cattails. (This was absolutely forbidden as the season was early and the blind had to last till December.) We hadn't been sitting more than a few minutes after John finished putting out the decoys when suddenly there was the whirring of wings over our heads—even Charlie noticed. It was still too early—we had five more minutes.

Finally, "Mark left" was heard and Fred took the first bird. Charlie was straining to go—right through the front of the blind. I finally sent him out the side. "Fetch!" He turned into the high marsh to the left and disappeared. John Sony had started to leave also to get the bird. I asked him to stop and let Charlie do it. I stood up in the blind on top of our seats to see where the duck went and to direct Charlie. The direction of the fallen bird was all that I could determine, as it had fallen in the cattails. The wind was at our backs, so the dog did have a chance—Charlie has a good nose and the bird was upwind. Shortly we heard him making his way through the cattails as he came back to the blind and wanted to come through the front. He had the duck in his mouth—a nice black! I got him squared away and he gave me the bird and then jumped in from the end.

Then for the next two hours as we filled our limits, Dr. Fred, John Sony, and I watched Charlie retrieve thirteen of fifteen ducks. They all were blind retrieves, as Charlie never once saw the bird fall. The job he did was All Hunting! The two he didn't get landed at John's feet, so he picked them up. For me, there was a great thrill in watching my dog Charlie (Charles of Marchmont) do a great job!

It Goes to Show You Never Really Know

DAN C. HOWLEY

It's nine-thirty A.M., we are in T-shirts now, the temperature is seventy degrees, I haven't seen a cloud in the sky since sunup, and you guessed it—the wind is calm. Ideal weather conditions for bonefishing in the Bahamas, but unfortunately this mid-October morning finds my father, his champion black Lab Rip, and myself in the Cherry Island duck blind at the Ottawa Shooting Club.

We haven't heard a single shot fired since we arrived at our blind over three hours ago. The term "crazy duck hunters" was coined for guys like us, just sitting there waiting for nothing to happen.

At nine-forty-five we take a vote as to whether we should call it a day. The vote is two to one to leave at ten if a single duck hasn't been sighted by then. My father casts the only negative vote. He wants to stay until noon. But the vote shows that Rip and I can take only another fifteen minutes of this.

One minute after ten A.M. I am unloading my gun when a single Canada goose is heard in the distance. The bird is so far behind us that I continue to unload my gun, but my father, never one to give up, starts calling on his goose call.

Within a few minutes there are several geese talking to my father and the sound is getting closer. My father is loudly whispering to keep still as I scurry to reload my gun. Soon five beautiful Canadas come over our back about three hundred yards to our right. They make a large circle in front of the blind and then set their wings for an approach from our left. Twenty feet off the water and twenty yards straight out we stand for the kill. Being at the left side of the blind, I put my sight on the fourth goose and pull the trigger. To my surprise both the fourth and fifth geese fall. At the same time my father bags the head goose. With a limit of five geese apiece in those days, we come to our senses quickly enough to each fire one more shot, bagging the remaining two geese.

Rip takes his time retrieving our game, but once they are all in the blind we understand why. Four number six magnum shells had killed five giant Canada geese. The smallest weighs slightly under twelve pounds, the largest just under sixteen pounds. Over sixty-five pounds of game!

Immediately there comes an outcry for another vote to extend our shoot until twelve noon. The result was two yes and one no. Rip is tired; he wants to go home now!

Fritz

FRITZ NEUBAUER

My name is Fritz Neubauer and I'm fifty-eight. As hard as it is to believe, I've made my living hunting, trapping, and fishing for forty years of my life (my wife says, "that's a living?") right here in Ohio within thirty minutes of Cleveland. I had my first duck hunt with my uncles on the Danube in Austria, I got my first bluebill with my air rifle at Gordon Park, and now I operate my four-thousand-acre Duck Marsh. I have approximately thirty-five club members and am very lucky that they're all sportsmen and respect my work and judgment of how to operate this dream of mine come true.

I would not exchange these times with anyone for anything. I've hunted animals all over the world, and there's just nothing that sets my blood racing like the sight of a smart flock of mallards wheeling. I'm just as glad when some trigger-happy guy can't wait any more and opens up at eighty yards and naturally misses and gets nothing, as when they set into the decoys and we bag a couple.

I'll never forget my first wild *Ente Jagt*—that's German for a wild duck hunt. I was eight years old and had been raised by my uncles, who were gamekeepers. Till then all I'd known was upland-game hunting. My job was to take care of the dachshunds. They would surround a piece of cover and I'd walk through with the dogs and rattle a can with a pebble in it. Those dachshunds brought out everything—deer, rabbits, quail. Every hunter had a Drilling—a double with a rifle barrel underneath. Duck hunting was done by simply walking the river banks or sitting in the willows. I had never heard of decoys.

The first morning began with a bitter cold clear winter dawn. We boarded a train outside of Vienna and headed for a small town along the bank of the Danube River. I was bug-eyed with excitement. We were on the river bank at daybreak, walking along the edge. The river was still open. At my Uncle Ernst's old German cry, "*Achtung Enten*," my heart came right up into my mouth and I almost wet my Lederhosen.

Since then I've seen millions of ducks and thousands killed, but so help me I'll never forget that first flock of ducks (I believe they were widgeon) that came winging up that river just as the morning sun hit them. When they saw us they flared to the other side, but they still dumped three on the other bank in the snow. I was peeling off my Lederhosen for a swim, I was so excited, when my uncles grabbed me and said, "*Zu kalt*, Fritz" ("too cold, Fritz"). They went into a huddle, and then they put me back on the train, which they flagged down. It took half an hour to the nearest bridge and two hours of me running and bumming a ride with an oxen-drawn woodcutter's wagon. But it was worth it when I ran up to the ducks and heard my uncles yell, "Bravo, Fritz!" What I wouldn't have given for a Lab, though. Needless to say, it was quitting time when I got back. I carried those ducks all over the village all evening to show the mayor, fire chief, and all the other hunters. I'll never forget that day.

After leaving Austria, next came America. For a farewell party my grandpa had the millstream shut off and let me and my buddies club brown trout, which went up to twenty pounds.

We made our home in Cleveland near Gordon Park. At first I spent a lot of time looking for Indians behind every tree along Lake Shore Boulevard and Gordon Park. I became a real loner. Imagine not being able to speak one word of English and moving into an all-Irish neighborhood (St. Aloysius) and going to an almost hundred-percent-Jewish school on 105th and St. Clair. I was still in my Lederhosen and was put back from the fourth grade to the first. How mad my teacher used to get when she'd catch me reading German hunting magazines inside my English Literature book.

I spent most of my time along the breakwall off Gordon Park. What a fascination those rafts of bluebills, buffleheads, and goldeneyes had for me. I'd lie in the rocks and watch the bluebills and listen to those whistlers by the hour. The shotguns booming on the breakwall used to get my blood boiling. I'd wait for hours at the boat dock just to look at the decoys and ducks when the gunners came in. I got to be well known at the boat house. "Christ!" they'd say. "That little kraut kid gets a real charge out of this duck hunting."

At ten I had another high point in my life. I got my first BB gun. I was the scourge of the neighborhood. Many an Irish kid had a sore rear end from "Fritzie mit the BB gun." Those were Depression days, so rabbits, squirrels, pigeons, quail, and so on really came in handy.

I got my first duck, a drake bluebill, after lying in the rocks for a couple of hours, with a cold northeaster blowing. I almost drowned retrieving him, with a big audience from the Bratenahl Country Club. Outrunning the Bratenahl police was quite a feat too, but I shook them by using the Coit Road sewer under Lake Shore Boulevard. I finally made it home with my prize, only to find out it was so oil-soaked we couldn't eat it.

Anyhow I was so proud of it I took a course at the Northwestern School of Taxidermy and after a week's work I finished mounting it. I was so pleased with the results of my work that I toured the neighborhood to round up all my buddies to show it off. By then they thought I was a complete nut; they couldn't figure out all that outdoor stuff. They had more fun stealing cars and robbing fruitstands.

The next day I came home and my mother and sister met me with a "I know you will think this is the end of the world" look on their faces. My sister's cat had torn my prize bluebill to pieces. Needless to say, it took hours for them to calm me down, and believe me my sister's and many another cat has paid dearly for that torn-up prize bluebill! I became a confirmed cat hater.

At fifteen I put enough money aside from my muskrat and opossum hides to buy a 20-gauge single at Sears. That twelve dollars was a fortune then. I got ten cents a day for lunch—five cents for a hamburger and five cents for milk. I'd skip the milk and buy a Peters H.V. at the Five Points Hardware (my mother would have killed me). Shots were far and few between, thank God, for no one had money for shells anyhow.

We always knew the rookies when they came on the wall. It was approximately 150 yards across the lagoon. After a couple of days of shooting with a strong northeaster blowing, the crippled bluebills would swim to the center and stay there. It always gave us a laugh when a few guys on the wall would start blasting at the cripples on the water. They would just shake the BBs off. Every once in a while one would flap his wing, like thumbing his nose.

If someone built a blind too close, we'd shoot at their blind instead of at a bluebill. They soon moved. It took skilled shooting, when they were really flying, to get your shots off and duck your head back in between the rocks, so you wouldn't lose an eye.

I wish I could shoot as well now as I did then. Many a time other hunters would hand me their guns with a "Please kill one for me, Fritz." Bluebill shooting with a strong northeast wind took a special skill. Few guys realized that at fifty yards a shot string would be pushed five to ten feet by a strong wind. There was many a time when the wind and spray hit you head on, and froze on you. When you did get a shot you were too cold to pull the trigger. Or your eyes were watering so badly you couldn't see a thing.

Very few of us had decoys. Store-bought dekes were unheard-of. We used cans, jars, driftwood, corks—almost anything. Ten one-pound cloth flour sacks, soaked in linseed oil and dyed black, with the necks tied to look like a duck head, worked wonders with bluebills. Mallards were rare. When someone got one it was big news and we'd all run up the breakwall to look at it with our mouths watering.

Listen to this heartbreak. In those days shooting time ended at four P.M. We had a Cuyahoga County game warden, Bert Cannel, who, as the saying goes, would pinch his own mother. He'd walk up and down the wall at quitting time checking. This one day I saw him coming down the pier looking at his watch, and as I knew he had pinched two guys the day before for not having their guns unloaded at four P.M. I hurriedly broke mine and shoved it in my burlap bag. No one had a watch, for that was a real luxury. Suddenly all the sheepshead fishermen started yelling at me, "Fritz, watch it!" Honk! Honk! I damn near died, for there twenty yards out and coming right along the wall was a lost Canada honker looking for company.

In those days this was unheard of. To bag a goose would have made me a hero for years. As I watched the goose go by with tears in my eyes, the warden walked up to me with his watch out and said, "What's the matter, Fritz? Don't you like goose? You've got five minutes to go till quitting time." Every once in a while you hear about hunters and fishermen throwing a game warden into the drink. Don't you think I had a good excuse? As it was, it wasn't in the books that I'd kill a goose for another twenty-five years.

Needless to say, my hunting and trapping (by streetcar and bus) at Shaker Lakes, Rocky River, Euclid Creek, Bluestone Quarry, Bratenahl, etc. was driving my mother and sister right up the wall. But somehow something saved me every time they were ready to give up on me. Once it was a mink from Rocky River and then two raccoons from Shaker Lakes. We didn't even know how to skin them, but I looked it up in *Fur, Fish and Game*, and when the check came in (twelve dollars for the mink and six and eight dollars for the coons) I was a hero again. Depression days . . . we lived a month on that. Another saving fact was that my buddies were getting caught stealing and were being sent to bad boys' school. Every time my mother was about to give up on me, she'd meet up with the mother of a boy who had just been sent up and she would have to listen to how lucky she was to have an outdoor kid like me. She would come home appreciating me, even though my fish oil had exploded and sent twenty families out of the apartment onto the streets at four in the morning.

Now came the big change in my duck-hunting life. One of my buddies (who wasn't jailed) bought a car—a Model A Ford. I was on cloud nine (big change to now when you watch kids go zipping by in new models). Now we could head out to hunting places we'd only heard of but never seen. To hell with the breakwall and dodging Nicholson and Hanna ore boats in the fog during that mad dash from the break-wall to the lighthouse. Why we never drowned is beyond me. We used to have two guys bailing and one rowing and still wound up with the boat half full of water. No more cussing the darn fishermen who always started swinging their throw lines when a flock started wheeling in. No more dodging the Cleveland and Bratenahl cops when you came inside the limits to look for cripples. No more eating ducks that tasted all fishy. All that was behind us, for we were going to hunt ducks such as we had read about, such as we'd seen pictures of on calendars. You know—putting out the dekes with thousands of ducks winging over in the sunrise, with a Lab posing by your side. It was a new ballgame, we thought!

We found Lake Aquilla, at the mouth of the Chagrin and Mentor Lagoon, in the spring of 1935. I was sixteen then, we were spring rat trapping, and the spring flight was in full swing. It was supposed to have been a bad year for ducks. Believe me, the summer of 1935 dragged on forever. I saw more ducks in an hour in the flooded waters of Lake Aquilla and the Cuyahoga than I ever thought possible. And what ducks—mallards, blacks, woodies, widgeon, you name it. Well! You all know what a good spring flight looks like when the rivers are flooded into the cornfields and woods. (I learned that lesson so well that spring that my whole Duck Marsh right now is set up to follow that pattern.)

We got permission to tear down an old boathouse on the boat-livery farm of Ward Roberts. We built three elaborate blinds in the button brush along the edge of the lake. Duck counting in the evening, while bluegill fishing, I'd sit and watch those local mallards and woodies pour in to roost. I didn't think opening day would ever come.

During the summer I found another outdoor income to keep away from the part-time factory job my mother was planning for me. I started hunting snapping turtles. Believe me, it paid well. Every beer joint on St. Clair from 9th Street to Nottingham served turtle soup on Fridays. Times were still tough, but you know the old story. Those Irish, Germans, and Polish would slop down buckets of this when they'd get loaded. Twelve cents a pound for live weight made me feel like a millionaire. A ten-pound snapper would bring at least a buck, and there were a good many twenty-to-forty-pounders that I brought in. My record was a fifty-eight-pound turtle caught in Punderson Lake.

So after gas money and other expenses I had enough left for another Sears special, a 16-gauge double, and four boxes of shells—high-velocity Sears extra range (I should have stuck to Peters H.V.). Also a dozen mallard decoys, a duck call, a camouflage outfit, the works. At long last, Opening Day!

With our new outfits and five gallons of gas in our Model A, we left the Glenville area for that grueling fifty-mile drive to the lake, after a sleepless night and still reeking of Hoppe's No. 9 (never were there cleaner guns). Once we were beyond the hill over the Chagrin River we knew we had made it. The three of us were on our way. We pulled into the boat livery and then got the shock of our lives.

All spring and summer we had hardly seen a soul, and now it looked like the opening day at the stadium for the Indians. We finally found a parking place and headed with our equipment for our boat. It was a good thing we had locked it up, for about a dozen guys were trying to uproot the tree it was chained to. Undaunted, we headed to our blinds. I heard my buddies say, "Look at all the ducks in front of our blind." When I heard this I pulled all the harder on the oars. When our light hit them through the fog and darkness, my heart sank. I could see they weren't riding right for live ducks. They were decoys.

Well, after hearing "Bull————, first come first served," and daylight coming fast, I said, "Come on, let's get over by those black willows and sit there." The only comfort there was hearing the wings whistling overhead in the dark.

We got out by the willows when a strong voice at my elbow said, "Hey, buddy, aren't you moving in a little close?" So help me, in the dawn's early gleaming, with guns starting to boom all around us, here were a half a dozen Amish men from a nearby farm, hanging in that willow tree like squirrels in a hickory tree. All with beards flapping in the wind. Naturally we excused ourselves and moved out, and not knowing what to do next, we rowed out on the lake to watch the show. As long as I live I'll never forget that Opening Day!

My comment, "Please take me back to my breakwall and the fish ducks," set everyone roaring. By this time the fireworks had really started. A lot of you have seen this, I know—Opening Day of the duck season on a public marsh. Please, if you have never witnessed this sight, go and see it once. You'll quit your complaining when you sit in a private marsh and the birds aren't coming in right and you only get half a limit. Since that day I've looked a few dissatisfied club members in the eye and said, "Try a public marsh!" Some took me up on the suggestion and came back whipped.

Well, back to Opening Day. As should be the case on all Opening Days, the air was full of ducks. The poor local young woodies took the main beating, even though the woodies had a closed season. What few ducks came down went into the marsh, where it was impossible to retrieve them. We watched more than one hunter try it, and their buddies had their hands full pulling them out of the marsh. Lake Aquilla marsh is one of those duck hunter's nightmares, a floating bog. Labrador retrievers were practically unheard of in those days.

One big drake mallard went down in the open water in the middle of the lake. He was the only one out of a flock of twenty that went up in the middle at a hundred yards. But so much lead went at them from both sides that we stopped counting around three hundred. It sounded like D-day on Saipan; all that was missing was the artillery. When that crippled bird hit the water, it dove under—you all know what that means. From all sides came what looked like the Spanish Armada, converging on the splash mark. My buddies, yelling, "Look, Fritz, look," proved to be the biggest laugh. The hunters who took over our blind, our pride and joy, that was built on fence posts spiked together and elevated three feet above the water, had four guns. Well! Two of the guns had jumped into their boat, which was tied to one of the uprights. In their hurry they forgot to unhook the chain. One of the men gave a tremendous shove with his oar and the whole damn thing came down in four feet of water and mud. God! What a sight. I wanted to yell, "Serves you right," but when it looked like they were going to drown in their waders we went over and helped pull them out and took them to the landing.

Meanwhile that smart old drake was still diving with half the boats on the lake after him. That old boy was really working for Du Pont. Cries like "Watch out, the BBs are bouncing off the water" after a shot filled the air. One cry, "I don't give a damn what you say, it stings like hell," made us decide to get out of there fast! I don't think they ever got that drake.

On the landing we had another laugh. Here was Forrest Tuttle, the old Geauga County game warden. He was busy as all hell lining up the hunters. He had caught a few early shooters, but most of them had their "crested teal," which were all young woodies. He had a lineup that looked like an Army chow line. We listened to such statements as "What's a plug?" and "What's a Duck Stamp?" We were just about to depart when he walked over to me. I don't know what it is, but whenever a game warden walks up to me the hair on the back of my neck starts rising. I wonder why? I guess it's only natural! But he merely greeted me—we'd gotten to know each other fairly well, and until the day he passed away, I considered him one of the best friends I had. He looked at me and said, "Stick around, Fritz." That had me wondering. By then things had quieted down considerably in the marsh, and all the unhappy hunters, cursing the "damn sky busters," etc., were leaving, naturally empty-handed and out of shells. Forrest was loading up his hunters to take them up to the Chardon Court House. It was noon and a real bluebird day. He left with a parting remark that took me by surprise: "Go and watch the marsh behind Charlie Olson's." One of my buddies said that there wouldn't be a thing moving on a day like this, but as he finished saying it we watched a lone hen sneak in and land in a far corner of the marsh. She was soon followed by a few more singles.

I believe that that is what makes a sportsman, whether he be a fisherman, hunter, trapper, or whatever. The surprise! Just as you are ready to give up, the unexpected happens. I got my first mallard that afternoon. A beautiful greenhead that I jumped from behind a rat house. I'll never forget him! His green head was shining in the sun, and in my excitement I missed him with my first shot and crumpled him with the second shot. I sat on that rat house for an hour just admiring him. We picked up a half dozen more that afternoon that way. We learned a real lesson on how many can be lost in a marsh without a dog. We tore the marsh apart looking for the cripples. The game warden's remark, "Best bag in the marsh," really made me feel like an old dyed-in-the-wool duck hunter.

When I got home my mother greeted me with "At Last!" For she was used to mallards in Austria and was getting damn tired of fish ducks. This also helped in my switch from the breakwall to the marshes.

I bagged a lot of mallards that fall by this method. I waited till everyone was gone and marked them down and systematically walked them up. You can never shoot when they are circling. If you do hit one it is almost always lost, either a cripple or too hard to find.

I know this will start an argument, but I found that for jump shooting, the best load was seven and a half low brass in the right barrel backed up with six high brass. Always move in with the wind at your back so the jump, which almost always is into the wind, shoves them into your face.

All those nice mallards to eat, and the muskrats I started bringing home at a buck apiece, finally convinced my mother that I was not cut out to be a factory boy, and believe it or not, she gave up on her crusade.

Naturally I hated school (don't let my kids hear this), so my mother wrote me out a working permit, and I quit—to go trapping. (I got my high school diploma in the Army, so I'm not a complete dropout.) I was getting a little big for the streetcar trap line, so I moved out and stayed with a trapper at the mouth of the Chagrin River, till the war came. There again we hunted, in a different way. The river was at its best when it froze. Then it was bedsheets in the snow lying next to the open rapids. There were mostly blacks. There was one great open hole where the river went into Lake Erie and another by the Ohio Rubber sewer outlet. Those two never froze.

Later, in the service, I used to hear the guys bitch about what they left—most of them worked in factories, stores, etc. I would just smile to myself and think what I had left—and I had volunteered.

Follow Instructions

R. O. A. HUNTER

At the age of twelve years, my son John joined me for his first duck-shooting experience. While he had fired a small-caliber rifle in target practice, he had not fired a shotgun. Because of his age, it was necessary to get a beginner's hunting license, which involved fairly detailed examination by police authorities.

With the natural excitement of anticipating his first duck shoot, we joined a relative at his shooting lodge at the peak of the bluebill flights. Our host arranged for us to be on location at nine-thirty A.M.— a treed point with a wild-rice marsh to right and left. Our decoys were placed ten to twenty yards out front and we awaited, along with our host and two other guests, the bluebill flight.

Within an hour and a half, we had several birds down among our decoys awaiting a pickup when we went in to lunch. As there was a lull in the flight, I gave my Winchester pump to son John and suggested he pick a spot in the wild rice and take a shot so that he could experience the recoil—which he did without falling over.

Fifteen minutes later, a flock of twelve to fifteen bluebills came into view quickly and I gave my gun to John with the instruction to hold aim and fire until I gave the word. As the flight passed from left to right, the other members fired, with no noticeable results. Within split seconds they were passing in front of John, and I said, "Aim," and then, "Fire." Down dropped a bluebill, very dead, and my son's exclamation was, "I got him."

Fifteen minutes later we were picked up by boat and proceeded to pick up our bag. In the course of all the maneuvering, John did not lose sight of "his" duck when they were being claimed.

At a cocktail party some months later, one of our fellow guests was being questioned on his shooting skill, to which he replied, "Not as good as Hunter's son John, who when given a gun and one shell and the instruction to aim and fire, did the only thing he could—namely, shot a duck!"

Wind and Tide

CHARLES G. CAROTHERS III

For once the weatherman hit it right on the button. The rapidly moving front would bring with it gale-force winds, which, coinciding with the full moon, would cause severe coastal flooding in the Duxbury area, a small town located on the South Shore midway between Boston and Cape Cod.

It was December 29, 1966. This was the year that the Fish and Wildlife Service conducted an experimental season for taking black ducks only from December 16 through January 8 in coastal waters of Maine, New Hampshire, and Massachusetts. Its purpose was to try to determine if these hardy blacks were a discreet population whose numbers were unlikely to venture farther down the Atlantic flyway regardless of the severity of a New England winter. An intensive banding program the previous winter and spring preceded this late season.

Tides in this area have a normal average fluctuation of perhaps eight feet, and as low water was early, it was midmorning before Konrad and I (Konrad Gesner, currently a Ducks Unlimited National Trustee and State Chairman from Massachusetts) drove down the barrier beach separating the coastal marshes from the stormy Atlantic. We had not reckoned with the wind's effect on that madly rushing incoming tide. Although it was several hours before high water, the water was flooding over the marsh and beach far in advance of schedule.

We simply couldn't navigate farther toward our destined shooting location, and thus parked the jeep near a jungle of scrub oak and beach plum which also was feeling the savagery of the wind and the pelting salt spray.

Yes, we did take our limit of birds, but more lasting will be our memories of drifting and lost decoys and the struggle to retrieve birds caught up in near surflike conditions. Remembered too is my "Don't shoot!" advice to Konrad as slightly long birds milled overhead struggling to make headway in the gale only to drop one at Konrad's feet a fraction of a second later, when several birds swooped overhead at incredible speed in a *Prairie Wings* "ducks-never-do-that" maneuver. Windblown words complaining about this shoddy treatment of a friend reaches me in more ways than one! And lastly, we'll remember the lovely picture of one black duck alone among ten pintails suspended over our decoys for several moments before disappearing downwind. While not a rarity, pintails are infrequent visitors to our wintery New England coast.

That it was a memorable and stormy day for waterfowling was later confirmed when the Weather Bureau reported that gusts measuring up to eighty-five miles per hour had been recorded.

Reminiscences of an Ohio Dog

OAK HARBOUR TAFFY
(as told to R. Dugald Pearson)

There is probably no one area in northern Ohio that is better known to duck hunters than the Sandusky Bay area. Bordered on one side by the city of Sandusky and the other by the city of Port Clinton, this has been the duck factory of Ohio ever since Quagmire was renamed Lake Erie. Little known to most hunters is the fact that close by is the birthplace and home of some of the finest hunting Labradors in the United States.

Oak Harbour, a town not far distant, is the center of a hunting dog breeding area that at times past has had no equal. Blacks, yellows, and chocolates have received nationwide recognition, and even some of the finest English breeding stock has been introduced into the local Ohio strain.

Unfortunately now most of the breeders are gone and the exploits of their former residents merely a memory. There are tales told, however, in the few duck clubs that do exist and among the few hunters that still hunt the marshes that warm the hearts of many an old-timer.

Memories grow faint with time and old-time hunters drift away like the flight of a black duck at the close of day. Tales and stories of the hunt seem, however, to be kept alive from father to son and hunter to hunter and punter to punter. One of the classic stories of the Sandusky Bay area is that of the kennel.

The kennel, just as easily called by any other name, was a well-known spot where many a hunter rested his dog either in between the morning and afternoon shoot or after the evening shoot. It consisted of a large white house with an Anchor Hocking fence around it with a system installed whereby each hunter as he arrived was announced by the ringing of a bell as he proceeded through the gate. The kennel's hours were from one P.M. to late in the evening, and a most restful spot it was. The furnishings were Victorian and "early Salvation Army." The accommodations furnished were ample, and each hunter and dog were received with a warm welcome.

I had just reached my fifteenth week when I was introduced to my master. I will never forget the day. It was in November, clear and cold. I along with twelve of my brothers and sisters was placed in a pen, and then the boys and girls were separated and placed in separate pens. I, being a girl, joined my four sisters in a separate pen. It wasn't long before the man who fed us appeared with two strangers at the gate. All of us being in rare form, we put on our best performance, jumping, yapping, and dancing around to the best of our ability. The strangers stood at the gate and examined all of us. It was clear that our owner was discussing our respective attributes—all, I hoped, to our benefit.

Suddenly the gate opened and we all made a mad dash for the outside.

The next thing I knew I had been seized by the scruff of the neck and was snuggled comfortably in the crook of an arm that smelled of strange odors and promised excitement. My comfort lasted only a short time and then I found myself in a cardboard box with an old glove for company and suddenly realized that I was being taken away from my brothers and sisters.

After a short interval the box was placed on the seat of what I later learned was a station wagon and off I went on my first journey into the world.

The initial journey was short; before long we arrived at a white house that I later knew to be the kennel. The first sound I heard was the clang of a bell, and then the car stopped and I was lifted from the box and carried to the kennel. Up the steps and into the parlor—my, what a sight! An overstuffed couch in one corner, floor lamps that looked like a funeral parlor, and several standing ash trays, placed between overstuffed chairs that sagged from use and comfort.

Needless to say, I was received with wonder and affection. After all, being a golden ball of fluff with unbounded energy, I was ready for anything. After much fondling and petting, I was treated to a bowl of milk and devoured it as much from excitement as from hunger.

My comfort was short-lived, and back in the box I went and back in the wagon and back on the road. Like all moments of pleasure, mine was short-lived—but fortunately to be repeated.

The next year was spent in learning the ropes of life and some of the finer points of dog education. Having passed my undergraduate courses with merit, I was once again soon in the duck capital of Ohio.

Fall is the time of year that stirs the soul of every hunter—the low overcast; the swift flight of the teal as it flashes by the decoys; the slow and methodical flight of the great Canadas as they move from the bay to the cornfields; the dipping and darting flight of the wood duck as it comes in and out of the canals; the flash of iridescent green on the head of the drake mallard as he darts by in the early dawn; the white on the breast and wing of the black duck as it flares out of range at the end of day; the constant movement of the large flights of sea gulls rising and falling in the calm areas of the marsh; the frequent flight of redwing blackbirds that come and go and wane as the colder weather moves in to the marsh from the north; the great white herons that sit like statues awaiting their dinner that moves below the surface of the pond; the gray cold dawn shrouded in the mist of the morning, gradually warming to a bright and sunny day or changing to a gray and cold wet snow; the sunsets that never last long enough; the hunt that is over too soon— these are moments in life cherished but yet quickly lost in the mist of yesterday and dawns of tomorrow. I am grateful to the man who picked me up that November day, and I am glad that he was my master and companion, and the moments that we have shared will be long remembered.

I am probably the only girl in Ohio who has been in every motel in the Sandusky area and never been asked to register. This includes the Island House Hotel that now excludes all of our kind due to the behavior of some of my brothers, sisters, and cousins, not to mention our masters! I can well remember the day when three or four of us would occupy the prime spots under the tables in the grill room of the Island House—what succulent morsels of perch, steak, and roast beef would be diverted our way and relished by us all. On some occasions, even an olive or cherry would suddenly appear, only to vanish as if by magic!

We drank nothing but the finest spring water from gleaming white porcelain, which was flushed frequently and refilled at our demand. Our beds were the thick carpet, hardwood floor, or now and then a pile of well-worn hunting clothes that testified to the deeds of past hunts and the promise of those to come. A stray feather often found and savored in some hidden nook and cranny of a coat—memory joggers, each having a history of its own.

I guess the hunt that I will always remember best is the one in the early days of my youth. Lucky Pierre, Bull Moose, and Bad Bill made it all possible. Things started out well enough, commencing with a quiet, pleasant trip from Cleveland to Port Clinton in Bull Moose's brand-new Ford station wagon. The car smelled new, and, indeed, less than a hundred miles had been registered before this momentous trip. The day was beautiful and warm, and into the Lakeland Motel pulled our wagon to be greeted by Bad Bill, the Moose (not to be confused with Bull Moose), and others, who for the purpose of avoiding any litigation will remain nameless. After a pleasant cocktail hour during which an uninvited guest crashed through the glass storm door (due to my "friendly" approach) all of us took a short walk to the grill room of the Island House. Steaks, fresh perch, and the coldest beverages soon soothed and calmed the group, and a retreat was made to our quarters for the night.

During the long night awaiting the dawn, I suddenly saw a shadowy figure appear in the doorway and at once raised the alarm, only to discover to my chagrin that I had cornered Bull Moose in the necessary room, and after a dressing-down from my master, I returned to my spot on the floor between the beds. Some time later I was invited to share the deluxe mattress with the party who had been trapped so skillfully by me at four A.M. Needless to say, no hard feelings were held by either, and I must say he was a most forgiving companion.

The day dawned bright and clear and with promise in the air. A short trip was taken to the Island House to awaken our partner for the shoot, who for some reason had failed to answer the call to arms. Unfortunately, the three of us had no better luck at accomplishing the arising of Bad Bill than had the desk clerk. The door was locked and guarded by a big black Canadian dog, named Can, and no one had the courage to enter and accomplish the feat of resurrection. Thus, without further adieu we retraced our steps down to the lobby and left a message with the desk clerk, who at this point was busy answering calls from guests on the floor we had just left; they had been awakened by what must have sounded like the biggest dog fight in history!

On to the marsh, and the closer we came the more promising the day became. Down the highway past the rest ponds and off on the long dirt road, provided by Sandusky's Jackie Mayer. We left the wagon at the end of the road and walked excitedly back to the boat landing into the boat, and then along the long boardwalk to our blind for the day.

We had hardly settled down when a sight to behold appeared. A huge flight of ducks, by conservative count, seventy-five, was headed straight for our pond. On they came in a long low sweep in and over the decoys with a swoop. The magnificence of the scene was one seldom seen since the early 1900s. Back they came over the decoys, split, and then came in on either side of the blocks. The sight of so many retrieves sent me into high gear and my antics soon put them all to flight. Not all was lost, however, as I overheard the shooters declare that no true sportsman ever flock-shot and if the birds were scared out without shooting, they would return in smaller groups, which is the proper way to bring game to bag.

Sure enough, it wasn't long before a small flock could be seen on the horizon. Exactly at that time a lone figure of hunter and dog could be seen trudging the dike in our direction. On came the hunter and on came the ducks. It was inevitable that their paths must cross. On they came, and at the last instant the flock broke and swung over the blind. Six reports split the morning air and five ducks folded in flight, Bull Moose with a triple and Lucky Pierre with a double. I couldn't make up my mind which bird to retrieve first, so I picked up two at once and towed them to the edge of the blind and then made a mad dash for the others. Each one seemed to be bigger than the one before, magnificent game for the bag.

This activity served to increase the urgency of the hunter traveling the dike, and the big black dog dashed forward. In no time at all, the hunter was in the blind, and as Bull Moose and Lucky Pierre had quit for the day, Bad Bill prepared to meet the next flight. It wasn't long before in swept two beauties, bearing down on the blind like a flash. Up came the gun and three shots roared forth, and on flew the ducks unscathed by nary a pellet. The emotional impact of this operation was such that all that could be heard was the retching of a very upset stomach, and the loss of a wonderful opportunity.

The game was gathered and off we all went for the long row and walk home. On the way, however, I discovered, along with Can, a magnificent pile of two-week-old dead trash fish that had been waiting for me down the dike. Oh, what a time was had as we rolled and romped, a sheer delight on such a cold day. On to the car and away to the pluckers with the prizes. After about fifteen minutes in the warm car, the strangest thing took place. An odor not heretofore smelled permeated the air and fought for dominance over the new-car smell. Needless to say, it won, and it was a one-sided victory not soon to be forgotten.

It was with great interest that we watched the antics of Lucky Pierre, Bull Moose, and Bad Bill as they each took turns blaming the other for what we both knew was a fragrance of our own creation. As all good things must end, they suddenly realized who was responsible for the foul deed, and into the bathtub at the Holiday Inn we went, followed by Sargeant's Flea Soap and Pine Spray, all of which failed to mute the deed of the day.

By this time have been thoroughly chastised, back we went to pick up our prizes. Woe, the trouble had just begun. Upon entering the home of our pickers, we were confronted by not one but two game wardens—a young state warden and the federal warden. Everywhere one looked lay ducks. The top of the deep freeze was covered, the tables and all the chairs. After establishing that no shooting over the limit had taken place, the shooters were confronted with the new state regulation that required all game to be tagged. The ducks, of course, were not tagged, as no one had a pencil or paper. Notices were duly written and served by the state warden on Bull Moose, Bad Bill, and Lucky Pierre.

A close examination of the summons, after the shock of a thunder storm which put out all the lights (and my attempt to sneak out in the dark was thwarted), revealed that the charge was shooting snipe and gallinules—an error made by the warden in selecting the wrong section of the game laws to be applied to the situation in question. The summons contained a trial date, and the big bad three were headed for Sandusky Municipal Court and the swift justice of Judge Miller.

Due to the fact that Lucky Pierre and Bad Bill were practitioners of the legal and illegal arts, an attorney was obtained, one Dick Kruse, of the Sandusky bar, to plead their hopeless case. Much planning was done and an all-night meeting held at a waterfront location in Huron, Ohio, far from the eyes and ears of the law. A defense was formulated and the next day the guilty proceeded to the day of judgment.

After a lengthy confrontation with the powers of the law, the charge of shooting those strange and exotic birds known as snipe and gallinules was changed to untagged ducks, to which the big three copped a plea, to use the vernacular. They were duly found guilty, fined, and discharged to consider the error of their ways. The judge, being an understanding and gracious dispenser of justice, ordered the return of the ducks to the hunters and ordered the matter closed.

The ducks, during this stay of legal proceedings, had been reposing in the deep freeze in the Old Folks' Home in Oak Harbour, Ohio, and the violators of the law, seeing the error of their ways, made sure that each resident of the home had a duck dinner the following Sunday.

I now spend a lot of time reminiscing about the hunts of yesteryear. You see, by the human calendar I am eighty-four years old, arthritic and retired. Yet every fall I feel the call and the urge to hunt. I am with my master in mind and spirit but have retired to the warm comfort of my home provided to me by my grateful master, surrounded by friends and the dreams of the hunts past and those to come.

Ottawa Duck Hunt

DAN C. ARMBRUSTER

"Hello, Dan. Lee Howley here."

"Hi, Lee. How are you?"

"Fine. How about a duck hunt on me at Ottawa?"

This was the beginning of a really enjoyable waterfowl hunting trip. Yes, this was the first time in my life to hunt on a Lake Erie marsh. My imagination started to run wild. I could picture heated blinds such as in ice-fishing shanties on Lake Erie.

I arrived at the Ottawa clubhouse at about six P.M. on Tuesday for the hunt the next day, had a few drinks and a good meal. After dinner, we discussed duck hunting, regulations, and a few complaints on the season. A little later Lee showed me the room where I was to sleep and told me they go to bed early.

The following morning I knew why—I heard a rap on the door. "Dan, get up."

I said, "Lee, you must be out of your cotton-pickin' mind. I just got to sleep. What time is it, anyway?"

Lee said, "Four-thirty."

I firmly believe that even though I was a farm boy I should always work the midnight shift because I love to sleep in in the morning. The reason I didn't sleep well the night before was that I was thinking of the duck hunt.

Well, I finally got out of bed half asleep, had a hard time getting my hunting gear on, and went downstairs to the dining room. There, sitting at the head of the table like an English country gentleman, was a good friend of mine, Henry Schmidt. He picked up a little bell near his plate and gave it a ring. In came some nice ladies and asked what I would like for breakfast. I don't think I have eaten ten breakfasts in twenty years, but I said, "Eggs, please." Through a sleepy haze and eggs, I heard Henry and Lee talk about the Upper and Lower Marsh. About that time, Lee's punter came in and announced, "We're about ready to go."

It was still dark as a cave, rather chilly. About this time, I was awake. The three of us and Lee's black Lab, Doc, got in the boat. The punter started the motor and we were on our way across the marsh. We came to a dike. Lee was out first. I figured we would walk up the dike—not so. We portaged here, pulled the boat across the dike and were off again.

Finally, we arrived at the blind. I don't know which one had built-in radar, but there we were. Before I knew what was going on, Lee grabbed an armful of decoys and was setting them out. Ducks were rising off the water. I had a thought that they had scared all the ducks away and shooting would not be any good. Lee and the punter were talking, but I don't remember about what. Lee and I got in the blind with the guns and gear.

Lee and the punter started calling ducks on their duck calls. I thought to myself, I can do that since I started practicing about a week before. I blew a few calls and they both looked at me—even the black Lab had a funny look in his eyes. I said, "Okay, fellows, I'm sorry." I imagined what was going through their minds—we have an inland dude that can't call ducks and I wonder how he shoots.

About that time, a flock of mallards was in the air. Lee gave a blow on the call. "Get down, here they come."

Now how in the hell can one get down lower in a blind than sitting down? But I soon found out—when they mean down, it can't be far enough. Like a dude, I turned my head to look up at the ducks and they flared.

Lee and the punter were very nice. They spoke softly, wonder why those ducks had flared. They knew what had happened. Lee said, "Check your gear to see if there is anything shining, and Dan, don't look up until you're ready to shoot. Those damn ducks can see your eyes."

It was just a matter of minutes till more ducks were coming in. Softly they both said, "Down."

All of a sudden, two shots rang out. Lee had bagged a mallard. "Fetch," Lee yelled to Doc.

That wonderful dog took off like a shot out of a cannon after the duck. Lee looked at me. "Dan, why didn't you shoot?"

"Hell, Lee, I was still programmed to get down." He gave me the Howley chuckle with a few raspberries.

"Down," the punter whispered. "More ducks on the left coming in." They flew over the blind. Lee said, "Shoot!" I did—three shots—but they kept on flying. In came Doc with Lee's duck, laid it down, and seemed very anxious to return for more ducks. I heard Lee softly say, "Down, Doc. He missed the whole flock."

Lee said, "Dan, pick out a duck and lead it about four to six feet." Then he excitedly said, "Down! Here come some pintails coming straight into the blind. Now shoot!"

I did! I aimed at the drake and dammit, I got the hen. Then for the next two hours, those pintails stayed out of range. We got a few more ducks and then it was lunchtime.

Lee got out the Thermos of beans. About this time, I was getting hungry. He poured two big cups, and they were hot. About that time, Lee looked back. "Here they come." They were mallards. We both turned to see the ducks. They didn't get within range. I turned around to pick up my cup of beans.

There was Doc, the black Lab, eating those hot beans.

"Lee, I know you're the national president of Ducks Unlimited and you invited me up for this duck hunt and that dog of yours is great, but do I have to eat those beans?" "No," he said, and he gave me his beans. We both laughed because that dog still had hot beans in his mouth.

This was one duck hunt I will never forget.

Flyway Farm

PAUL H. SWETLAND

In 1969 I purchased a plot of ground of about seventy acres in Newbury Township, Geauga County, Ohio. My desire was to live in the country and my interest in waterfowl prompted this move. The land, in general, was low-lying, had a stream running through it and a sugar bush that was planted some seventy years ago, containing about three acres. However, most of the last was scrub, with the exception of one area of one acre that was a former filtering bed for a gravel pit that had been abandoned upstream some years before. In that area, I would spread about a bucket of corn and go and check the following day and find that it was all gone. This gave me the idea that there were some ducks about and that there might be the possibility of establishing some type of waterfowl refuge in a fast-urbanizing area. That fall, with an excavator, we staked out a pond of about three acres and went to work. While the pond was nice, it was not complete habitat for waterfowl. We decided to repair a dam at the old settling basin and flooded approximately three and a half acres. This area had an average depth of about eighteen inches and was covered with cattails. Therefore, a good deal of work had to be done in thinning the cover to allow potholes and various areas of open water. The middle of March the first spring, when we discovered six Canada geese settling in on the pond, we knew we were on the right track.

In learning about pond management, I have found that the life of a pond can be as short as ten years from its inception to its death, and the life of a marsh is much more critical, due to the intrusion from shoreline growth, the sedimentation, and the decay of vegetation within the marsh. Since a marsh is a more complete habitat for ducks, we decided to flood an area to the north of the first lake of approximately eight acres. This required a dam of close to five hundred feet in length and eight feet in height. When this area was filled, the average depth was about two feet. The first year, I drained the area and planted millet and duck wheat, and when this matured, I flooded the area again. However, I found that blackbirds would get the seeds long before the ducks were in the area. This left the only alternative of importing submerged plants such as sago pond weed, wild celery, duck potato—both deep and shallow water—plus coontail and various bullrushes.

After building our home on this acreage, we found that the first lake was not quite large enough and there was a possibility of extending it and flooding a wooded area in the rear. So, in came the bulldozers and we went to work again building another seven hundred feet of dams and a spillway with a drop pipe of about six feet in diameter. The first dam we cut down to a level of eight inches below the high-water mark so that the first lake could be drained, or the whole area could be drained and the first lake would still retain water. We could chemically treat the first lake, which was near the residence, so that it would be free of aquatic growth. Now that it is complete, we have approximately twenty acres under water, twenty-nine wood-duck boxes, and five goose-nesting platforms, plus numerous mallard nests on various islands in the lake area. This past year we had an egg count of over four hundred, and probably a hatch of near three hundred wood ducks. Wood ducks will not nest and rear their young in an area that does not provide suitable cover. Therefore, the marsh land with cattails and the flooded woods seems to provide an ideal setting.

We had three families of geese that hatched in the area and find that the birds return year after year. The hunting in the general area has improved over the past few years; there are more birds and they are not driven off completely since they have a few refuges that they can drop into for sanctuary. Since a flyway is the migration route of avian travel from breeding grounds to winter quarters, we named our place Flyway Farm. Waterfowl tend to adhere to their ancestral route year after year. At Flyway Farm, we do not believe in trying to hold the birds over the winter and do believe they should migrate as nature intended.

We have counted some twenty-five species of ducks and geese. While only a few of these stay and rear their young, it does provide a place for them to rest during their migration periods, and it also shows the need to preserve whatever wetlands we can on these routes. To do this there is a need to provide some incentive to the landowner. The Federal Water Bank Program is one method that tries to preserve wetlands and should be extended to other areas than those on the main migratory routes, because we are fast losing our open space and wetlands to the developer and the plow. I feel that the Water Bank Program should be carried on in more than the few counties of the thirteen states that are now involved. The purpose of the program is to conserve surface waters, to preserve and improve habitat for migratory waterfowl and other wildlife resources, to reduce runoff, and soil and wind erosion, and to contribute to water control.

If we do not preserve the wintering grounds and the intermediate stopover places for waterfowl that do not fly nonstop, all of the money that we spend in Canada for nesting grounds will be for naught. As this habitat disappears due to man's encroachment, so will the birds.

Ducks On Ice

WILLIAM S. HAWGOOD

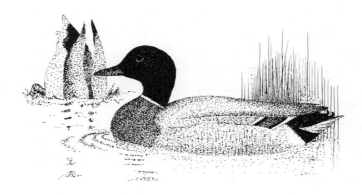

A few years ago, two days before the end of the split season, my son Lary, his shooting buddy Dave, and I decided to give the Sandusky Bay area a last effort on the closing day.

There was sufficient daylight that late afternoon of our arrival to see that the marshes and bay were frozen tight. Lots of ice fishermen, but not a duck did we see in the last light.

We checked the city pond in Castalia, which remains ice-free all winter because of the great volume of water that the Blue Hole provides. We found duck, probably more than ten thousand—blacks and mallards with a few widgeon and pintail. This gathering was so dense on this three-acre pond that you couldn't see a spot of open water. We concluded that all the late ducks were loafing there and feeding in the cornfields early evening and before sunup. We had expected ice, but optimistically thought there might be some spots of open water near the outer bay.

We had shot a sandbar earlier in the season that lies between Bay Point and Cedar Point. It is a great spot for mergansers and an occasional black or mallard in early November.

Two hours before sunrise the following morning we left our snug motel in Bay View and drove to a parking area near Marblehead Point, and our adventure began.

The two young men and my two Labs were moving about with great enthusiasm as we dragged our "toboggan" down to the ice. The so-called toboggan was a ten-by-five-foot piece of heavy polyethylene sheet on which we had curled the edges and fixed a sled rope. It comfortably carried sixty duck decoys, seven goose decoys, three guns, two bags of charcoal for the canister heater, an ax, a one-man crosscut saw, a large Thermos of coffee, and plenty of shells. At least it was satisfying to be so well equipped as we easily glided along over smooth ice that appeared to be nearly six inches thick. We were travelling parallel to the Bay Point shore, which broke the strong southwest wind.

Our objective was probably close to a mile and a half, but could we find it when we got there? If the bay had frozen at high water it would be well submerged.

With a little light now showing in the east, it all seemed like a nice outing, but I thought there was a slim chance of warming any barrels. We passed the tip of Bay Point and a quarter-mile beyond was our sandbar with nearly three acres exposed. The great surprise was to find two acres of open water adjoining the off side of the sandbar.

There was a strong current of water flowing out of the bay along the east edge of the bar that kept it open. With the early light we could see no more open water in any direction. There were thick chunks of pressure ice piled on the west side of the bar, which we fashioned into a very rough ice fort.

The temperature at the motel had read twenty-four degrees when we left, and that southwest wind was really beginning to blow, coming straight down the bay with nothing to interrupt it.

I got the scotch stove going and put in half the first bag of charcoal. We set out the goose decoys on the high point of the sandbar and were setting out the duck decoys on the upwind edge of open water when we were suddenly aware of quacking overhead.

A flight of several hundred blacks and mallards was passing overhead eighty yards high, flying directly southwest into the wind. Within seconds, probably twenty of them peeled off and landed with one swoop right among us. Most of them were within fifteen yards of us, which was ten times closer to us than our three empty guns, which were still nesting on the toboggan.

At any rate, it was an exciting beginning.

Now we were ready, huddled behind our few ice blocks, stoking our little stove with the remainder of the first bag of charcoal, and waiting for a repeat performance.

Two hours later we were still waiting. The second bag of charcoal was nearly consumed, burning like a blast furnace in the driving wind.

Greedy for the fringes of heat, we did nothing to baffle the wind, and let it burn.

Small flocks of goldeneye whistled overhead well out of range as the coals cooled and our blood congealed. Lary and Dave "volunteered" to walk to the Bay Point shore and pick up driftwood to sustain our fire.

They had just returned when we saw a dozen honkers flying low over the ice into the wind and heading directly toward us. Their ground speed seemed near zero as the minutes passed. They veered slightly as they saw the goose decoys, dropped to less than ten feet, and continued their struggle into the wind.

Now we were ready, now we were warmer, and so were my Labs as they charged out of our ice house when the geese were fifty yards short of the decoys with their landing gear down. Not a shot fired except the verbal abuse from the three of us.

A short while later, we saw a red fox heading toward us in a straight line and at a fast trot, coming on a line from the coal docks in Sandusky. He reached the far edge of the open water, about a hundred yards away and certainly too far for our number fours. He visually surveyed all of the open water area, turned tail, and trotted away on his backtrail. On watching him disappear from view, I recollected the stories of foxes "working" rafts, salvaging the lead sick ones. An old-timer had told me of witnessing a raft of duck on the bay ice with six baldheaded eagles standing on the ice patiently encircling them at a slow walk, expecting when they were spooked there would be a few sick ducks remaining. (Nature isn't mild, but it is efficient.)

It was now midmorning and the only thing that was moving was the wind. Prepared, we thought we were, with sufficient clothing—but we were wrong, and I have never been so cold.

The boys had gone ashore for more wood and I was jumping around on the ice to sustain life when I saw four ducks coming in low over the ice from the direction of Cedar Point. In an instant they were over the decoys and cut downwind.

At that split second I saw they were drake canvasbacks. At this moment they were traveling in single file; I swung ahead of the leader, fired, and the end drake folded. I will have to blame that reverse lead on my crystallized joints.

The shot brought back the boys in a hurry. They had barely returned when a huge flight of ducks started coming from the north. They were passing directly overhead at about a hundred yards. They were quartering into the wind and making reasonable headway. The next five minutes were the ultimate. Small groups of mallards and blacks curled out of the big flight and swooped toward the decoys. The boys did well, as did the Labs, and they filled out their limits, mostly in greenheads.

Suddenly it wasn't so cold and we were headed home with our gear and limits, easily sledding across the ice and carrying within all of us quite a bunch of exciting memories.

Warm-Weather Bluebills

ALAN G. HAID

As we were driving down Interstate 75 somewhere in Georgia in January 1973, the talk was about bluebills. We were on our way to Charlotte, Florida, to try out some Yankee tactics on the Florida bluebills. The year before, when Tom Winstel and Bob Dwyer, my two companions from Cincinnati, were on a combination fishing and sunning vacation with their families, they had seen large rafts of blue-bills in Charlotte Harbor—"thousands of bluebills!" They had managed to shoot a few off points of land jutting out into the harbor. Since that time we have speculated as to how our two-man layout boat would work in Florida.

We had been layout shooting for a few years on Lake Erie and Sandusky Bay, but the shooting had fallen off and that overnight trip from Cincinnati was a killer. When Lake Erie was too rough all the layout shooters went to Sandusky Bay, and by actual count I had spotted twenty-five different layout rigs set up in the bay on one day. It doesn't take the bluebills long to discover that Sandusky Bay isn't the place to ride it out on a windy day. With layout-shooting opportunities in Ohio dwindling, it was logical to turn elsewhere. Florida seemed to have the best possibilities.

Would bluebills in Florida react like northern bluebills? Would they trade back and forth? Would they decoy to our rig? They are the same ducks, we told ourselves; it is only later in the season. Bluebills were a ten-point duck in Florida, so ten bluebills per day provided plenty of shooting opportunity. In thirty hours we would know. We had done our homework well, we hoped. We had painted our layout boat a "wet-rust" color to match the brackish color of the Peace River as it enters Charlotte Harbor. The color is a far cry from the steel-gray color of Lake Erie. Our layout boat, which we were towing behind the car, was a two-man style built by master layout builder John Kalask of Gibraltar, Michigan. His boats are the standard for Detroit River and Lake Erie layout hunters. John does a super job of building a seaworthy craft that is as light as possible. We had proved that in some of those eight-foot rollers that suddenly come up on Lake Erie.

As far as we knew from talking to other duck hunters, there wasn't anyone using a layout boat in the state of Florida. So there was no one to ask for advice as to how to set up, how many decoys to use, when the birds would fly, weather conditions, tides, etc. It would be quite an experience to see how the bluebills would react.

The layout boat was crammed full of exactly one hundred home-made diver-duck decoys. They were our own design—mostly cork bodies with our own or Herter's heads. All of the decoy lines, each holding twenty decoys, were carefully wrapped on the spools and were ready to go. The single decoys had their lines wrapped around their bodies.

The dawn broke and the sun started its climb as we crossed the border into Florida. Soon we stopped for gas and to stretch our legs. While we were parked in the service station, some of the elder local citizens strolled out to look at what we were towing behind the station wagon. They speculated as to what it was, where the motor would go, how fast the waves would sink it, and why it had no seats. We did not justify our cargo. We simply climbed back into the car and continued down I-75.

When we arrived in Port Charlotte at noon, we called Roy Aires, a native fishing guide, and asked him to meet us at the boat ramp where Florida 41 crosses the Peace River. As we crossed the bridge to the ramp we scanned the water with our binoculars to look for bluebills. They were there—thousands of them. They were on both sides of the bridge, the river side and the harbor side. Nothing helps duck hunting like ducks—and there they were!

Roy soon arrived and we discussed our strategy for the morning. He had a fourteen-foot johnboat and a nine-and-a-half-horsepower motor. That limited us to hunting in the river. Roy said many of the bluebills rested in the harbor overnight and flew up the river to feed in the bays in the morning. Toward noon, they would fly back out to the harbor or the wider areas of the river. We decided to set up on a sandbar in the flight path. Tomorrow's high tide would be at seven minutes past eight, so the bar would be covered with water, and we could set up our spread by walking on the sandbar with our waders on. This would save much time over setting the decoys out from the boat. We left Roy's boat and motor tied up in the water and agreed to meet at five-fifteen A.M. This should give us ample time to get set up and be ready to shoot at the seven-o'clock sunrise.

That night at dinner we proceeded with the formalities of deciding who would shoot first in the layout boat, with the third man staying in the tender boat with Roy. It was a foregone conclusion that Tom, with his luck, would shoot first; but I had a chance against Bob for the other starting spot. When we cut the cards, the three of hearts told me I would start the day in the tender boat with Roy.

We arrived at the landing promptly at five-fifteen and saw Roy already in his boat with the motor running. After varied experiences with some fifty or more guides across the North American continent, a sight like that gives you a real warm feeling inside. We quickly launched the layout boat, piled the decoys inside, and started our tow up the channel to the submerged sandbar. I rode in the layout boat to make sure that it didn't bump the tender boat. Canoe paddles do come in handy.

As we started out to the channel, the light wind was drifting the fog across the water. It was a chilly forty-five degrees, which is unseasonably cool for this part of Florida. One by one, the channel markers came into the light from Roy's flashlight. After he carefully counted five channel markers, we turned sharply to the left, crossed in front of one island, and Roy announced that we were over the sandbar. We threw out the anchor of the john boat, and the three hunters jumped into the water to position the layout boat and put out the decoys. The water was about waist deep and the tide was still coming in. Roy advised us to shuffle our feet on the sandbar so we would not step on sand sharks or sting rays that might be lying on the bar. I tried not to think too much about what he said.

The trip from the boat ramp had taken about forty-five minutes, so we had to hustle to get set up in time to shoot. Tom and I set up the long lines that had twenty divers on each line. Bob stood in the layout boat and threw out the singles between the lines to break up the pattern. We could see the lights on the bridge over Florida 41 and occasionally heard the sound of wings. We positioned the layout boat at our backs, so the birds would be landing into the wind and provide good shots. We occasionally could see birds now. Bluebills—all bluebills!

It was just seven when we put the last decoy bags in the tender boat. Tom and Bob climbed in the layout boat with their guns and shells and Roy and I started for our spot out in the channel downstream a quarter of a mile away. I knew Tom and Bob were getting themselves ready to shoot, pulling that "wet-rust"-colored tarp over their bodies and lying flat on the boat bottom.

As I looked over Roy's shoulder, I could see the bluebills starting to move from the harbor up the river. Then I heard shots, and I knew some were flying close to the boat. When we anchored, I watched through binoculars and I could see birds actually decoying into our spread. There were lots of shots now, and occasionally I could see one of them jump out of the boat to retrieve a downed bluebill. I even saw three birds fall at once!

Eight o'clock was the designated time to shift, so Roy and I started out to the layout boat. We cut across and proceeded upstream. We picked up five dead birds the tide and current had washed out. We also shot two cripples for them, making seven. They had eight birds in the layout boat. Those fifteen birds were half our limit and I hadn't fired a shot! Since Bob had shot the most birds, he left with Roy to take up the tender position downstream.

I climbed into the layout boat and lay flat on my back so that I could hardly see over the end of the boat. The hundred pounds of lead ballast in the foot of the boat dropped it to just the right angle. All of a sudden, there was a drake bluebill roaring into our spread. My side— my shot—and I took him! There were more behind him. Tom and I each dropped one more before that group left. Then more came, and more. If you have never shot bluebills from a layout boat, you have missed a real thrill. They come bearing in like a P-38! Not like a cautious black duck or a flighty pintail—just straight in, as only blue- bills can do. Their wings never stop and they keep coming. They fly on Charlotte Harbor just as they do on Lake Erie!

The rest was history. We had our thirty-duck limit—all bluebills— by ten A.M. A super day, a super shoot—our Yankee tactics had worked on these "warm-weather bluebills."

You've Got to Be Nuts

ARTHUR CLARK

Most folks think that *Non illegitimus carborundum* is Latin for "Don't let the bastards wear you down."

They're wrong! It really means: "All duck hunters are dumb bastards." If you don't think so, ask any waterfowler's wife. Including mine!

After a generation of wedded bliss (except during the all-too-brief waterfowl seasons) my wife still marvels that I can be in a coma until midmorning all year long, then be up and alert, bright-eyed and bushy-tailed, at four o'clock any morning from mid-October till year's end.

Why? There are many reasons: the joy of starting out at thirty degrees, with snow, sleet, and rain slashing into one's face; wading through slop and muck with the water an inch or two below wader tops; sitting in a blind, not moving a muscle, as atrophy sets in from the inaction; exclaiming "What a perfect day!" as the wind whistles and the shooting glasses become opaque from snow and rain.

At long last, a flight comes in to the blocks. I knock down two ducks. One falls in open water and is quickly retrieved by my Labrador. The other lands way over in the cattails. The Lab can't find it. Over I go to help him. As the search goes on, a large flight sets down in my decoy spread—but too far away for a shot.

Another time, in the metal canvasback sink blind well out in the bay, the wind has been gaining speed for thirty uninterrupted miles across the lake. Back at the dock the thermometer reads eight degrees. But out here, the chill factor has got to be sixty below. I'm not freezing because I'm wearing my winter flying suit from World War II. But the glass eye in my left socket feels like a red-hot poker.

Arriving home long past dark and bone-tired, love's labor demands spending another half-hour or so down at the river bank, cleaning the birds by flashlight in the bitter cold, tearing skin off knuckles cleaning out the carcass, missing half the pinfeathers in the dark.

Finally, getting in the house, shucking the wet and muddy gear, reaching for a warming toddy—only to be told by my dearly beloved that the freezer is full, so why not give those birds away in the morning.

The sad story of a duck hunter's travail was well stated by these lines from our friend Anon.

A duck hunter belongs to a crazy breed
A hole in the mud is all they need.
A place to watch for a flying duck
In ninety acres of smelly muck.

It's almost wicked for a man with a brain
To risk his health in fog and in rain,
To tempt the fates and sell his soul
Just to squat in the mud of a slimy hole.

Would I run the risk of enduring strife
By getting in bad with the little wife,
Just to sit in a blind, suffering pain,
In snow and wind and sleeting rain?

Would I waste my money, and my time,
To sit cramped and wet in stinking slime?
Would I do these things no sane man should?
Brother, you're right—I certainly would.

Canine Pirate

ASA SHIVERICK, JR.

A few years back on a beautiful duck day, I was shooting out of Blind 2 where no ducks were interested. My companions were shooting out of Blind 1 having lots of action.

Each time they shot a duck, having no dog, one of them would get out of the blind, wade out to where the duck had fallen, retrieve the duck, bring it back to the blind, and toss the duck behind the blind while they proceeded to wait for the next flight.

Meanwhile, my dog and I were waiting patiently for ducks to come into our decoys. My dog in his anxiety would slip away, go to the other blind, and bring me their ducks each time after they had shot and retrieved them.

As a result, at the end of the day, it was quite embarrassing when I came in with a double limit not having fired my gun, and they came in empty-handed and, needless to say, mad as hell.

All The Way

W. RAY KROMER

When I was thirteen years old, I traded twelve car washes to a real-estate broker in a small town in Minnesota for a 12-gauge single-barrel shotgun. The men in town, the barber and his friends, were very helpful in getting me started. They would take me out in the sloughs around Bird Island, Minnesota, of which there were many, and there were plenty of ducks during the season.

On one occasion, on the way back from early-morning shooting, the driver said he had to stop at the garage and have his Model T Ford checked over. The garage was on the Yellowstone Trail outside of the main street, so they loaded the ducks on my shoulders and I proceeded up the street to the barber shop to drop off the ducks.

I was met at the door by the town marshal. He asked me for my license, which I did not have. I learned afterward that it was planned that way, and after a kangaroo court, they all chipped in and bought me a license, which I think probably cost them about ten cents apiece.

I shined shoes at the barber shop every dance night, and every dime that I got, I took to the hardware store where they would sell me shells at five cents apiece. So I got enough shells to shoot, but very carefully.

I graduated from duck hunting in Minnesota and spent several fall duck-hunting seasons in South Dakota in the hills in the north-eastern part. There, my brother and I and my uncle continually did pothole shooting. One time in particular, I remember that my brother and I saw ducks in a pothole. He went around the outside and I crawled up through the rushes. I was waiting for him, and waited and waited until finally the ducks became excited, and so did I. I stood up and all of a sudden there were like a bunch of stars in the water, and instead of taking a duck, I just shot blindly. My brother got up and said, "What the devil are you doing? Didn't you see that bunch coming in? Those were the sparklers on the water." There was another group of ducks coming in that were bigger in number than the ones on the water.

My uncle and I went pass shooting on several occasions. There was one pass south of Eden, South Dakota, that was between two lakes, one of them called Stink Lake. My uncle used to say, "Raymond, watch those humpbacks. Those canvasbacks are the best eating. Take them before the mallards."

In regard to goose shooting, I have had some very good experiences, and some that were not too good. First, I'll take the better ones. Before they started feeding geese in Virginia and Maryland, we used to have good shooting in North Carolina, at Mattamuskeet and Currituck Sound. I made several trips there with friends and we never failed to get our limit, especially in Mattamuskeet in the bean fields surrounding the lake. The swans bothered us. They would come in about ten or twelve feet high over us, and the geese did not follow them. We caught up with them in the bean fields. They had geese in Montana in the northern part, about thirty miles from Shelby. They were mostly all snow geese, but we would dig in and use paper decoys, and along before sunup, it really got cold. I was shivering constantly until the ducks or the geese came in. We had a very successful shoot there on two different occasions.

Not many people have seen geese resting in trees or lighting in trees. I have, in northern Australia, about 150 miles west of Darwin. I was there for water buffalo, which were not hard to get, and after getting a good trophy, we went goose hunting and fishing. The geese would come in on the river, which was not sluggish. After shooting, they would get up and land in the trees. I found out afterward that they had two or three toes and wondered whether or not they could swim, but I found out they could. This was quite an experience. They were roasted in an oven that was fired up earlier and placed in the oven after the fire was dragged out.

There are Canada geese in New Zealand. I was there on a hunt for chamois and deer and I was awakened in the morning by the honking of geese. I couldn't believe it, but upon going outside I saw flocks of Canadas circling the upper end of Lake Taupo. I bought a shotgun and with Gary Joll collected more geese than we should have for the capacity of his freezer. We enjoyed two goose dinners before I left New Zealand.

On one of my hunting trips to Africa, we saw ducks flying on the lake quite a ways from the camp, and with a little persuasion, Bryan Coleman and I went over to get some ducks for the camp. We had a number of seven and a half shot for guinea fowl. I was surprised at the number of teal and pintail that were in this lake and nesting there. About the middle of the morning, several geese came by, and they kept flying around. I knew that the small shot would not bother them until they came in very low, and I could hear the shot scatter off their feathers, but it never fazed them. We did manage to collect one or two of the geese that were nesting in the lake.

My best goose shooting has been on the Eastern Shore of Maryland. I've been to eastern Maryland on two different occasions, to Chesapeake Bay on a blind out in the water. The blinds in the eastern area are the best shooting. Our best shooting was in blinds next to bean and corn fields. In Maryland and on Chesapeake Bay it was not difficult to obtain your limit and be into camp before lunch.

I want to recount two experiences that I had which were very unsuccessful. One was in Mexico, south of El Paso. I had read in the sporting magazines about the great goose shooting in northern Mexico, plus sandhill crane. After two years, I wrote and they gave glowing descriptions of the number of geese that were available. In one week, I fired two shots without getting a goose or a sandhill crane. They had been shot up so much that you just had to take a suicide shot on the last day.

The second disappointment was up in Canada near Hudson Bay. A camp up there, with headquarters out of Toronto, gave glowing reports on the geese. I met a friend from Los Angeles in Toronto and we stayed together at this lodge and followed an Indian guide all over the terrain where the scrub pine was about up to your knees. He was continually looking for goose droppings to establish a blind, which he made up of scrub pine. There were geese in the area, but they were very wary, and in one week my friend and I each got two shots and we came home with two geese, one of which he mounted. These were snow geese and not very large.

There is some humor in that while we were waiting behind the blind for some geese to come in, the Indian guide came over most hurriedly. The tide was out and we could hear a slop, slop, slop coming in toward us. He said "Shoot, shoot, shoot!" He was referring to a polar bear that came toward us. I put my hand on the shoulder of my friend and said, "Don't shoot. He won't bother us if we don't bother him." He went within a hundred yards of us and went up on a rise behind us, turned around, and looked at us. But I have never seen an Indian turn white before. The same thing happened two days later. I don't know whether it was the same bear or another one, but he tried to dig himself into the ground.

That trip was an experience. It taught me a lesson not to go to a place unless it was recommended by a friend or another hunter as being good. I received a folder from this outfit recently and believe it or not, my picture was on the front of the cover of the folder with the two geese over my shoulder. It certainly is misrepresentation, and I hope none of my friends take it as a recommendation.

Now for duck hunting. I think all of us remember certain duck hunts that were outstanding and that we never will forget. One of these was in Montana, where I was teaching school between getting my degree. The agriculture teacher and I roomed together in the small town of Warden, about twenty miles from Billings. Of course, we went into Billings every Saturday night that we could afford, and one Sunday morning on returning, about eight miles from town we saw greenhead mallards resting in an irrigation project. The fields were flooded periodically by irrigation, and this was in the Huntley sugar-beet project. The water was about six or seven feet deep, and these ducks must have flown quite some distance, because they seemed to be tired and enjoying a good rest and not feeding.

Ferguson and I hurried back to our room, got our guns and ammunition, changed our clothes, which was fortunate, and returned. We had to crawl down an irrigation ditch which had recently been used and was full of mud, but as Ferguson put it, "Two good duck hunters don't mind a little mud." So we crawled up this irrigation ditch until we were opposite the center of the swamp.

On the first rise, Ferguson and I got two apiece. We thought that was it, but the ducks circled and landed right in front of us. We came back to town with our limit and brought ducks into our landlady, who was feeding the school teachers. We had several good duck dinners.

There was other duck hunting on the Yellowstone River about a mile from town. However, that was really good shooting. Another one was in the northern part of South Dakota, north of Sand Lake, which is a duck and goose preserve. Bob Gorder and I went out, getting permission from a farmer to dig some shallow pits in a cornfield just adjacent to a stubble field. We had good success day after day, and on the last day of the season, Bob said, "This is the last day—we had better go out and see what we can do." We dug our shallow pits and I put some decoys out in the stubble field. We got several speckled pheasant and a couple of good Canada geese.

Then a few ducks came in. I left the blind and went over to pick up a greenhead. I had just two shells in my gun. It started to snow heavily and ducks came in all around us. I could even see the sparkle in their eyes as they came in. I fired at a drake, and this is the first time that I ever got a triple in one shot. A hen and another drake fell right behind him. I got another duck with the second shot. I let him lay and hurried back to my blind for more shells. They kept coming in, and whether I was standing up or not made no difference to them. They were going to sit down, and Bob and I had our limit within fifteen to twenty minutes. They kept on coming in. We stood there and watched them settle in among the decoys and in the cornfield. Evidently the snow had brought them down. I have never seen anything that equaled that flight of ducks.

I did have one more experience on goose shooting where geese returned. I was in a pit in a bean field and two geese came over. I got the lead goose. We had no decoys, so I got out of the pit and took a couple of sticks and put them under the wings of this goose and under his head for a decoy. My partner, over in another blind, said, "Ray, the second goose is coming back." He came right back over and I learned later that if you get the lead goose, the others will frequently return, to their sorrow.

Believe It or...

HAROLD D. NORTH, JR.

The oddest waterfowl experience I ever had was my first goose hunt. George Gascoigne took me to Outer Islands Lodge in Nags Head, North Carolina, to hunt geese miles from shore in the shallow water in Chesapeake Bay. We had to be taken out by jet boat and were in a sink box that had four ropes so that we could raise and lower the heavy frame that supported the waterproof canvas and keep the top just 2 or 3 inches above the level of the bay. Of course, we had to change it approximately every hour as the tide rose and fell. We were surrounded with a lattice wave breaker and an enormous quantity of duck and goose decoys both on the lattice and floating. We had been told that we would never get a goose if we had our head so that our eyes were more than two inches above the top of the box and that if we so much as winked when the geese were within a quarter of a mile of us, they would see it and be spooked. Having always heard how wary geese are, I believed all this, and George and I, facing each other on the bench seats, were trying to live up to the instructions.

It was a bluebird day and early in the morning one flight of geese had appeared way to the north of us and that was all. About eleven in the morning it was time to adjust our box. George and I each manned a pair of the ropes. Something went wrong and the thing got away from us so that the top of the box dropped under water and it was gushing in and flooding us. We had to let go of one side, both pulling on the ropes to cleat them, and then turn back and raise the other side, and finally we got the thing under control with only two feet of water in the bottom.

You can imagine the yelling and cussing that went on through this procedure.

George was finished cleating the ropes and I turned around and looked at the decoys. Incredibly, I suddenly realized that seven of the decoys had slightly longer necks and were moving away from the blind between twenty and twenty-five yards up the wind. You would suppose that I yelled, "Mark." Actually, I yelled, "My God, George, they're real."

He said, "What's real?"

And I said, "Seven geese in the decoys."

Mind you, through all this yelling, they were just slowly swimming away. And so we both grabbed our guns and didn't know what to do because they did not spook into flight. Finally, we waved our arms and yelled and the geese took to the air. In our excitement we both fired both barrels. I dropped one on *George's* side, and he dropped one on *my* side. Great teamwork! Off went the other five.

After retrieving them and congratulating each other and wondering what to think about all those years we had heard about the wariness of the great bird, we finally settled down and took a look around. About a quarter-mile to the side there was something that we could see flopping. In excitement I waded in the slightly over knee-deep water as fast as I could, hoping not to land in the ship channel, and sure enough found we had killed a third goose, which expired just as I got there totally out of breath. Of course, we will never know which of us killed that goose, since we each fired twice. We have recorded it together as a goose and a half each.

The incredible sight of the geese in the midst of the hullabaloo we were kicking up trying to save our sink box will make me wonder forever how sometimes these birds can be so smart and how in heaven's name they could have been so dumb that morning. But needless to say, my first goose was the most memorable goose I will probably ever shoot.

The Legacy

JAMES E. KEHRES

My father, Ed Kehres, gave my brother and me a great love of hunting and the outdoors. In all modesty, he was one of the finest duck shots and hunters with whom I have ever had the privilege to hunt. He used his grandfather's Winchester Model 97 pump hammer gun with a thirty-two-inch full-choke barrel—not a very fancy gun but in his hands, a deadly weapon on ducks. Oddly enough, he was a miserable skeet shot. If he got fifteen or sixteen targets in a round he considered that pretty good, but in the duck marsh he was something to watch.

Quite a few years back, my dad and I were invited to shoot at the Magee Marsh. If my memory serves me right, it was about the time cars went from floor shift to standard shift on the column. We owned a 1939 Chevy, and the gear shift on those cars was operated by a vacuum system.

When we got to the Magee Marsh, which is located on the western end of Lake Erie, we had no sooner parked the car when the equivalent of bellhops took all of our luggage, hunting clothes, guns, and other equipment and put them into our respective private rooms. I was a lad of about thirteen at the time, and we had a rather sizable springer by the name of Kip. To a youngster that age, the lavishness of this duck-hunting camp was something to behold.

The following morning we were up about five A.M. and, after a gluttonous breakfast, Dad and I and Kip headed out to the blind with our punter. The blinds were constructed of wood, closed at one end, with the other end left open for access. The outside of the blind was covered with cattails to blend in with the rest of the marsh area. Dad and I got into the blind while the punter was putting out the decoys.

With the blocks out and our blind ready for business, I was put at the closed end of the blind. Kip was next to me, then Dad, and the punter on the end. Since I was thirteen and obviously new at the game, Dad wanted me to shoot first. There were ducks all over. A pair came in over the decoys, and I stood up and surprised myself by knocking one down. However, there was one thing we hadn't taken into account. The three of us could see the duck on the water, but the dog couldn't, because of the height of the blind. Now everyone knows that when a good dog sees a duck fall, his instincts are to fetch it. That is what Kip did! However, in the process of getting the duck, and there being only one way out, sixty pounds of springer spaniel sailed over my father's lap and hit the punter square on. He did the most beautiful belly flop into the pond, while his gun sailed through the air and landed perfectly straight up and down in the muck, with the butt in the air. Needless to say, the soaking-wet punter made it quite clear that that dog was not getting back into the blind.

Kip was then assigned the top of a muskrat house as his base of operation. It was interesting that he wouldn't bring any of the ducks back to the blind. He would take them instead back to the muskrat house. On one occasion, he brought back a cripple that was quite lively. He put it on the pile with the other ducks, and each time he'd lay it down, the duck would get up, walk off the muskrat house, and start swimming. After that happened two or three times, he dug a hole in the top of the muskrat house and literally buried the duck.

Another time, while shooting with Dad at Nielsen's Marsh, he and our punter, Chet Nielsen, had one of their raging spelling bees going. Dad had a degree in law and Chet hadn't gone much past grammar school. Anytime a word was misspelled, the winner was rewarded with a quick nip. It was a slow morning, and the two of them had been thoroughly engrossed in their battle, which seemed to me to be a draw.

Meanwhile, I was sitting there perched down because of the closed lid on the blind, with my ears on the contest and my eyes peering through the foot-high slit looking for ducks. Sure enough, along came this big drake mallard just hanging out over the decoys. Without bothering to lift the lid, or to advise my dad and Chet, I stuck the gun through the slit and let blast.

With Dad and Chet having had a few nips, and eardrums ringing from what sounded like a bomb in the partially enclosed blind, they instinctively jumped up and added to their misery by whamming their heads on the closed lid. To add insult to the whole affair, after having waited most of the morning for a shot, I had missed. You can well imagine how sternly I was told how to conduct myself when that situation happened again.

You'd think that with all my hunting experience with my father, I would have learned a few lessons. Later on in life, however, on one occasion my brother Charley and I, accompanied by my new bride, Marcia, took off on a beautiful sunny day to shoot at Henry Schmidt's place, just across the dike from the Ottawa Shooting Club. Hunting is not one of my wife's fortes, though she had handled a gun before. She proceeded to settle herself comfortably on the dike, propped up against a punt boat, and engross herself in a book, while Charley and I took off into the flooded corn with our Lab to do some teal shooting. We were having a "Hey Rube," as the teal were plentiful, and within an hour and a half needed only one bird to finish our limit. With the two of us blasting away, Marcia appeared on the scene to see how we were doing. With only one duck to go, I asked her if she didn't want to take a shot. With an affirmative reply, she took my gun and within a few minutes, two teal zipped around the corner. She let go a single shot and, low and behold, down dropped a duck. She was as tickled as a kid in a candy store with a pocketful of change.

Since the duck had dropped beyond our sight in the rows of corn, I sent the dog out to bring back the bird. A few minutes later my black Lab, Cal, came slopping back through the flooded corn with the drake greenwing. As the three of us stood waiting, Cal brought the bird into our midst and dropped it at Marcia's feet. The duck then proceeded to get up unsteadily on his own feet, with his eyes looking straight up at my wife, and blood flowing copiously from his head. Marcia turned ashen. I immediately picked up the duck and hustled into the corn to end its agony. I was, however, too late. My wife's duck-hunting career was over. She has yet to this day not forgotten those little eyes looking up at her.

One time when Dad and I were shooting Nielsen's Marsh, he said to me, "Jim, there's a big difference between duck shooters. There are many, many fine duck shots who have no idea how to hunt their quarry." I can recall many times how he would move the blocks with every little wind shift. I well remember his magic with a duck call, and his walking the dikes looking for crippled birds. But especially, I will never forget how much he enjoyed the camaraderie of hunting with his sons and friends and finally his great delight of an epicurean duck dinner, with wild rice and all the trimmings, at the end of a day in the marsh.

All of these things made up his duck-hunting "package," the legacy he left me, for which I am most grateful.

Duck Hunt

J. ANDREW KUNDTZ

Orion stalked boldly into the west as the punt boat lurched into total darkness, painfully pushing the new ice aside. Cal, a half-breed, sweatily leaned into the pole and muttered, "It's colder than a whore's heart this morning." Will, just fifty, sat forward in frozen stillness, thinking that one false move would send all over into the black water, something he feared his heart could not stand. In the center of the ice-encrusted skiff squatted John, instinctively trying to quiet Will's nervous two-year-old Lab, Lady.

"Just ahead," puffed Cal as he steered the punt down the narrowing channel through man-high cattails. Looking straight forward, Will's eye focused skyward on the Pleiades, and he knew they were pushing due west now after having struggled for twenty minutes through the blackness. "Must be approaching the far end of the marsh and the high blind that's a stone's throw from Lake St. Clair," he thought to himself. Even though Will had hunted this marsh for years and was one of the founding members of the club, Cal would never tell him the blind assignments for the day. It was always the same morning command, only the time changed to coincide with the present day's sunrise: "Six o'clock; time to go—if you want any ducks, God damn!" Now, at six-twenty A.M., a full forty minutes before sunrise, Will relaxed, let the cold air cut into his lungs, and felt good as his mild hangover quickly vanished in the morning chill. "Plenty of time to set the decoys and get ready. See any action?" barked Will. "Too early," replied Cal, knowing that this much ice in the marsh in the middle of November was bad.

As the punt slid to a stop, John turned his head as far as he could and felt the hood of his hunting coat shave his stinging cheek. His right eye caught Cal's bold silhouette and beyond the gray glow that announces dawn's soon and swift arrival. "Out," directed Cal, and John youthfully lifted his wadered leg over the side and slid into the knee-high muck. He had hunted since he was a kid, but never on Mitchell's Bay. Now, at age thirty-five, he had his chance. As he pulled himself up and through the last few feet of water to the high ground, he wondered if he had brought the right gun. Maybe his Winchester 21 that his dad had given him over twenty years ago would not keep up with Will's new 1100. "Oh, well," he mused to himself, "Will's the best duck shot around, so what's the difference!"

Before Will had deposited himself in the sturdy little blind, Cal was in the middle of the pond feverishly shelfing ice. "Damn, that will delay us at least ten minutes. John, get a weather report," ordered Will. John obediently fumbled with the Japanese pocket transistor radio for a few seconds, and finally out of the squawks and squelches came a clear and quick voice:

"Good morning, people. This is WCAR, Detroit, 1130 on your dial. Time to wake up, and here is your seven-A.M. instant weather report: Partly cloudy this morning with sixty percent chance of precipitation likely today. Last night's low was twenty-five degrees and a high today in the upper thirties—"

"Turn that damned thing off! That's no kind of help. What does he know about ice in the marsh? And, for Christ's sake, what about the wind? That will make the difference today," said Will. As he rambled on, the sky grew lighter by the second and the wind did stir. There were birds awing now, high and far, and just a few minutes before sunup. Cal finished slinging the decoys into some unknown configuration in the open water and slushed toward the blind. "I've quit trying to tell him how to set the blocks," muttered Will. "I think it depends on whether he wants to shoot or not. He's got the hole wide open this morning, probably because of the ice."

As Cal slipped into his hide behind the blind, a thick layer of low-lying clouds rolled overhead and the first snow was felt. Along with the front came a fast circling flash of birds. The wind was now strong from the west and at their backs. Cal started to call. The first notes were rough and varied, but he quickly steadied and the birds listened. On the second pass they suddenly dropped and flopped into the pond before anyone could react. It was well past opening time and a few muffled reports could be heard from the open lake.

As they pondered the placid birds, six more circled by. Everyone froze and waited. As they flew behind the blind John could hear their wings beating boldly into the wind. He caught sight of them as they came around to the right. Cal whispered, "Ready." And then, "Take 'em, boys!"

John and Will rose in unison as the birds set their wings over the pond. As they let fire it was difficult to tell what happened with all the panic in the air and on the water. Will quickly counted three on the pond with legs up and a fourth feebly attempting to swim away. After he dispatched it, he released Lady with a bold "Fetch," and she, much to his surprise, burst outward and to the left on a direct line toward the decoys. After several commands of "Over," he realized that she was heading for a big greenhead that Cal must have picked off from the jumping birds.

"Thought you might want a little help this morn," offered Cal.

After John commented that he was sure he had shot his bird twice, Will thrice reloaded and unconsciously rubbed the sleek D.U. emblem on the receiver of his new Remington. "It was worth it," he thought to himself. "Three for three for openers."

Cal kept working the call whenever birds were near. Will again observed his strong face, black hair, and dark eyes. The weather had aged his skin, but he was still vigorous and healthy at age fifty-five. He had confided in Will over the years and told him of his father's coming from England and marrying his mother, a Potawatomi, whose tribe now resided on nearby Walpole Island. He was raised on a farm not two miles from the marsh, but preferred the life of his cousins on his mother's side. He fished in the spring and summer and hunted in the fall and winter. He had his own family now and was a little sad that his children did not follow his ways mainly because the wilderness of land and sea was fast disappearing from around them.

Cal's tone was strong, full, and confident by now. He was down to a fine chuckle and completely invisible as he hunched over in his hide. Neither Will nor John saw the birds until they were right upon them at two o'clock. They stood together, leveled their guns, and pulled repeatedly. The ducks flared and never lost a beat. Cal also shot to again test the range of his rusty Model 12. "Too soon," blurted Cal, and a long silence followed. "More shells," he commanded, and Will and John silently passed back their plastic tribute to one of nature's noblemen.

The wind was stronger and they had no fear that the pond would refreeze. The snow was heavy and wet and at times made seeing difficult. The last excitement had put some humility back into Will, and he had reluctantly decided to follow Cal's call even though he didn't like the idea. He glanced over at John on his right and, before he could speak, his eye caught sight of two low-flying objects approaching with great speed. No time to wait for Cal to give the word; no time to alert John; time only to stand, release the safety, and fire at the mile-a-minute diving ducks that apparently were diverted off the lake by the snow squall. He had to shoot before the gun was fully mounted and the recoil ached in his biceps. As the lead bird pinwheeled down, he used every bit of strength and coordination his adrenaline could muster to push thirty inches of steel in his left hand far ahead and up on the now-flaring bird. Hoping he had at least six feet of daylight between bead and bill, he pulled and pulled again, almost falling over from recoil and swing.

Lady had to be held back after the retrieve of the drake canvasback, because she was already bleeding in several places on leg and paw from ice cuts. Cal had been gone for what seemed an eternity, but was in reality about fifteen minutes. Will was feeling bad for having shot at the second bird when it was beyond the pond, knowing it was almost impossible to find a cripple in a frozen marsh, especially this marsh with its thickets and tangles of snake grass and rushes. As they waited, Cal's figure slowly emerged out of the tall cover, and he held the trophy on high for a second until Will's eye caught sight of the fine white feathers of the hen canvasback.

"I know you and I could have spent the rest of the day in there and never have found that bird, John. If he has an ice cut in his waders, I'll have to buy him a new pair, but I don't care," said Will.

As the hours passed they had good action. Following the whispered instructions of Cal and working together, sometimes backing each other and at times shooting together, Will and John easily bagged eight more mallards and blacks. That made their limit, and they relaxed. The last of the coffee was shared as the snow continued more furiously.

As they completed storing shells and gear and the ducks were strung in readiness for departure, a lonely, familiar, but out-of-place sound was heard. No mistake now—it was the plaintive cry of a Canada goose. The snow was blinding and they could hardly see across the pond because of the heavy wet flakes of plastering white. More out of fun than anything else the two happy hunters started to respond to the lonely honker. No one expected the big bird to come very close, but at least John kept himself prepared as he nervously fingered the two shells in his left pocket. The honking seemed to fade a little, and Cal and Will gave up interest as they went back to their evacuation chores. But their calling as muffled through the snow was too good, and the old gander, without mate and probably carrying a little lead, took a direct route to the pond. Surely he must have thought there was a whole harem hidden away beneath the blinding blizzard!

John's right hand nervously rubbed the last of the bluing off the trigger guard of his otherwise immaculate 21. Then his left slipped two magnum fours into the sleek double as his eyes caught sight of the low bomberlike figure appearing in and out of the devilish sleet. All in one movement he snapped shut, released safety, and mounted the beamy gun. His heart beat and as he calculated his lead, he silently cursed himself for not bringing the number-two goose loads that he always carried while duck hunting—just in case. Instinctively he pulled the trigger, advanced his lead, and fired again. Will was now alert and, as he armed his 1100, he could see the first shot plunge into the body of the powerful bird. He aimed at its head and saw that slight but certain jerk in its neck as John's second shot reported out. Will knew the honker was mortally wounded and decided to let it die like the monarch it was. He relaxed the stock of the gun and waited for the strong heart to stop. Without warning the gander's wings quit, and it fell like a stone into the water not five feet from the decoy-retrieving Cal, who let out a great oath after the jacket-soaking splash. He picked up the twelve pounds of Thanksgiving feast by the neck and flung it into the punt boat. Cal then swiftly completed his rounds and returned to pick up his now snow-covered wards.

The return was difficult, but no one seemed to mind the extra burden of channel ice and blanketing snow. Will passed his flask of brandy forward to John, who timidly tilted and drank several sips of the warming liquid. He looked straight ahead and caught a few cooling snowflakes in his mouth. "It was a great morning," he thought to himself, "a truly exhilarating experience with nature at its best. And now to return to a warm camp with friends, a good meal, and a little rest."

Will drank slowly and savored each sip. He was proud and pleased with the hunt and his companions. "Stop a while, Cal, and have a drink, but don't take too long. I want to get back and call my office before noon."

He handed the half-empty flask to Cal, who took the opportunity without hesitation. Still standing, he leaned heavily on the pole and gulped heartily. The moment of rest and strong drink revived his strength quickly. As he lit a cigarette, Cal spoke. "Good work this morning, but time to go in before the storm gets too bad." Silently the punt again surged forward into the blinding snow.

Recollections

E. J. (BUSS) RUFFING

Along about 1968 or '69, I was invited by a group of Ducks Unlimited friends to join them on a waterfowl hunt at their Lucy-Timber Hunt Club located near Swan Lake Refuge in Missouri. The invitation was extended by Jim Shull and John Westfall, but other members of the club included at the time were Dan Bray, Ralph Botsford, John Cleveland, and Bud Craddock. I had just been with Ducks Unlimited as a staff man for a short time, so this was an opportunity to experience some Swan Lake duck and goose hunting and get better acquainted with some of the members of the Kansas City/ Western Missouri Ducks Unlimited chapter.

My home was originally Columbus, Ohio, and I spent nearly all of my life there on a small farm outside of town. Central Ohio has got to be one of the poorest waterfowl-hunting areas in the country. There was no goose hunting, and duck hunting was pretty much confined to jump-shooting wood ducks, mallards, and blacks on the rivers and small streams. Consequently, most of my hunting experiences were associated with poking shots at cottontail rabbits in the brush and weedy fields around my home place. I had never shot a duck over decoys—had never even been close to a goose.

I was, therefore, looking forward with much anxiety to hunting waterfowl in what was purported to be one of the better waterfowl areas in the Mississippi flyway. Since I was a wildlife biologist, I knew something about the Swan Lake area but had never had the opportunity to obtain firsthand experience. So I packed up what limited hunting gear

I had and oiled up an old Browning automatic-5 12-gauge that used to belong to my dad. I had since I was twelve years old shot a 20-gauge Browning auto-5. In fact, that was the only gun I had ever shot. I had experienced some limitations with the 20-gauge on jump-shooting water-fowl, so I figured I had better try the old 12-gauge that Dad, who was ill, no longer used. I reasoned that I could stand all the help I could get.

So I went to Kansas City. John Westfall picked me up at the airport at about two or so in the afternoon. John, then in his sixties, was one of the founders of the Western Missouri D.U. chapter in Kansas City. We collected my gear at the baggage claim and headed toward Swan Lake, Missouri. John quickly explained that if we'd hurry, we could get in the evening shoot. His intentions to get there in time became more obvious as the three-hour drive progressed. You'd have thought that John hadn't taken a shot at a goose for twenty years.

I reminded my host that I would have to procure a nonresident hunting license. He assured me that would be no problem—we'd stop along the way. Our first stop was in a small town where John wanted to pick up that special deep-smoked country bacon. He explained this was absolutely a must for breakfast and substitutes were simply not accept-able. Well, we got the bacon all right, but we got no license—seemed they were sold out. So we proceeded to another small town enroute and stopped at a couple of places there and still no license. Well, the sun was beginning to ease down a little bit in the west and I could see that good Mr. Westfall was getting a bit nervous about the amount of time remaining in this precious day. The last place we stopped assured us that we would have to go to the court house in Carrollton to get the license. Of course, our immediate concern was if we would get there before the courthouse closed.

Away we went toward Carrollton. With John having a firm grip on the steering wheel and a heavy foot on the accelerator, we arrived at the courthouse and, with no place to park, John let me out and said he'd circle the town square. I ran up the marble steps, taking about three or four at a time, and was able to procure my license just ahead of the closing time. I ran back out, caught John on the first swing around the square, and jumped in (he never stopped for me—just slowed down a bit). So away we went, license in hand, heading out of town.

We got about a block and a flashing red light appeared and a siren blast convinced us that the strong arm of the law wanted to speak with us. The officer walked up and explained that we had just run a stop sign and were exceeding the town speed limit. "Where the hell are you going in such a big hurry?"

John explained, to my astonishment, that we were simply trying to get in the evening shoot at Swan Lake! The officer commented that he certainly didn't want to stand in the way of anything that important but would we please take it easy until we passed the city limits. So away we went again.

We got to the clubhouse, met Jim Shull and four other members, put on our gear, and hastened down to the marsh. Less than one hour of shooting time remained. An L-shaped levee separated two four-acre ponds. We spread out about twenty yards apart in groups of two at the bend in the L. The blinds were sort of a halfhearted effort. One was a small stock tank full of water and therefore unusable, and the other was nothing more than a board on a couple of chunks of wood with a few giant ragweed stems stuck around here and there.

I was put on the end next to John. I loaded three high-brass Remington Express number fours in my dad's old Browning and watched my friend John Westfall jam in some three-inch magnums in his Model 12. I had never seen shells that big.

I recall to this day sitting there on my haunches on that levee looking out at the sky pondering my move if a duck or goose should appear from this direction or that. I was unfamiliar with the heavy old 12-gauge Browning. I found it a bit clumsy, having toted a 20-gauge all my life. I was also reminded that I had no experience at this type of hunting. I was trying to figure the proper lead should something fly across. I was quickly reminded that most of my shooting had been dead-away shots regardless of the type of game I had hunted, whether rabbits, ducks, or an occasional ringneck. The few pass shots or crossing shots that I'd ever had, I remembered that I would always miss. I had read about shooting head-on shots at game flying toward you but, of course, had never had the opportunity to try such a shot. So I was expecting the worst if the opportunity for a shot presented itself.

The more I thought about all these possibilities, the more apprehensive I became about the whole deal. But, anyway, things were kind of quiet and we just sat there visiting a bit. Pretty soon, John spotted a big honker way off and took out the goose call and began calling. He told me to keep my head down so I didn't really know what the hell was going on, except the tempo of John's efforts on the goose call appeared to be picking up. Pretty soon John said, "This one's yours, Buss!" My God, me! The entire specter of this setup rushed before my eyes as my heart pumped blood to my veins at a rate that would short-circuit an EKG machine. Here were six seasoned Missouri goose hunters and veteran D.U. committee workers and me, a rookie D.U.'er and a novice waterfowler! I could see these old-timers waiting to see how this new-comer that D.U. had hired would perform. My, how I wished I had told them how inexperienced I was!

I remembered that the safety on Dad's gun was not the crossbolt type that I was accustomed to but was located inside the trigger guard. Soon John dropped his call and calmly whispered, "Take him, Buss." I looked up to a sight I shall never forget. My God, he was huge and bearing down like a B-29 *head-on*! I eased off the safety and, having mentally rehearsed this maneuver a few moments before, I brought the gun up underneath that magnificent bird and when he was about ten o'clock high, squeezed it off without stopping the gun. Straight down he came, looming ever larger as he descended. Good heavens, he's going to land right on top of me! Well, he missed us by only three feet. "Cemetery dead"—with a single shot! Cheers and applause went up along the levee from my newfound D.U. friends. "Great shot, Buss!" I'll never know how or why, but I kept a calm composure and eased that old, uncomfortable Browning back on safe. I recall making some comment to Mr. Westfall that it was the name of the game, as if the whole exhibition was an everyday occurrence with me.

Well, everybody limited out their one goose that evening, and we returned to camp, poured ourselves the usual after-hunt drink, propped our feet on the fireplace, and commenced to recount the events of the day. As the evening wore on, events of past days and past years were intertwined. Nowhere in this conversation did I give any indication that this was the first goose I had ever shot at.

Well, the year wore on and I had subsequent meetings and conversations with these and other members of the Western Missouri D.U. chapter. One evening, after a meeting, we were discussing the hunt that we had had earlier up at Swan Lake and someone remembered the nice shot that I had made on that goose. Well, I couldn't resist any longer, so I confessed the true story. Out of the corner of my eye, I saw a broad grin appear on John Westfall's face. He had called in for me my first goose! I could sense what this meant for John. I could feel a special friendship developing between us—not particularly close, just special.

Through the years when I would meet the Kansas City D.U. crowd —whether at a Kansas City D.U. function, a national convention, or whatever—there'd be that frequent opportunity for John Westfall to introduce me to a stranger. The introduction would always be that same one-liner: "This is Buss Ruffing from D.U. National—I called in the first goose he ever shot." And a smile of contentment would appear.

Over the years I've had, I guess, two or three opportunities to share a day on that levee with John and others, and that memorable moment when John called in that first goose for me always appears in the conversation. And I am reminded of the good feeling I got on that special day and how my association and warm friendship with John, Jim Shull, and the other members of the Western Missouri group all began.

Message to a City Slicker From Those Who Know

J. K. (BARNEY) BURRY

I believe it was the fall of 1970 when I received an invitation to three days of duck shooting in southern Louisiana just off the Gulf Coast.

My host invited me to drive down with him, but because of the time factor involved, I flew down and was to meet him later. When I arrived at the airport, I was greeted by two men, father and son, who had earlier been described to me, and we had no trouble introducing ourselves.

While in the car proceeding to the rendezvous point with my host, the father and son were in the front seat exchanging remarks, some of which were in Cajun French, which, of course, I couldn't understand. I remembered my host had warned me about this and advised me not to ask any questions.

We arrived at the farmhouse, and much to my amazement a rather small Brittany spaniel jumped out of the front seat. She was introduced to me as Money Belle, and she would be our retriever during the hunt. I immediately said to myself, "My God, I have traveled seventeen hundred miles and taken four days of precious vacation time to shoot over a Brittany while hunting ducks and geese. You have to be out of your cotton-pickin' mind!"

By now, my host had arrived, and after a succulent dinner prepared in typical Louisiana style, we hit the sack early in anticipation of a good hunt the next day.

The next morning while having breakfast, my host and I were asked what kind of ducks we preferred to shoot that day—large or small ducks? Maybe some woodies? Or would we care to shoot some geese, perhaps? Again, I said to myself, "Seventeen hundred long miles, four precious days, and here I am in fantasy land with a bunch of quacks."

I chose to go "goose shooting" and was paired off with the son. We entered the blind about five a.m., complete with our so-called retriever. As I sat in the blind, I couldn't help but giggle, looking at the Brittany huddled under a camouflage blanket and again deciding I was a complete idiot to be here.

I would love to give the details of that day's shoot, but first to summarize. We bagged ten geese—four specklebellies and six blues. I saw Money Belle execute two double retrieves, pick up four crips, and do beautiful water work on the rest. I am now a firm believer not only in a Brittany as a retriever, but in the use of Cajun French in dog commands.

The next day, I was again given my choice of shooting, and this time chose the woodies. At four-thirty a.m., I found myself wading out to the blind in pure blackness, with tree-stump obstacles up to my hips. The going was tougher than the imagination can imagine, except for Money Belle, who seemed to be having a ball. It was so damn dark that even an owl would have been scared. I wondered if I would ever get back to Shaker Heights, Ohio, again to make another mortgage payment and see my buddies for lunch at P.J.'s.

We finally found the blind and I immediately communicated with the Good Lord, thanking him for getting us there and also asking for early reservations for a safe trip back.

Dawn was breaking and we could hear the ducks all around us. It sounded like hundreds. My guide by now could see his watch and gave me the nod to start shooting any time. He started things off by taking a double with the smoothness of a Cutty on the rocks. As I gathered some courage, I put my over-and-under on a pair and executed the most beautiful dutch known to man. Again my partner shot his automatic and three more woodies splashed down. At this point, I had recovered from the ordeal of wading out to the blind and began engaging in some really good woody shooting.

By now the sun was shining and I could see the area in detail. We were in an elevated blind, perhaps six feet off the water, with an open-water area in front with trees surrounding the entire area. What a gorgeous setup. At this time, I again heard some Cajun French commands and out went Money Belle for the first time. We figured we knocked down twenty birds and she brought back nineteen—every one a woody. What a day and what a dog.

The next day, I went small-duck shooting with the father and had a fabulous day shooting teal and widgeon. In fact, the whole trip was fabulous—seventeen hundred miles and four great and ever-to-be-remembered days.

The Lady Got the One on the Right

BARBARA DAVIS

The facts are that this incident *did* take place and it began several years ago at four-thirty A.M. when Bill picked me up in Cleveland and headed west in predawn dark for Nielsen's Marsh. We arrived in due time at the West Marsh. Cy Nielsen was there to meet us and to punt us out to Blind 16.

We are now in the blind. Bill is on the left and Cyrus is on the right, which leaves me in the middle. We have a ton of food with us, which I bought the day before. Also, a bottle of brandy, because it is late in the season and it is cold.

Anyway, all these ducks come in. Bill has put one thing in my gun—what do you call it—one bullet in my gun and has said to be sure to keep the safety on. I mean I've had the long talk on safety. So I have the gun upright between my legs with the safety on and instructions to keep it on until Bill tells me to stand up, take the safety off, and shoot.

Well, finally, either Bill or Cyrus announce: "Here come some at nine o'clock." Then Bill says, "Stand up, stand up and shoot!" And he gets all excited. I stand up and pull the trigger and nothing happens. I have forgotten to take the safety off.

So Bill says, "You forgot to take the safety off, but don't take it off now. Okay? Safety's on? Now the next time I tell you to stand up, take the safety off immediately." So I say, "Okay."

We then sit there for what seems like hours. It is cold and we have a little brandy. Oh yes, I have to go to the bathroom, too. What a job climbing out of that blind. Cyrus has to give me a boost. You know, I've had to go in a lot of outdoor places.

Finally, somebody says, "Here comes a pair at eleven o'clock." Bill says, "Stand up; you take the one on the right and I'll take the one on the left." I do remember to take the safety off. I look out at the one on the right and go boom. Bill goes boom, boom, and a pair drop.

Then Bill turns and says, "Well, I'll be damned, that was my fourth pair of doubles this season." With that Cyrus, good old Cy, says, "The lady got the one on the right."

It really is a true story, and Bill hates it, but right then he said, "She did not!" We had quite an argument about it but now he thinks its sort of funny. It is interesting, though, that he doesn't ask me to go duck hunting with him very often any more.

Blue Ribbon

JAMES WEITZEL

etriever trials can be very exciting to some and very boring to others. Having been involved with spaniels and retrievers in the field-trial business for some thirty-five years, I find it is similar to teaching school and coaching—I had spent fourteen years as coach and athletic director. One never could predict from one week to the next what young men were going to do under a given situation. If you cannot predict what an eighteen-year-old will do, how can you predict what a dog is going to do? When a prediction can't be made as to the outcome, this gives me the feeling of excitement, but to others, who expect perfection in everything they do or are connected with, mistakes can be boring unless they realize they are not dealing with a computerized machine. If that's what they want, it would be better to have a robot made by I.B.M. to retrieve their birds. It wouldn't cost anything to feed and they certainly would not have to clean up after it.

Mistakes are expected in a field trial as they are on a football field. My job as a professional dog trainer is to help eliminate the mistakes during training sessions and to put a dog into many different situations during his training so that when that situation comes up at a trial he has had some experience with the problem and can complete the test with the least amount of difficulty. The fewest mistakes win the trial just as the fewest mistakes win the football game.

The judges at a retriever trial are the same as the officials on the football field. They have to make snap decisions at the time of an infraction. They are human, even though they would like to be thought of as something more, and they, too, make mistakes. They also make the "sports" what they are —exciting to some, boring to others.

The best decision I have ever witnessed came some eight years ago at the Wolverine Retriever Club's Licensed Trial held at Milford, Michigan. The judges were Paul Provenzano from Texas and John McAssey from Colorado. The Amateur Stake was going along very smoothly with dogs separating themselves by their work. For the fourth and apparently last test the judges had set up an angle-entry water blind to the right. The line to the blind paralleled the shore the total way. The line was no more than fifteen yards off the shoreline, and the total distance of the blind, including the starting position on land, was in the neighborhood of a possible 175 yards. A very demanding blind, with several points along the right shore which looked most inviting to the dog. Of the twelve dogs called back for this test, the first three landed on the shoreline at the first point and were subsequently picked up after many cast refusals. The fourth dog was sent very wide from the line to the blind and with seven or eight whistles was put on the blind. This becomes the question on a blind of this nature. Do I go for the correct line or do I play it safe and send the dog out to sea, away from the inviting shoreline, and direct him from there? Many of the amateur handlers, knowing that they could not control their dogs that tight to shore, did the latter, and all three completed the test without too much of a problem but completely avoided the hazard.

Then John Nash of Gates Mills, Ohio, one of the early founders of retriever trials in the Midwest, came to line with possibly one of the finest lining retrievers that I have ever worked with, Amateur Field Champion and Field Champion Marelvan Mike of Twin Oaks. Previous to his turn on line I said to John, "Go for the line, he'll do it." John, sure enough, sent Mike on the correct line, and Mike kept the line until about fifteen yards short of the muskrat house, where the blind had been planted, and then veered to the left. John blew the whistle, Mike turned for directions, and John gave him an angle right back cast. Beautiful! The dog responded, went to the muskrat house, grabbed the bird, and came back the quickest way, which was by shore. As he approached John, some twenty feet away, he set what he had in his mouth down and shook the mud and water from his coat. In regrasping his burden he realized that he had no bird—he had a mouthful of muck from the muskrat house! I don't know who looked more startled—Mike or John.

However, the boy who was planting the blinds had seen Mike pick up the bird and had already planted the bird for the next dog to run. It was at this point that the two judges showed the value of experience and the ability to make snap decisions. John McAssey asked John to heel his dog and immediately threw a bird into the open water and asked John to send Mike for the retrieve. The point was made that he was willing to retrieve a wet pheasant.

I wouldn't have written this story had it not been one of success. Needless to say, Mike was the winner without having retrieved the bird he was sent for. "Mitigating circumstances." With much criticism accepted, the judges made a decision concerning the work of the winning dog. They quickly figured that in going for the bird on the muskrat house Mike had grabbed the bird, covered with a clump of muck, and in returning with the bird it had slipped out of this clump of muck. Sure enough, upon examining the shoreline they discovered the bird where it had slipped from Mike's grip. I have to give those judges a lot of credit for exhibiting their many years of experience not only in judging trials, but also in the duck blind and for making their decision on this basis.

Bluebird Day

RICHARD P. THEAKER

Even the last hours before dawn held little promise. Only a feather-light puff of balmy air occasionally came up from the south, and then scarcely enough to even ripple the top of the water.

As we pushed off from the rickety wooden dock, a hopeful glance upward found only bright stars dancing in a light night sky.

Up Cedar Creek we went, past summer cottages and fishing shacks, empty now in late October, and looking forlorn and lonely in the shadowy half-light, half-dark of a false dawn. There were no sounds except the gurgle and pop of our small outboard motor, and an occasional half-hearted bark from a farm dog disturbed by our passing. There were four of us in the boat: Ed Davis, Carl Baer, and myself, eager but novice waterfowl hunters from a small Ohio city, and our host and guide John Miner. John is the grandson of the late Jack Miner, pioneer in waterfowl banding and founder of the famous Jack Miner Goose Refuge at Kingsville, Ontario.

We had met John the April before while seining for smelt at Point Pelee and had been more than intrigued by his stories of the fine goose shooting to be had at his blind on Cedar Creek. So we had at that time made arrangements to come up in October; however, as so often happens when you must make plans so far in advance, it appeared we had made a bad choice and were going to have what a waterfowl hunter dreads most—a "bluebird" day.

Also in the boat was another character who was destined to play a part in the events of the day to come: John's old black Lab, Queenie. She rode quietly now, sitting on the bottom of the boat, her huge head cradled in my lap, nearly asleep, but thoroughly enjoying the occasional pat on the head I gave her.

Finally we reached the part of Cedar Creek where it forms huge gray sticky mud flats before flowing into Lake Erie. And through the darkness we could just make out the silhouettes of John's spread of decoys. To save time he had placed them the night before, great over-size cork decoys painted as no particular species of waterfowl, just shades of gray and charcoal black, but guaranteed, as John said, to decoy anything from greenwing teal to Canada geese.

The decoys lay in loose formation off a prominent point of land jutting into the river, and as we came closer, we could perceive the outlines of John's box blind blended well into the underbrush along the shore. Quickly we unloaded the boat and carried into the blind enough equipment for an army campaign: guns, shell bags, rainwear (not a chance), containers of coffee, and a bag of delicious-looking sweet rolls from the local bakery.

After taking the boat downstream a hundred yards and concealing it in the brush along the shore, John returned and, after donning waders, carefully waded among the decoys, changing a block's position here and there until they exactly suited him. Thus went the last few minutes of darkness.

Back in the blind, with all prehunting details complete, guns loaded and ready, we watched the sky with high anticipation. And then came the dawn—slowly at first, with the gray of the eastern sky giving way to pinks and orange; then more rapidly as the orange faded and the sky was bright blue. The light took away the shadowy shapes and turned them into stark reality—we had our bluebird day.

The decoys lay as lifeless as logs on a millpond. The only wings we heard were some hardy mosquitoes revived by the warm sun, and even a few bees buzzed by. And so the morning went. High anticipation turned to frustration and was only revived briefly when a trio of mallards paid us an unexpected visit and stayed after a volley of shots from the blind.

Back at John's house in the very early hours of the morning, we had enjoyed a real hunter's breakfast with ham and eggs and coffee, and toast with that delicious Canadian strawberry jam. But that seemed ages ago, and when someone suggested a sweet roll and a cup of coffee to break the monotony, it sounded good. However, a search of the boat resulted in our finding a torn sack, and a Labrador just licking the last of the frosting from her chops—Queenie had eaten the whole dozen rolls! We settled for a cup of coffee.

It was nearly ten in the morning now and heavy coats had come off in the warmth of a bright October day. Suddenly we were snapped out of our drowsiness by a single honk coming from behind the blind. And there they were! A flock of a dozen or more Canadas lazily flying inland. We shook with excitement, but unfortunately no amount of passionate pleading from John's expert call even wavered them, and with heavy hearts we watched them sail to a landing in a cornfield a half-mile away.

With little hope for success in his voice, John asked if anyone was interested in trying to make a stalk on the geese. In desperation Carl and Ed volunteered to go, for it surely looked as though the day would be a blank anyway. I felt the chance for a successful stalk was nearly nil, and was in no mood for a "wild goose chase," so I decided to stay in the blind. The three stalkers set off.

To keep Queenie from following her master and possibly spoiling their effort, I tied her to a corner inside the blind. A seemingly endless time went by, as it so often does when you're hopefully waiting for something. But suddenly both Queenie and I were brought to attention by a volley of shots from the cornfield, and the Lab began to fuss and whine, for there they were! The flock of geese flushed from the cornfield was heading directly toward the blind! Noting my excitement, Queenie became even more agitated and began to whine loudly, tugging at her rope. That's when the blind became a one-man beehive of action. While nudging at Queenie with my knee, pleading with her to keep quiet, I was also trying to change the duck loads in my gun to goose loads (at least I had remembered the duck loads were in, left there from the action with the mallards earlier) and at the same time locate the goose call to give a couple of reassuring honks to the oncoming geese. So there I was— kick the dog, change a shell, blow the call, kick the dog, change a shell, blow the call! I managed to get the goose loads in, and give a couple of weak honks when the geese decided to make a pass in front of the blind. Three quick shots sent two honkers tumbling down, including the leader of the flock, which only wing-tipped, scaled off to plop down on the mud flat across the river. Leaderless, the flock went only a short distance up the river and turned, headed back toward the blind. Quickly I reloaded, and as they made the second pass, left to right this time, managed two clean kills with my three shots. Four geese down! I was jubilant! And then, much to my surprise, I saw that two of the remaining geese in the flock had lit beside their wounded leader on the mud bank across the river.

About this time the shuffling sound of men running while crouched over signaled the return of my hunting companions. "What's all the shooting about?" they asked. And when I told them about the four geese, they were unbelieving but delighted. Their foray in the cornfield had not been so successful. Something had spooked the geese just as they reached the edge of the field, but luckily the Canadas had come pouring out right over them.

John and Ed had unfortunately both concentrated on the same goose for their first shot, and it fell like a rock, at least two ounces of number twos heavier. This flustered them, and they missed with the rest of their shots. Carl admitted "flock shooting," with the result of not touching a feather. Even with birds as large as Canada geese flocked together, you must still concentrate on a single bird with each shot. As a result, they had just one goose to show for their effort.

A peek out of the blind showed three dead geese on the water, one wounded on the mud flat, and two very much alive and alert ones standing near it. A council of war was held, and it was decided that since I had had some good luck and they had not, I would attempt to reach John's small double-ended duck punt, which was hidden a few yards from the blind (he used it to help Queenie retrieve downed birds), take it, and try to circle behind the geese on the mud flat.

Crawling on all fours I reached the punt, and carefully stowing my gun aboard, managed to shove off without disturbing the two geese on the mud flat. Keeping as low as I could, I paddled upstream to try to get behind the geese on the flat, hoping that when they flushed, they would go over the blind and give Ed and Carl a shot.

Halfway across the river the situation drastically changed; the excited honks of a large flock of geese filled the air. And then I saw them coming across the river from the blind—a flock of twenty or more huge Canadas. And now John's excited calling from the blind was pulling them directly to us. I put my nose in the bottom of the punt, trying to get my silhouette as low and inconspicuous as possible, but I had to peek up to see what was going to happen next.

On they came, heading right for the blind, calling loudly, never wavering for a second. And now their landing gear were down and they were hovering over the decoys. My question "Why don't they shoot?" was immediately answered by three shot volleys from the blind. Geese were dropping and flaring everywhere. A single passed thirty yards in front of me and I rose up on my knees and dropped him cleanly. I had the fifth goose of the liberal Ontario five-goose limit! I couldn't believe it!

But when the excitement died down, I realized that I didn't have the fifth goose, for there it was, still standing on the mud flat. I was going to have to go get it. Paddling the small punt up to the edge of the mud flat, I gingerly stepped out of the boat and promptly sank above my knees in the stickiest gumbo I have ever seen. Every step toward the wounded goose was a herculean effort. I had to pull each leg high out of the suction of the mud, move it ahead, and then repeat with the other. And now as I came closer, the wounded goose was starting to walk away from me! Queenie could not help me, either, for she would only have wallowed in the soft muck.

There was only one way to stop the goose from walking away from me, and a load of fours aimed at its head solved that problem. Now the painfully slow process of dragging myself through the muck to pick the goose up began. At last I reached it, and picking it up, started back toward the punt, each step becoming harder in the now stirred-up mud.

The laughter from the blind at my predicament soon became quieted with concern as my pace became slower and harder. Some ten yards short of the boat I hit an extra-soft spot and found myself trapped. I couldn't move. I was exhausted and getting dizzy. My longtime hunting partner Ed Davis noted my predicament, and with the big boat came over to my rescue. By shoving the canoe paddle from the punt under my boots he was able to break the suction, and then I walked out, stepping on the paddle as I went.

Back at the blind, we rejoiced at a large bag of Canada geese, including my one and only five-goose limit. A bluebird day had turned into a blue-ribbon day!

Baby Mallards

ROBERT SINGLETON

Almost without exception, every wildlife biologist recalls many humorous field experiences. Some of these are personal, while some originate with other sportsmen. Several such memories will be with me always.

One of these, while related to deer hunting, rather than waterfowl, happened in a small crowded county courthouse one very hot July. In fact, the weather and the conversation were both very hot! The courtroom, where regulatory proposals were being explained at a public hearing, was not air-conditioned, and thus all windows were up, with the hope of catching a breeze. The particular subject being discussed, in a less than cool and calm atmosphere, was the harvest of antlerless, or doe, deer. Most of those at the hearing were landowners and most were violently opposed to any regulation which would permit the legal harvest of doe deer. Biological data on sex ratios and reproduction, as well as size of deer and carrying capacity of the land, were as useless and unacceptable as a hand crank would be to a 1976 automobile.

The climax of the meeting took place when one of the landowners questioned the validity of our biological data by asking, "How would you all know anything about the deer population in this county? Why, one of your biologists was up in an oak tree to count deer when he went to sleep and fell out of the tree!"

Of a more personal nature was an exchange between myself and a group of duck hunters back in about 1948. One of the large coastal ranches had opened nineteen thousand acres to public or day hunting.

I was at the only exit gate from the marsh and was checking hunters' bags to collect information on species, sex, crippling loss, etc. Gizzards were being collected, if the hunters okayed my request, for food analysis.

A group of four wet, muddy, and cold hunters from Houston had a limit of greenwing teal. After taking the data which I wanted, I remarked that they had a good bag of teal. An immediate response came from one of the party: "Man, don't you know your ducks? These are not teal, they are baby mallards!" Further attempts to establish their identity as teal were to no avail. "Just look at the heads of these ducks. See that green color? These are baby mallards and the green is just beginning to show."

So, four wet but happy hunters headed home with a limit of baby mallards.

The manager, and one of the owners of this ranch, Joe Lagaw, would frequently make a quick hunt in the marsh on those days when the weather was bad for people but good for ducks, and hunters were few and far between. Sometimes I would hunt alone. One day hunting was not at its best, and being in a hurry to get my limit so I could get to work, I bagged a pair of spoonbills. Knowing that Joe would kid me about taking spoonies, I hid the pair behind the seat of my pickup, prior to returning to camp headquarters. Joe and I were enjoying a cup of coffee when he noticed that his big straw-colored Chesapeake retriever was sniffing at the door of my pickup and trying to get through the window. Overcome by curiosity, Joe went out, opened the pickup door, and his retriever immediately stuck his nose and as much of his head as possible behind the seat. I'm sure that Joe had already figured that I had hidden some ducks, so he pulled the seat forward and found my spoonies.

To be done in by a retriever, even a good one, is no honor.

Specklebellies at Twelve O'clock

THOMAS A. WINSTEL

"Every specklebelly, Canada, and snow goose in Alaska will pass through here in a twelve-day period beginning about the third week in September!"

Those were the words of a game biologist in Alberta that had brought us two thousand miles by plane and a hundred and fifty miles by four-wheel-drive vehicle and four hundred back-wrenching, blood-sweating yards to the blind site Alan and I were now occupying.

This story actually began approximately two years before when, one evening, two longtime duck-hunting friends, Bob Dwyer and Alan Haid, and myself were sitting at the table and trying to decide just where the best duck and goose hunting left in North America might be. With Alan being an engineer and applying some strong parameters of critique and Bob Dwyer being the biggest pessimist the world has ever seen or will see, we had a sounding board that rejected perhaps twenty-five locations in North, Central, and South America where a couple of fellows could still put together their own hunt and enjoy the sights and sounds of a multitude of ducks and geese as described in the books of yesteryear. Two were not rejected, however. Those were the Athabaskan River Delta and Hay Lakes staging areas. From all of Ducks Unlimited reports and U.S. Wildlife and Canadian Wildlife studies, these two areas were still remote enough not to have been commercialized but yet were still collecting points for at least 20 percent of the continental waterfowl population.

The logistics involved our bringing all the equipment we would need for a ten-day shoot with us from Cincinnati, Ohio. Sounds easy until you think of the multitude of items: guns, gun parts, clothing, and backup gear you need to prevent any one mishap ruining your hunting. After many hours of condensing the baggage, the day we had been waiting for arrived, and we were on our way.

Everything went smoothly until we reached Edmonton, Canada. At that time it was necessary to cross the city to another airport for connections going north. After arriving at the small airport, the smiling ticket taker for the small airline we were using informed us all baggage was being handled at an additional cost of fifty cents per pound. With this, the negotiating team went to work and after a half-hour and a bottle of Canadian Club, we arrived at twenty-five cents per pound and our baggage now labeled as freight.

After shaking hands and smiling, we walked to the airplane, where we were informed by the nice little hostess with the pretty smile that we had another problem. It seems that a coffin had to travel with the flight, and due to the additional weight, something had to be left behind. That's right, friends! Back to the conference room. This time we convinced our Canadian brother that the gentleman in the pine box, having been born in Canada and lived his life on the frontier, certainly would wish us a good hunt and would not mind waiting on this, his last trip across the prairie.

Goose and duck decoys, guns and shells arrived as scheduled! Hallelujah!

I'll never forget the next three days. God, the ducks, thick as a locust plague, were everywhere. Teal by the thousands, pintails so thick that when they came off the water, the noise was like thunder. Although they weren't there the first several days, the mallards soon started to arrive in just endless strings. Hunting was never so easy. It consisted of shooting the first four or five ducks that flew over, propping their heads up on sticks, and *voilà*—instant decoys! Lord how those ducks did like the spread. There was action every minute from the time you set out. No sooner were ducks down than a new bunch would be working the rig. Smoking guns were soon put away and the cameras brought out. After going through a case of film, it became apparent we were missing a key item on the agenda: Where in the hell were the geese? Although we had seen them trading back and forth in the sky and had picked up an occasional snow goose and specklebelly goose in the decoys, the mass of the specklebellies we were seeing were not using the same lake area we had been hunting, and that area encompassed approximately fifteen square miles!

That night after another fabulous dinner by our little Indian cook, we sat down with our maps to speculate where the specklebellies were feeding and resting. A little note on that Indian cook: He who primes Indian cook with rum for better dinner had best be prepared for consequences in the event of overdose.

It was the consensus of opinion that we had to have an airplane to scout this half-million acres if we were to hunt geese while we were here.

Lo and behold, the next morning a missionary landed in the small airstrip adjoining the Indian mission and, as Bob Dwyer happily put it, "There is a God after all!" That poor little old missionary never knew what happened to him. For the next moment he had two Yankees with maps on board and the search was on for lost souls and geese. Salvation was not far off! About fifteen miles from where we were staying, we found this wild rice marsh with about an inch of water on top of four inches of muck, and what a sight to behold. There must have been fifty thousand geese using the field. Specklebellies, Canada geese, some small Canada subspecies, and here and there the snow geese were beginning to show up in groups of fifty or one hundred with more flying in. Getting there was not to be easy. After finding and repairing the only outboard motor within four hundred miles, and bargaining with the Indians for the usage of the tribe's freighter canoe, we were on our way.

We had been traveling up the river since three A.M. and now we began to see the first light of dawn. As we pulled the canoe over to the bank, we could see small bunches of honking Canadas coming in high and heading in the same direction we were. After what seemed to be an eternity, but was probably only half an hour, the six of us had the freighter canoe unloaded. After dividing into groups of two, we headed out into the marsh, which must have been five miles wide by twenty miles long, with small groups of geese as close as three hundred yards from the edge of the river feeding in preparation for their long migration ahead.

Alan Haid and I had paired up for hunting that day. Experience had shown that from a concealment basis and with our hunting from canoes, two people were the most practical number for hunting conditions. Loaded up with decoys, shotgun shells, shotgun, cameras, and lunch, we left a small stand of birch trees bordering the river and headed out onto the ricefield plain stretching before us. Two members of our group were heading out from our left to a small willow clump they spied about five hundred yards away.

The two remaining sports, Tom Baker, our silver-tongued Florida migrant, and Bob Dwyer, chubby as they were, were going to "blind up" in some willows approximately a hundred yards directly in front of us. Alan and I decided, while putting our act together, to head upwind about three hundred yards and then cut about a hundred and fifty yards out in the plain to a small bunch of willows we could see in the distance.

Walking at the edge of the birch thicket was easy, but when we got out into the muck of the wild rice, each step necessitated the careful extraction of the back foot, else the boot would be left behind in the mud. Now if you have ever walked much in waders, I am sure you can foresee the splattering result of an untimed footstep.

We finally made it to the willow clump. By this time we were seeing some small Canadas flying by in singles and doubles, fighting against the wind and passing around two hundred yards in front of us and then to what appeared to be a large concentration of feeding birds about a half-mile to our left. Out of breath with the sun coming up, we were putting together the silhouette decoys when off to our left, we heard the first gunshots of the day. It was Bob Dwyer and Tom Baker. A small string of six Canadas were coming over from behind them as we saw first one fall, then two, then again two more. Five out of six—wow! Were they going to be hard to live with!

By this time, we had our two dozen silhouettes rigged out downwind from us and rearranged a small willow clump into a blind. Down on our knees and gun butts in about two inches of water, we were crouched and awaiting. A single got up in front of us, then two, but as they approached us they seemed to go to our left about two hundred yards and then pass on beyond us upwind. More waiting. . . . Then Alan said those words I'll never forget: "Specklebellies at twelve o'clock!"

Like a small whirling tornado they got off the plain, first twenty-five, then fifty, then a hundred, and then it seemed as if the earth opened up and thousands of them rose into the sky. From where we were, it sounded as if every specklebelly goose in Canada had to be cackling in that flock. After swirling around for a minute or two they settled back down with small bunches of five or six in lines one hundred to two hundred yards apart now leaving the main concentration and coming toward us. Like the group that came by before, the first skein passed approximately two hundred yards to our left.

Did somebody have their face up? Was there something shining? Were they seeing our profiles? Knowing Alan as I did, I doubted if his face was any higher than mine, which was only scant inches from the water. We scanned the plain and noticed that our willow clump and the other one that Bob Dwyer and Tom Baker were in were the only two out in the plain. Perhaps it was the willow clump!

I suggested to Alan we move another two hundred and fifty yards out. Without waiting on an answer from him I grabbed my shotgun, filled my pocket with a box of shells, grabbed six of the decoys, and started slugging another two hundred and fifty yards. I can remember after two hundred yards those twenty-five shells became heavier and heavier.

Damn, I thought, as good a shot as you are, Winstel, you know you only need eight shells. Should I leave the others behind? No, only a hundred yards more to go, fifty yards . . . Is this good enough? No, I said to myself, let's do it the right way and go all the way right to the very same spot that last line of geese passed over.

I finally reached it. What a relief! I sat down for a minute to recover my breath, and when I looked up I saw that big bunch, that cloud, was getting nervous, starting to raise in small bunches. Watching that huge herd I soon forgot how tired I was. With adrenaline racing, I got to work.

With six decoys now set in front of me, I saw about eight geese leaving the big flock and heading my way. With waders on, head down, some grass pulled in front of my face, and knees ever deeper in the mud, I sensed them coming and coming—two hundred yards, one hundred yards.

Words cannot describe the cackle of a specklebelly. All I can say is it makes your blood boil and your head pound and your grip on that gunstock get even tighter. Seventy-five yards, and only ten feet high, and heading my way.

I counted to three slowly and then I came up. The geese were startled, almost twenty-five yards away. Heads now rearing back, they were fighting their forward momentum as they tried to gain altitude. The end goose on the left had probably the biggest whitest-speckled breast I have ever seen, and as I pulled the trigger, I can remember hearing the snap as the shot ripped through his wings. As his wings collapsed, I was thinking, Hot damn, my very first specklebelly. Then, coming to my senses, I saw the second bull goose to his right boring through over my head. Swinging backward and nearly falling, I swung past his head and folded him with a shot that must have been fifty yards.

What a feeling, what excitement, what a double! Running out to pick up the first goose, I noticed the big herd of geese in the distance now starting to rise again. The wind was picking up as I glanced to my right, hoping that I could call Alan and have him join me. I should have known better. From that very first shot, our precision-minded, cold, calculating engineer had turned into what looked like a Japanese guerrilla fighter, galloping on hands and knees through the wild rice, shotgun in one hand and shells bouncing from his pockets. It's amazing how a forty-one-year-old man can move sometimes. He plowed in beside me, trying to keep his oxygen-starved lungs still and his red face down.

Alan and I waited on the next groups coming across the plains. As their predecessors, they came on ten feet or so above the ground and straight toward us. At thirty-five yards Alan and I both came up out of the grass and took our shots. Four shots then . . . doubles!

Fantastic day!! Both of us had doubled on specklebellies. As the geese were falling to the ground, we noticed two huge white bellies among them. These two fine "ganders" were a third larger than the rest of the geese. What were they? A different species?

We'll never know—all I can say is they were the biggest specklebellies Alan and I ever saw or have seen since. Alan and I finished picking up our limits that morning, finishing out on the early-arriving Eskimo geese, as the natives called them, that started to work into the plain. Like the specklebellies, they seemed to want to trade back and forth with the wind from one end of this carpet of goose feed to the other end, and there we were right in the middle.

Sorry to say, the camera was left at that first blind site, but as we agreed when we gathered with the group back in the birch forest over a roaring log fire, if we should never hunt again, we could say we have seen the best North America had to offer.

Memorable—
But Once is Enough

RICHARD E. URSEM

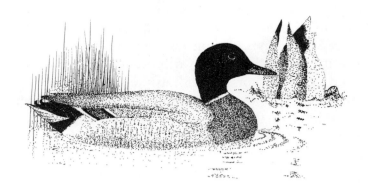

The month was November, the year 1973, and the place was the Sandusky Bay area near the mouth of the Sandusky River off Lake Erie.

Every fall for the past several years, some friends and I rent a cottage at Bay Breeze Cabins and set up headquarters for the duck and goose season in Ohio. We hunt the waterfowl by use of a layout boat and decoys together with a motorized tender boat for the retrieving of the game and getting to and from the middle of the bay.

We talk about the special nature of layout-boat hunting and the many happenings which occur to us that the blind shooters just can't fathom.

The planning for this particular day began when my friend Jack Templeton came to Cleveland from his old home in Denver, Colorado, to start a new job. I asked Jack if he would like to take a crack at layout-boat duck hunting. With a little prodding he accepted.

We left Cleveland on Monday evening and made the short (one-hour) trip to the bay cottage. We unpacked our gear and hit the sack, as we planned to be up about five A.M. the next morning.

Morning arrived only too soon and we donned our chest waders and other cumbersome gear and took to the bay. The bay was calm and there was only a slight breeze. It looked like a day which could be too good weather for good duck hunting. We launched the tender boat with the decoys and the layout boat aboard and headed across the bay to the mouth of the river. This was usually a good spot to catch the flight of the ducks from their trips to and from the open Lake Erie to the marshes of the rest area in the bay.

We set up our boat and about sixty decoys, and I put Jack in the layout for the first shot. We usually alternate places in the layout boat and the tender boat, which anchors about one-quarter to one-half mile from the spread. The man in the layout gets about one hour or until he gets a duck down, and then we change places. Well, Jack had only been in the layout boat for about twenty minutes when I saw a double approach and set their wings for a landing. Jack sat up, took up the shotgun, and blam, blam, blam went the three shots. On the final shot, one of the greenheads folded up and hit the water. I started the tender boat and headed out to retrieve both Jack and his first duck via the layout-boat method.

We exchanged the words and backslapping that take place on such occasions and then traded places, my turn in the layout boat. During my stint in the layout, I began to notice that the wind was picking up and there was some chop to the bay. I also noticed that it should be getting lighter, as sunrise had passed, but it was quite dark instead. I sat up in the layout boat and looked around. Behind me was a line of snow squalls that really looked ominous. I motioned to Jack to come out and get me, and he pulled up anchor and started out. By the time he got to me, it had begun to snow and blow. The bay, being quite shallow, was now rolling with about three-to-five-foot waves, all this within about fifteen to twenty minutes. Jack picked me up and we began to take in the decoys. Each decoy has about twenty feet of line and an anchor attached, and it must be wound for each decoy we picked up. This process was very difficult, as the waves grew larger and the storm became more intense. I was in the bow of the boat and Jack in the stern. I was unaware that we were taking in water until I looked down at my feet and saw the water at my ankles. The waders made it difficult to feel the water until it was too late. We had taken in too much water and the battery was now submerged. Then the motor quit and would not restart. Before we knew what had happened the sixteen-foot Starcraft had filled and was sinking.

We pushed the layout boat overboard and both jumped onto it. We watched the Starcraft roll over and sink to the bottom. The flotation kept the bow overturned but bobbing on the surface of the bay. By now the air temperature had dropped to thirty-four degrees. It was cold! The wind was pushing us and our layout boat away from the shoreline. We had to make a difficult decision. Whether to leave the boat and walk to shore, or stay with the boat and let the wind take us to the opposite shore, which was two miles away. We felt that the water was warmer than the outside air and chose to abandon the boat and walk for shore, which was about three-quarters of a mile away. The water depth was about five feet, but with the waves we were continuously hit in the face with the water.

We later learned that the water temperature was forty-eight degrees and that we had indeed made the right judgment. We made for the shoreline and about twenty-five minutes later we were about a hundred yards from shore when we were spotted by some other hunters. They assisted us to shore and we were taken by ambulance to Fremont Hospital, where they gave us brandy and blankets. Everyone told us how lucky we were and that we only had minutes left before we would have been unable to function in the cold water.

Most of our gear, the Starcraft, the layout boat, many of the decoys, and yes, Jack's first Ohio duck, were recovered. I had the duck mounted and presented it to Jack, and he still has it on his office wall as a reminder of Sandusky Bay layout-boat duck hunting.

It Could Have Been a Harder Lesson

SAM HERN

I don't know exactly how many years I have been hunting ducks, but I'm sixty-two years old and began pretty early. I did a lot of hunting in early times on the Ohio River, and one of the hot spots before the river channelization came along was Madison, Indiana, which is downriver from Cincinnati around sixty miles, and upriver from Louisville around thirty miles. This one morning we put our boat in at Madison. We always attempted to go in just at sunrise, or rather just as the day was breaking, because there are tow boats on the river and things like that and we like a little visibility for a safety factor. We put our boat in and started our motor.

On the Indiana side of the Ohio River a lot of red willows hang out for the first three miles or so below Madison. This morning was kind of an unusual one. It was foggy, there was an abnormal amount of ducks moving out of the red willows, and it was very cold, I'd say somewhere about ten degrees above zero. We had no intentions of doing any shooting, so we had our heavy gloves on and our life jackets and were motoring down very slowly because it was just getting to be light enough to see where we were going. As we proceeded down, these ducks kept agitating us by coming out in twos and threes and sixes and tens, you know, and so it wasn't long till we shut the motor down, folded it up, and loaded our shotguns with shells and let the current take us on down.

One fellow was sitting in the front seat of our fourteen-foot boat, and we always had a rule that when we floated, the man in the front seat sat down and the man in the rear stood up. Since I was operating the motor I was in the back.

It wasn't but just a few minutes until a nice bunch of ducks took off out of those red willows and the hunter who was with me—his name was Bud Doyle—knocked a double down. It was so cold that I failed to remove my glove from my hand. When the next group came up, I stood up, slipping my finger into the trigger guard. I didn't feel the trigger at all, and you know what's coming up next.

Yep. Right through the bottom of the boat. I pulled that trigger and put a hole in there about as big as an unhulled walnut.

Well, here we had Old Faithful geyser right in the boat, and I put the gun down in a hurry, put the motor back in the water, and started it up, and with the water rushing up I inserted my thumb through the hole in the boat to keep the water from gushing in.

We went in and hit the shore with no difficulty and I got to thinking about it. If I'd hit a floating log or it had been extra shallow, I'd not only have had a hole in the boat, I'd have lost my thumb to boot with it. So, we put a stob in it. Now, a Yankee doesn't know what a stob is. A stob is a wood dowel or wood plug when you're down in old Rebel country. So I put a stob in that dude with some cotton rags that I had there and we finished our day of hunting.

But believe me, we made a new law. Whenever you handle a boat in a floating operation, in that boat the glove comes off immediately before you ever start any floating at all. It could have been a harder lesson, but it's great to talk about.

One of the things that happened to me that was really unusual is that I killed a true albino hen mallard. It had a pink eye, and was totally white. No speculum whatsoever, and the bill had definite markings of the hen mallard, the orange and the little brownish-black running through the bill. This bird was flying with all-wild ducks. We were far enough away that there couldn't have been any tame ones around. Plus it was verified by our taxidermist here in Cincinnati. But it was quite an experience.

It was on the big Miami River just below Hamilton, and at this point the river is totally surrounded by cornfields. It always was a very fine haven for ducks. We spotted this duck on a day's hunt that we were on and noted that it had to be flying and feeding locally, with the ten or fifteen ducks that were with it.

It was late in the evening, so the next day my partner and I separated and set up decoys about half a mile apart, which we figured would give us a better advantage and a little more percentage of getting a shot at this duck.

Well, it so happened that this duck came along and I got my shot and on my second shot it fell. It was very cold and the ice was frozen in the river, except for the ripples, and there was no way that I could get to that duck on that ice floe. So we rambled on home to pick up a light boat and put it over the hill. My hopes of that duck being there were not too high. I could see where the muskrats and polecats would be out on that ice just tearing that duck up, plus we do have a lot of crows in this particular area and they could have been picking on it.

But as luck would have it, when we got back there the next morning, there was the duck, frozen to the ice solid. I chopped out around the ice, put the chunk of ice with the duck frozen to it in the boat, brought it on home, melted it out, and took it to our taxidermist.

I still have it mounted in a complete glass case, and it is in perfect condition.

Down in Arkansas, in the Stuttgart area, we were hunting the rice fields one particular day. There were six hunters in the group—three in each blind. Our birds came in and we got a number, I can't remember anymore, but I would say about four or five out of the bunch. This one cripple flew off, I would say approximately two hundred yards, and fell. We'd been watching this old eagle sitting up on a big tree practically from dawn—I guess this was somewhere around eight o'clock in the morning. When he saw that bird fall, he immediately came off his perch and made a dive right for it. He snatched it up. I don't know why, but he kept on a straight line and right for our blind. Actually we were kind of in shock, all six of us.

As the old eagle came closer and closer and closer, I figured there was only one thing to do if we were going to get that duck away from that eagle and that's just fire a shot. So I pointed the gun out the blind parallel to the water and pulled the trigger. Boom! And I guess it shocked that eagle, because he dropped that duck—and believe it or not it was within ten feet of our blind.

Now when it comes to retrieving, I think that's a retrieving story that will really amaze a lot of hunters. I never heard of anybody having that happen before, but it was all through the Stuttgart area that year. That's all you heard was that eagle story. But it was something to see. It really was.

Man and Dog

W. R. (RUSS) BOSTON

Kris, as Karl F. Bruch was called by his family and friends, was a gentle man and a true sportsman.

Waterfowling was an activity that held his interest long after he had retired from industry. For quite a few duck seasons he shared his marsh fun with a Labrador retriever named Buster. It is Kris and Buster that prompt this nostalgic splash.

Kris first saw Buster at a field trial. The dog's trainer advised Kris that Buster was available and that while the dog had shown some promise as a future trial dog, possibly he would be more adaptable to the marsh—far away from the trial circuit. Upon watching Buster "break" in the first series (with joyful abandon), Kris concurred with the trainer's appraisal and, so to speak, freed Buster of his indenture.

For this heady new status, Buster—in his own inimitable style— agreed to seek and retrieve anything airborne that Kris downed, up to and including sixteen pounds of it, with vigor.

It was a delightful relationship that had an air about it of carefully planned disaster which, fortunately, never came to pass. Buster was, indeed, an explosively direct retriever. As a shooting guest of Kris's, one had to watch out for Buster. As you rose to greet an incoming bird, Buster also jumped to his feet, and this boisterous behavior could really foul up your act. However, once a bird was downed, Buster exited smartly—through your legs, over you, but never through the blind's entrance. Usually Buster's spirited effort was accompanied by a terse statement from Kris, such as "Oh, that damn dog!"

Good shooting for Kris and his guest usually meant leaving a drafty blind in need of immediate repairs. Rumor had it that the duck club's treasurer used an assessment notice, especially designed and worded, to cover repairs to the most recent blind used by Kris and Buster. It was a banner duck season if Kris received no fewer than a dozen "Buster bills."

It was not long after Buster left the scene that Kris hung up his Parker. Those long-past days spent with Kris and his friend Buster have a special place in our memory bank.

Five On Four

WILLIAM A. PAPENBROCK

The state of Ohio is not noted for outstanding goose hunting. However, now and then a duck hunter will luck out and run into some goose shooting which is comparable to that of any place in the United States. At any rate, whether you get any shooting at all, it sure beats working.

A few years ago, my law partner, Jack Naylor, had the good fortune to be drawn in a public drawing for a blind at the Ohio Division of Wildlife's Mosquito Lake Goose Hunting Preserve. Mosquito Lake is an inland lake located about fifty miles southeast of Cleveland. Jack had never been goose hunting in his life, although he was an accomplished pheasant, woodcock, and grouse hunter. While Jack did enjoy duck hunting, you could count on your two hands the number of ducks he had bagged.

Jack and I had hunted a lot together for upland game and always had fun playing hooky from work. Besides our close professional and social relationship, Jack also knew that I was a somewhat experienced goose hunter, having hunted geese at Cairo, Illinois; James Bay, Ontario; and Ungava Bay in upper Quebec. Consequently, I was not entirely surprised when Jack walked into my office, dropped his Mosquito hunting permit on my desk, and asked me if I wanted to take a long shot and try for geese at Mosquito Lake. Neither of us had previously hunted at Mosquito Lake or knew anyone who had been there, although we both had known of the Division of Wildlife's operation there for a few years. Naturally, I said yes to Jack's proposal, and that was the start of one of the more interesting days of goose and duck shooting I have ever experienced.

Never having been to the state's Mosquito Lake Preserve, I was somewhat apprehensive of what we would find when we got there. The regulations stated that we had to be there by five A.M. to check in, present our permit, and receive instructions. The regulations also advised that each hunter would be allowed to take only ten shells with him to the blind. This does not permit too great a margin of error when shooting waterfowl, especially tough, hard, high-flying geese. Jack expressed great concern and dismay at the ten-shell limit, but I confidently reassured him that we each should be able to bag our two geese with ten shells each—a total of twenty shells for four geese. Having shot boxes of shells at ducks and geese with often very little to show for the empty shell casings, I was not quite as certain of my statement as I had led Jack to believe (which is not too unusual for an attorney).

Jack was to pick me up at about four A.M. I cautioned him to bring his waders, because we probably would be shooting over water and I didn't think my five-month-old yellow Labrador puppy would be much help to us (especially since the pup would still be sleeping at my wife's feet when we left—dogs aren't as dumb as we think).

Jack was right on time. I threw my gear in the car, including my 20-gauge Winchester automatic, lunch, waders, clothes, etc., and we headed for Mosquito Lake. As we were enroute, I couldn't help but think of my dad and some of my other friends who also had taken the day off to go duck hunting at our favorite duck marsh at Sawmill Creek on western Lake Erie between Huron and Cedar Point, Ohio (which, in 1972–73, was developed into beautiful Sawmill Creek Lodge, much to my dismay and that of some of the other partners of that venture who loved the duck hunting in the marshes along the lake more than the thought of making money from the development of the property). I knew they would have good shooting on the overcast, crisp November day. I wondered to myself if Jack and I shouldn't have canceled the Mosquito trip and gone duck hunting with my dad at Sawmill Creek. I said nothing to Jack.

Being right on schedule, we arrived at Mosquito Lake about four-forty-five A.M. and located the Division of Wildlife check-in station without too much difficulty. We checked in and waited for final instructions and permission to head for our blind. We were given ten silhouette goose decoys and a map which showed where our blind was located. To our surprise, almost all of the blinds, including ours, were not on the lake, but instead were far inland in fields well away from the labyrinth of dirt roads which wound through the preserve. We were told where to park our car and that all the blinds were well marked so we should have no trouble finding it. Jack had brought a flashlight, so we were not too concerned. By about five-fifteen A.M. all the other hunters were present and accounted for, so the Division of Wildlife personnel proceeded to review the regulations, including the ten-shell limit, wished everyone good luck, and reminded everyone to check back with their geese and decoys after the hunt, which was to end at one P.M.

Jack and I got in the car and started off in the darkness down the winding dirt roads toward where we thought our blind was located. After a few wrong turns, we finally located the parking area on the map we had been given. Since we had no other boots, except waders, which was the result of my miscalculation, we put them on, loaded up with the decoys, guns, lunches, Thermos of coffee, etc., and headed off into the darkness with our map and flashlight in the general direction of our blind. Several other groups of hunters had parked with us, and as a result, we all sort of started off together in a group.

To this day, I am relatively certain that the guy that prepared our map must have been a bit sadistic. To call the map a map was extremely charitable. The blinds were well marked on the map as being in a row of standing corn between two rows of wheat, which were between more standing corn, which were between more wheat, ad nauseam. It looked great on the map, but when you started wandering around in those huge fields in the pitch-black darkness it became apparent that the only thing that map was good for was an emergency substitute for tissue paper. I stumbled and fell once, scattering decoys and my gear all over the wet mud. Jack didn't do much better stumbling through the fields, but at least he managed to stay on his feet. This went on for about forty-five minutes. By this time, we were exhausted and soaking wet from sweating in our waders, which were loaded down with mud. We passed two of the other groups of hunters who had parked with us and were delighted to learn that we were not the only idiots who couldn't find their blind. Each time we compared notes with the other hunters on what we respectively believed our maps indicated in relationship to where we had been. Each group lamented their predicament, sympathized with us, and went on their own way muttering.

After numerous sit-down conferences to regain our senses and energy and to determine where we were not, it was apparent that Jack and I would have to wait for dawn to find our blind. This was quite discouraging, because shooting time was a half-hour before sunrise, and everyone knows the first hour of shooting time is usually the best. As the heavy overcast sky started to brighten in the east, it was already shooting time and we were still sitting on our butts in the middle of nowhere. The regulations of the Division of Wildlife were quite explicit in that you were limited to hunting from your assigned blind. Thus, we couldn't shoot at geese before we got to our blind even if they were landing at our feet! About six-thirty it was finally light enough to see where we were. Before too long, we were able to locate our blind, which was well hidden in a row of standing corn. By six-forty-five, which was about thirty minutes after the start of shooting time, we had our decoys out in the field and were in place in our blind.

Both Jack and I were tired and rather unhappy with the difficult time we had had in locating our blind, but at least we were there. It soon became apparent that we hadn't missed much shooting in the first half-hour of the morning. As we stood in our blind and viewed the empty horizon all around us, the only other living thing we saw was a beautiful twelve-point buck which was casually strolling down a strip of wheat about forty yards away. As Jack and I marveled at the beautiful buck, we were also aware that we had not seen or even heard a goose the entire morning. I mentioned to Jack that after all we had gone through to get here, things didn't look too good. We couldn't even hear any shooting anywhere in the distance. Jack sipped some coffee and jokingly announced that he no longer was worried about running out of shells. Neither of us realized how right he was.

About seven-thirty, I saw in the far distance a large flight of ducks which were coming straight for us. I said to Jack that I thought we ought to take a shot at the ducks if by accident they came over us. Jack said nothing. I watched the ducks come closer and closer and finally they were in range. The big ducks were really moving as they passed over us. Having only ten shells, I didn't intend to unload three shells at the ducks, so I jumped up, picked out one duck, pulled, and to my satisfaction the duck folded and crashed to the ground in front of our blind. To my surprise, Jack didn't shoot. As I reentered the blind with a beautiful huge black duck, I asked Jack why he hadn't shot and he quietly replied that he thought they were out of range. I confirmed they were high, but still in range, and said nothing further.

It was now about eight A.M. and we had only one duck and one empty shell to show for our efforts. But now and then we could hear a few shots in the distance and occasionally we saw a flock of geese a mile or so away. By eight-fifteen, there were geese everywhere. Just as if someone had lifted the starting gates for a horse race, the geese started coming in large and small flocks, and low! Both of us were very excited, to say the least, at this point. I saw a flock heading directly for us on the deck, wings beating and honking and crying with their heads moving from side to side. I said to Jack, "Here they come, get ready!"

The Canada honkers came in and over to the left of the blind as I jumped up, picked up one of the lead honkers, led him a few feet, squeezed the trigger, and watched the large goose fold and fall to the ground. The flock flared, scattered, and escaped without any further shots being fired. I turned to Jack and asked him why he hadn't fired, and he quietly replied that he thought they were out of range. I went out and picked up my goose and returned to the blind. A few other flocks and singles and doubles came close, but not close enough. About ten minutes later, I saw another flock coming in and I told Jack, "Here they come, get ready!"

The honkers came in beautifully and swerved a bit at the last moment, but I jumped up, picked on one goose, laid my 20-gauge Winchester out in front, pulled, and watched my second honker drop like a ton of bricks out of the flock. The flock flared and for a few moments they looked motionless as they hung up in the air before they turned and gained altitude in the opposite direction. Again, Jack had not shot, and I again asked him why. Yep, Jack confirmed that he had thought they were out of range.

Geese are very deceptive targets, as anyone who has hunted them can testify. At times, the large Canadas look like they are barely moving and are close enough to bring down with an easy shot. The most common mistake in hunting geese is to shoot too soon while the geese are still out of range. Jack wasn't going to make that mistake!

I retrieved my goose and returned to the blind. I had my limit of two Canada geese and one large black duck on three shots. Not too bad, I thought. I looked at Jack and could see that he was rather dejected and unhappy with himself for not shooting at the flocks I had taken geese from. I told Jack that he shouldn't worry about missing a few shots because, if necessary, he could use my remaining seven shells as well as his ten shells to get his two birds. Jack confirmed that he no longer intended to wait for the geese to land in our decoys before shooting. Since I knew that Jack was an excellent shot, I wasn't worried about Jack killing his geese once he started shooting—assuming, of course, we would get some more geese to shoot at.

Within another five to ten minutes, we saw them coming. A flock of about twenty Canadas no more than fifteen yards high were coming right into our decoys. Jack whispered to me, "Let me know when!" I said I would as we watched them come closer and closer. The honkers set their wings to land in our decoys in the corn, but were still out of range and I cautioned Jack to stay down. As the geese dropped their gear it was clear they were in good killing range, and I forcefully said, "Now!" Jack jumped up and the geese immediately realized their plight. Geese filled the air everywhere above the decoys as they desperately tried to gain altitude. I watched Jack as he raised his Browning over-and-under —and fired once. For a moment, I wasn't sure what had happened with all the confusion in the air. However, in a split second the confusion cleared and two huge Canadas were heading down to the ground and eventually the dinner table.

To say that Jack was excited is an understatement. He put his safety on and raced out of the blind to retrieve his double in Canadas with one shot—his first shot ever at geese. When Jack returned to the blind, we looked at each other, and our bag, and laughed. We had four Canada geese and one black duck on four shots. Not bad at all, and it was only about nine in the morning.

We loaded up our gear and birds and headed for the check-in station. After checking in, we got in the car and had breakfast; a couple of beers and hamburgers in a friendly country roadside tavern. With our spirits high and it being only ten A.M., we decided the day was young, so we headed for the Sawmill Creek duck marsh where my dad was hunting halfway across the State of Ohio. We got there about noon and drove down to the marshes, where we compared bags with the duck hunters. My dad and my friends had done very well with a mixed bag of wood ducks, mallards, teal, widgeon, and gadwall, but not everyone had yet limited out. When we opened the trunk of Jack's car and showed them our four geese, one black duck, and four empty shell casings, they couldn't believe it. As for the rest of the day, well, both Jack and I got a few more ducks apiece, including a beautiful greenhead mallard. But it was all rather anticlimatic after that wonderful half-hour in the morning at Mosquito Lake which I will never forget.

Jack and I went to Mosquito Lake the next year and never shot our guns. We almost froze to death that day. However, we have been back since then and have taken geese. I am also happy to report that the Ohio Division of Wildlife has improved the marking of blinds. All in all, Mosquito Lake can provide some exciting goose shooting and represents an example of excellent management of waterfowl by Ohio's Division of Wildlife.

A Helluva Lot of Birds

CHRISTOPHER C. MORTON

When December comes to the St. Clair River flats and the adjoining islands on both sides of the St. Clair River, even the hardiest waterfowler is content in seeking his warm fireside along with its pleasant memories of balmy October and early-November shooting. It takes usually a single-trip down Johnson Channel to Johnson or Mitchell's Bay late in the season to convince even the most persistent of hunters that the season is over and the time has come to stow gear and total up.

This was pretty much our feeling as we spent an entire morning scanning an empty sky from our improvised boat blind on Johnson Bay. All the marshes in the area had been frozen solid for days, and still clinging to the hope of some late-season shooting, we had invited some fellow hunters from Maryland to try their luck on Ontario mallards, as the duck season had been so disappointing the last few years on the Eastern Shore. Our guests were quite anxious to see whether our glowing reports of the waterfowl shooting in this part of the country were accurate.

After a flightless morning, our guide decided we were wasting our time near the bay and urged us to try the cornfields on Ste. Anne Island, as large concentrations of mallards had been seen feeding there in late afternoon. Most of the birds still in the area had given up frequenting the marsh because of the ice and were resting up all day in the lake south of us where it was quiet. We planned right after lunch to head for the cornfields, but were cautioned to take very little gear with us as we would have to walk several miles to get into the spot our guide was thinking of. Our friends from Maryland had to be convinced, however, as they insisted they wanted to shoot over water. We finally persuaded them to try at least one afternoon in the cornfield, and after lunch we were off.

To get to the cornfield one must use a nineteenth-century ferry. The cars are driven up on a barge with no guard rail and with about eight inches to spare on either side. With a rusty wire and pulley, we were winched across to the island. Believe me, everyone's hand was on the door handle of the car all the way across.

We found that the cornfields were covered with a light crusted ice that broke under a man's weight. Then came a foot of water and ten to twelve inches of the blackest and slimiest mud any of us had ever seen. After five minutes, our guests from Maryland had had enough and decided that they would set up their blinds on a muskrat house. The four of us who were left started into the cornfield and with a full two hours' daylight left weren't in too much of a hurry, as the going was really tough.

The sun had been out all day and the thaw was clearly under way, which worsened the footing in the cornfield. The crust cut us right under the knee when we broke through, and within a few hundred yards, we were sweating heavily with shins badly bruised. We sat for one and a half hours crouching, trying to get comfortable, never really succeeding, and not doing much except getting covered with mud and slush. Several high flocks began working the field, but the sun was still high enough and bright enough that they wouldn't come near enough for a shot. With about fifteen minutes of light remaining, our guide yelled to be still and stay down, as the big flocks were just beginning to come over. We were not prepared for what happened then, as the sound of thousands of wings broke the absolute stillness of twilight. Enormous flights of ducks began pouring into the field, actually blotting out what seconds before had been a brilliant sunset. My first three shots dropped two black ducks which had been coming right at me and less than twenty yards overhead. I'll never forget trying to swing on the second bird, having forgotten about the mud which was holding me fast from the knees down. I bagged the bird, but ended up toppled over backward into the mud.

The next ten minutes were a real Chinese fire drill. It consisted of a sequence of shooting, half falling, and trying to slush and trudge through the mud and ice retrieving cripples. The flight of these northern birds consisted mostly of mallards and blacks and seemed to be endless. On the other hand, the hunting pressure from the field was absolutely staggering, as birds fell all around us, and yet the flocks, after flying off for a hundred yards or so, would come right back to where we were standing and the sequence would begin again. It was now dark, and although we continued to hear wings overhead and had a dozen birds piled up, we still had quite a few more down within a thirty-to-forty-yard circle. We began our search and very shortly realized how futile our attempt was. After twenty minutes or so of searching, it was obvious we were not going to find more than one or two of the downed birds without a dog. A terrible feeling of waste came over us and I myself vowed at that moment never to hunt ducks without a dog again.

This feeling of waste turned to absolute horror when I realized we couldn't even find our pile of twelve ducks we had collected. We trudged out of that field with a meager two ducks and a feeling in my stomach that I hope never to experience again.

It was so dark that we were lucky to find our car. We arrived back at the motel about eight o'clock to find our friends showered, on their third drink, and pretty skeptical of hunting in December. They had shot two ducks earlier in the afternoon and had driven back before dark.

Believe me, they had a good laugh when they saw the state of us, covered from head to foot with slimy mud and only two ducks to show for it. All during dinner that night and even breakfast the next morning, I could not eat, and the thought of all those ducks not retrieved preoccupied all our talking. We decided to try the lake a little early to accommodate our friends from Maryland, but agreed that if there was no shooting before nine A.M., we would stop for a sandwich and head for the same field we had been in the afternoon before. We were sure we would be able to pick up what we couldn't find the night before.

The following morning there were no birds, no wind and nothing but penetrating twenty-eight-degree cold. Our colleagues from Maryland insisted that they would come back that afternoon, as they still wanted no part of the cornfield, having seen us the night before. We stopped for lunch and a short nap and when we got up around 1:30 P.M. I was really sure that things had finally taken a turn for the better, but that fickle December Ontario weather provided us with still another cruel blow. Though we had only been sleeping about an hour, a howling nor'wester had dumped four to six inches of snow on the countryside. The wind was gusting to twenty-five knots and the snowflakes were the size of quarters. By the time we got to our cornfield, the visibility was down to fifty feet and heavy snow squalls were in full progress.

The drop in the mercury the night before had refrozen the cornfield, and to our amazement, we could walk quite easily down between the rows of standing corn. From that point on began the most fantastic duck shooting I have ever seen or heard of.

We first spent half an hour circling the area we had thought we were in the night before. Every time we discovered a duck-size lump under the snow, it turned out to be nothing more than a frozen cornstalk. We realized then that the snow had obliterated any chance of finding last night's shooting. We abandoned our search when we heard our guide calling several flocks which had begun working the field from the south. We discovered we did not even have to conceal ourselves or crouch down at all. By merely standing in the rows of corn, we could step out onto the frozen field at the last moment as the ducks came over and pick out the exact bird we wanted. These ducks were not in one enormous flock as were the ones the night before, but rather came dropping in out of the snow in bunches of thirty or forty. We were hidden by the snow and they couldn't see us until it was too late. In fifteen minutes all four of us limited out, taking out only mammoth greenheads and blacks. The birds were so close we would take turns calling our shot, and never once did a bird fall more than thirty yards away. A quick jog down the row of corn where the birds fell was all that was needed to retrieve even wing shots, and it gave us a great feeling knowing we didn't lose one cripple the whole day.

The continuing air show that followed throughout the rest of the afternoon cannot be described in words. Mallard, black, widgeon, and pintail dropped in and out of the snow so close we could have hit them with our hands. With all hands limiting out, with the exception of our friends, who killed one goldeneye on the lake, we drove home through the storm with a never-to-be-forgotten picture of thousands of ducks withstanding unbelievable hunting pressure to get to their precious corn.

As all stories should have a happy ending, this one will too. Out in the back yard at the moment are two black Labrador retrievers that were picked up after last year's hunting season. Between the two of them, they have retrieved several hundred ducks this past season, and both spent quite a little time on the Ste. Anne cornfield with me during the present season and I hope will do so again in the future. But the day last December when the ducks came in by the thousands is the day that

I'll never forget. Anyone who has hunted with a good retriever knows what I know now: that duck hunting without a dog is "for the birds."

I've got to tell just one other story. Every so often, even the oldest veteran has to stop for a minute and admit this story or that story really "says it all" for him. This one does it for me.

In 1973, while driving up to Canada for a weekend's hunting with two good friends known for their advanced cases of duck fever, I was recalling for their benefit my favorite Gene Hill duck-hunting story. Little did I know how close to tragedy one of them would come this weekend.

The story concerns an old waterfowler who on his death bed called in his family and said, "I want to apologize to you all. I know I haven't been a very good father and husband. I shamefully admit that I spent as much of my life as I could with my dogs and guns. I was rarely at home during the hunting seasons and I spent far too much time at the gun club." He paused here to rest for a minute, then continued. "I hope you all will forgive me." He paused again and looked around at his family gathered around him. Then he closed his eyes and a smile crossed his face as he said in a half-whisper to himself, "On the other hand . . . I *have* shot a helluva lot of birds!"

All weekend long we nearly doubled up with laughter trying out different variations of that story. For example, the hero of our weekend, whom we will call Bill (that's his name), would double on black ducks, calmly take out a Thermos of coffee, pour it slowly into a cup, take a long drink, and then look up and say with a casual air, "On the other hand, boys, I *have* shot a helluva lot of birds." This went on for two days, and we even managed a photograph of Bill on top of a muskrat house on one of those forays of relief from the blind, after all that coffee took effect. All in all, if I've ever had a more relaxing shooting trip, I can't remember when.

Sunday, on the trip home, Bill mentioned he had seen some blood in his morning stool and admitted he was really feeling lousy. We didn't give it much thought, because after a long Saturday-night celebration following a great two days of shooting, we were all a little pale.

The next day I was informed that Bill had been quite sick that night and now was in the hospital for tests. Twenty-four hours later, our friend Bill was undergoing major surgery for cancer of the colon. To say you are shocked just doesn't describe the feeling that comes over you when you realize that a buddy who the day before had lent you shells in the marsh is in the hospital now fighting for his life.

Finally came the news from Bill's family—he was okay. The operation had been successful, and although Bill would be laid up for quite a while, he was going to be all right. Later that week, we got the "frosting on the cake."

Bill's wife had gone into the recovery room after consulting with the doctor and found Bill still in the twilight zone, lying there with a snow-white face and no visible sign of life.

She whispered in Bill's ear, not knowing whether he could comprehend or not, that the doctor said everything had gone well and he thought he had removed all the cancer. At first there was still no sign of life. Then Bill's lips moved ever so slightly.

Two witnesses swear the first words from Bill's mouth were: "On the other hand . . . I *have* shot a helluva lot of birds."

Day of the Long-Tailed Ducks

WERNER D. MUELLER

"**B**lowfish," Jay grunted, squinting over the edge of the duck blind, "get off your banker's back side and see what Kinki and I see!"

I did, and seventy yards in front of Jay's popping eyeballs a sassy cock pheasant sailed downwind over the cattails of this northern Ohio duck marsh.

"Look at that tail and hear that rooster cackle," Jay said. "Maybe we're hunting the wrong game."

His sourdough-style mustache twitched, and he whispered, "You suppose that cock bird has lots of friends in this marsh?"

Of course, we were not pheasant hunting at all. We never even thought of pheasant when we planned this trip. We were *duck* hunting.

But as any veteran hunter knows, duck hunting is a funny kind of sport. Sometimes you go duck hunting and wind up pheasant shooting, and sometimes your retriever teaches you something about both.

Well, anyway, that's the way it turned out that morning. Brother Jay, from Alaska, wanted to see if Ohio, the state he had left, had any ducks or anything else worthy of the pursuit of a hunter, and he was also curious to find out whether I had been able to train a retriever, as I had claimed in our occasional letters.

Jay left Ohio twenty-five years ago on a summer vacation to Alaska, and liked it so much that he stayed there and got married and went into business and learned to fly a plane and worked hard ten months a year and hunted and fished the other two months. Having left Ohio and stayed in Seward's Ice Bay for reasons of his own, his curiosity drove him to check up on me, his kid brother, every five years or so, to find out what was up in the smog belt. I wanted to prove that we civilized folk had the best of two worlds—civilization and duck hunting. I also wanted to brag about my Labrador retriever.

We shared a blind with my Lab, Kinki von Hansel, who is now in canine Valhalla. He was named Kinki because his patrician features were married by a kink in his tail. He answered to the name of von Hansel, because his old man was Neubauer's Hansel, who was a legend in his own right.

That morning we had waded out to our duck blind in pitch darkness as usual, me charged with the extra hope of someone who wanted to give his long-lost brother a good show. The stars evaporated gently and were replaced by a golden glow from the east. Red-winged blackbirds flapped and gargled and gurgled and acted the way red-winged blackbirds act when they are about to fly south. Then mallards and teal and wood ducks started quacking and crying and trading all over the marsh, but it turned into a bluebird day and everything except the blackbirds flew halfway between our blind and the then unpublicized comet Kohoutek.

The sights and sounds were beautiful. But Kinki von Hansel frowned a deep black Labrador frown, because no matter how quietly he sat and no matter how much he rolled his eyeballs at feathers hurtling through the air, *there were no ducks.*

Kinki von Hansel sat for an hour, and then two hours, and then he said in very plain dog language "————you. We are going P-H-E-A-S-A-N-T hunting."

He swaggered off in that authoritative Lab way that says "Follow me." Jay and I hitched up our hip boots and followed him. Kinki, in turn, followed his nose, but suddenly he stopped. His ears cocked forward, his nose twitched, and his head pointed toward an inviting tuft of marsh grass, and I hollered, "Heads up!"

An almost black rooster leaped from the tuft of marsh grass, wings beating frantically to put distance between him and that overstuffed fox we called a Labrador, cackled four times, and crumpled in a cloud of feathers. Brother Jay lowered his Parker side-by-side and smirked smugly, the way Alaskans smirk when they have succeeded—as usual.

Jay was a member of the Alaska State Trap Shooting Team, and was an accomplished duck shot. Pheasants posed no technical problem.

Kinki trotted in with bird number one, and delivered it to hand.

Kinki grinned a big Lab grin that said, "Yes, I'm pleased with myself. I figured out there ain't no duck hunting, so now we are r-e-a-l-l-y going P-H-E-A-S-A-N-T hunting!" He pivoted upwind. His wagging tail told us to follow him and shut up. We did, and Kinki and Jay promptly bagged a second rooster—an exact repeat of the first.

To our utter amazement—for pheasant hunting generally hasn't been that good in Ohio since World War II—Kinki started making game again almost as soon as he had delivered the second bird. "Let's go," I muttered to Jay as soon as he had popped the bird into his game pocket. "You've got your birds, but you can watch me get mine, and incidentally see some first-class dog work."

As soon as that brag left my mouth, our aristocratic canine friend decided to go on a hunt of his own. He had been working ten yards ahead of us. All of a sudden, he decided *fifty* yards was more like it, and then he made game and raced through the cattails making figure-eights a mile a minute.

Pheasants jumped ahead of him wherever he went: cock pheasants, hen pheasants, big pheasants, and little pheasants. His master whistled and hollered and cursed, but Kinki von Hansel had a face full of scent and just kept on thrashing through the cattails on a hunt of his own.

After fifteen minutes of this nonsense, his great bragging red-faced master chased Kinki down and cussed him out and lifted him up by the neck and told him what he thought about a lousy Lab who went on a toot of his own fifty yards ahead of the guns.

"Kinki, *damn* you—who do you think you're hunting for?" I grabbed his neck skin and lifted him off the ground and shook him until his eyeballs waggled.

He just looked at me and waited until his feet were on the ground and I, his great master, said, "Okay, find the bird."

Off went a proud but obviously chastized Kinki. Minutes later, up went a cock pheasant and blam! Down he fell.

So what did Kinki do? He marked where it hit, sprinted toward the fallen bird, found it, placed one front paw deliberately on the back of the dead bird . . . then grabbed its tail and pulled out all the tail feathers!

This pleased him greatly. He looked up at his great master without flinching. Fire shot from his eyes, and then he went back to plucking out more feathers. He climaxed this exhibition by rolling over the now half-naked carcass.

"Kinki! Damn you! *Fetch*!"

Ha ha ha. Kinki von Hansel clamped down on the carcass, fetched it ten feet closer, and dropped it. He pulled out more feathers and then rolled over the poor bedraggled bird once again.

Brother Jay was laughing and chortling and choking and flapping his arms in the air and almost swallowed his chewing tobacco (which he learned to chew because now he was an Alaskan).

"What the hell's so funny?" I groaned.

"He's trying to tell you something," Jay said solemnly. "And maybe even you, my kid brother, are smart enough to figure it out." For punctuation, he spat out a huge gob of tobacco juice, Alaskan style, miraculously missing his sourdough mustache and billygoat goatee in the process.

So . . . we didn't get any ducks but we did learn something about duck dogs.

"Kinki von Hansel," I begged, "bring me that damned bird and I'll say I'm sorry."

Kinki von Hansel thought about it, picked up the cock bird, and dumped it at my feet.

I told him he was a good mutt and loved him up and rubbed his silky ears and touched my face to his face and told him he was right and I was wrong and I was sorry.

"Kinki, I'm sorry I roughed you up. I was wrong. See, I'm rubbing your ears to prove I mean what I say. So let's start over . . . okay?"

Kinki rolled his big brown eyes, rose quietly, looked into the wind, cocked his ears, and jumped back into the cattails.

"Kak—kak—kak," and up jumped a big old rooster with a four-foot tail. "Blam!" went the duck gun and down went the cock bird. Kinki piled on top of the rooster, picked it up, and delivered it to hand, with chin pointed at a forty-five-degree angle to the sky.

That finished our pheasant hunt, as Ohio has a two-bird limit, so we spent the rest of the day watching blackbirds.

As the sun sank into the western clouds, two men and a dog (with four pheasants) slogged out of the marsh toward a hot toddy and men's talk and cigar smoke and a charcoal-broiled strip steak.

And the two men were much wiser. An old black Lab with a dignified white muzzle had taught them that when ducks don't fly, you hunt pheasants, and that Labs aren't dogs—they're a special kind of people, who can teach a tenderfoot a thing or two about how to treat others—especially four-legged people with dignified white muzzles.

Buckeye Joe

JOSEF WOOSTER

How can a man that's spent the last thirty-five years squintin' down the barrel of a Model 12 practically every daylight hour from Indian summer's Opening Day till January's final numbing sunset pick out one day, one hunt, or one shot as being most memorable? Oh hell yes, I can remember the times I've traveled to some distant prime hunting ground, and enjoyed being entertained like a blue-nosed big-city sport, but Long Island's Great South Bay, Virginia's Chincoteague Island, Nebraska's winding river, and Maryland's Eastern Shore have damn little in common with the central-Ohio hunting I've known. Those jaunts, and the memories they conjure up, were more a busman's holiday than a true picture of what my hunting has been like, and if I am to select just one day from these years of cold coffee and frozen fingers, I'd like it to be typical of the experiences I've had seemingly every season.

Maybe I should start out by telling you that so far as waterfowling is concerned, I am a professional. No, not a professional market hunter, fer crissake; that went out with meat rationing back during the war. I am a full-time professional decoy carver; been one for years, here in Ashley, Ohio, a stone's throw from the Delaware Wildlife area, and while the average duck hunter might become enthusiastic for two or three months during the season, my interest in waterfowl lasts 365 days a year, and nobody can spend that much time at something without learning at least a trick or two. It's common knowledge I can set a spread of decoys with enough expertise to coax a wary ole black duck to set down inside a hula hoop, and while my lamps are nothing like they once were a few years ago, the chances are I can shoot backup for you all day and end up wiping your eye! I've hunted with hundreds of Mr. Average Duck-hunters, and discovered they damn near all shoot three feet behind the bird, and the spread of decoys they hunt over likely draws more "snake-feeders" than ducks. I've a healthy disrespect for amateur duck hunters that could well be called contempt, so let me tell you how a real bunch of experts go about this duck-hunting business, and no doubt you'll want to take notes!

The day I'll always have frozen in my memory, my dad, Paul Wooster, and a young fellow named Ron Fridley and myself were enjoying what remained of a too warm, too bright morning, remarking to each other during the lulls, "Sure a pretty day, isn't it?" We'd had a few blacks and mallards into the spread that dawn before the "smoke" burned off, and a mixed flight of bluebills and ringnecks had given us a pass or two before deciding things were a mite too hot for them at the mouth of the Whetstone. Ducks had all but stopped moving on the opposite side of the river, so now, with good light, we admired the birds we'd bagged, commenting on each as its turn came, "Damn, that's sure a nice greenhead," or joked, "Okay, which one of you pot hunters shot this half-sized black jack?"

The action had slowed to a halt, and only old Happy's panting from under the bench broke the still of nature's vacuum-like calm. Nature had, however, been sending me a different message, so I dug into one of Dad's sacks looking for the roll of paper I knew would be there. "You hungry?" Dad asked hopefully, because he'd been waiting for an excuse to start digging out the grub, now that the shooting had let up.

"Nope, just lookin' for the paper; I've gotta see a man about a horse!" I wisecracked.

"How about you, Ron, you gettin' hungry?" I heard over my shoulder, as I slipped out the back of the blind and headed for the trees in the middle of the island.

I laughed to myself as I made my way down the trail, "Wait till Ron sees all that food Dad brought along; he'll think we're stayin' all week!"

My father looked like a roly-poly carry-out boy that morning, standing on the porch in the dark, his two big sacks stuffed full of loaves of bread, lunch meats, boxes of crackers, cheese, mustard, horseradish, candy, and cans of this and that. Now, none of us needed the extra calories, but after thirty-five years of hunting with him, I've given up all thoughts of reform. Dad loves the eating as much as, if not more than, the hunting. His skill with his old Fox-Sterlingworth is amazing to say the least; if there's a better man with a side-by-side, I've yet to meet him. But what Dad can do to a quantity of food is absolutely indescribable.

I'd almost made it back to the blind when I heard the low-keyed quack of a drake black duck hanging over my head. I froze in my tracks, in spite of the fact I knew it was probably too late; not many black ducks get themselves killed with hunters out walking around the blind. Ron's automatic appeared above the outline of the roof and gave a single bark. I looked up in time to see the big black set his wings and start one of those slow, slow, mile-long descents.

"I hope to hell that was rock salt you shot him with," I needled.

"I'm not sure he even came down in this state!" Dad chimed in.

Ron by now realized that since he had shot the only duck in the sky, he was going to serve as our target. We heaped on the insults, as the three of us slid the kayak into the water from its hide behind the blind.

"Ron, have ya ever thought about shootin' in front of one of 'em?" Dad asked.

"Maybe if ya bent the barrel on that gas pipe it would help!" I offered as my parting shot, as Ron handed over the double-blade paddle, along with my pump gun, chuckling at being outnumbered.

"Stay!" I ordered the old Lab as they gave me a shove off. "Hap might have marked that bird a couple of years ago," I mused, picking up the rhythm, aided by the wind on my back. "He's just gettin' old, like the rest of us," I thought, as the sleek little boat knifed the water, covering the distance to the fallen black in a fraction of the time one might guess. The bird was still very much alive, and gave every indication he intended to leave the country, and as I've had "dead" black ducks fly off more times than I care to recall, I reached for the Model 12.

Still a good sixty yards, I figured, but the wind is closing the gap. He looks a mite too healthy to wait much longer! The black and the Winchester jumped within a wink of each other, with the results lying belly up, his red legs fanning the air. Two or three strokes, and I am alongside and heft the duck into the boat. "Heavy son of a gun," I volunteer, and I wonder if he's an early arrival of the big redlegs we usually don't see until the second half of the split; I decide his bill isn't yellow enough to be a redleg, as I turn the kayak upwind. It's tough going now, with the breeze in my face, so I look for slick water along the banks, as well as doing my best to stay in the lee of the island. No resting now, or I'll end up back where I started, the way I am being shoved around. I debate going through the rig to reach the blind, but veto the idea in favor of cutting behind the island and coming in the back way. "Damned wind is pickin' up," I mutter to my silent shipmate, while fighting to keep the kayak off the rocks, getting more of a workout than I bargain for slicing across the chop. The sand beach behind the blind is a welcome sight as I nose the boat onto it, then drag it out of the water, too pooped to go any farther. Chest heaving, shoulders aching, and wool shirt soaked with sweat, I half walk, half stumble up the sand toward the blind.

A couple of thumps of old Happy's tail greet my entrance into the snug shelter. "Boy, you guys are sure a big help," I announce, the kayak's weight through the sand still fresh in my mind.

"We didn't know you were back; hell, we figgered that ole black duck had whupped ya!" Dad fired back, as I leaned my shotgun in the corner, and bent over to add the big drake to the pile of ducks gathered in front of the doorway. BLAM!—the bomblike explosion rocked my lowered head with a deafening roar, the concussion jarring me ungracefully into the pile of dead ducks. Smoke filled the blind, making it impossible to see even the dead birds I was now in the midst of.

A million thoughts flashed through my brain, but foremost was my shotgun. Had I left the safety off when I sat that gun in the corner? Could it have fallen somehow while I was bent over, and gone off inside the blind? Old fears and a guilty conscience made me certain that was what had happened, and as the smoke started to clear, I got my first hazy look at what was left of my hunting partners. Both sat dead still on the bench, their heads and chests covered with a pinkish-brown gore! My God, I've killed 'em both, my shocked spinning brain concluded!

Remorse, panic, shame, and guilt swept through my body in waves, yet I was dumbstruck as to what I should do. "Pull yourself together, gawddammit," I cursed. No use going for help, it's twenty miles to the nearest hospital. Maybe I could stop the bleeding! Huh? What the hell? That's strange, I can't believe my eyes. I don't see any bleeding to stop; now I really am confused.

The rhythmic quake of my dad's protruding stomach caught my eye, shaking like a bowl of jelly, and I notice both "corpses" are beginning to move. Oh no, I must be losing my mind, because I'd swear it sounds like they're laughing. Nobody takes getting shot in the head that good-naturedly, do they? My dad's hand slowly moves up to his face, and using a forefinger like a windshield wiper, he removes the layer of gore from one side of his glasses, and by now their laughter is just short of hysteria.

I get my wits organized long enough to glance in the corner, and there, standing right where I'd left it, with the safety on, no less, was my trusty Model 12, and Dad's double-barrel, as well as Ron's automatic, both exactly where I'd last seen them.

The laughing from the two "gunshot" victims had not subsided, it had grown worse, and was now of the type heard only from the loud-speakers in front of a midway funhouse. Deep, sobbing wails, followed by more uncontrolled wild cackling. Dad composed himself just long enough to point a goop-coated finger in the direction of the five-thousand-BTU heater, and there, sitting on the expanded wire cover, its top and contents blown away, sat the lethal bomb—a can of Vienna sausage.

Memories of the Marsh

E. L. GARRIGAN, JR.

Whistling wings in the mist, anxious tremors of a golden retriever, a distant quack of a mallard and the thrilling call of a goose.

These are the ingredients that bind a man from his earliest recollections as a youth to his golden years as a devotee of the mystical order of waterfowling.

To reflect on a lifetime of outdoor experience recalls an endless multitude of memorable and pleasurable experiences, but there is always that one event that stands out above all others.

The particular incident that remains so vivid in my memory occurred on the bank of the Toussaint River, one November afternoon.

The goose decoys are set, the wind and weather are cooperating at their miserable best, and we are awaiting the afternoon flight of geese.

As is often the case in such a situation, one is inclined to drowse and daydream until that magical "honk" breaks the stillness, and inevitably it occurs. The geese are on the wing and the calling commences. By skill and luck they are turned in the direction of the decoys.

One's heart begins to beat faster, and the dogs shudder in anticipation. Emotion builds by the second. Man and dog are ready for that crucial moment when wings are set and the geese are in range.

You rise and fire, and a goose hits the water. The command to retrieve is given to Sandy, but for a moment she hesitates, apparently frightened by the size of the first goose she has ever seen. In that moment a more seasoned Labrador is in the water going for the retrieve; Sandy follows in hot pursuit.

She honors the Lab's retrieve, but in mortification at having failed, she swims into the decoys, picks one up, and proudly delivers the decoy to my feet.

Laughter runs rampant, but recognition of the spirit of her deed results in applause and forgiveness.

This was my most unforgettable hunting experience!

Ragu

JOHN E. SPENCE, SR.

In 1950, seven crazy duck hunters from Des Moines formed what is known as NoDux Unlimited. We leased some North Platte river bottom land near Bridgeport, Nebraska. Because this lease was six hundred and fifty miles from Des Moines, we felt it would be almost impossible to build a hunting camp and maintain it that far away; so we became very friendly with a motel owner by the name of Lee Golden. Naturally his motel was known as Golden Acres. Sounds like a permanent home. It is built on a little hill overlooking the beautiful Platte river bottom.

Lee is an old duck hunter and understood mud, feathers, empty whiskey bottles, etc. in his motel, but he used to get a little unhappy when some of our member's Labs tore the curtains from the rods and left yellow spots on the bedspreads.

It was always our policy to leave Des Moines with our station wagons full of guns, dogs, bourbon, and all the neat things needed for a hunting trip. We would drive somewhere along old Highway 30 where our two or three station wagons would meet, and we'd spend the evening playing cards and lying to each other about duck hunting. Then we would get up bright and early and continue on to our spot in western Nebraska.

It was a ritual to go to the motel, unload our luggage, go to the farmer's barn where we stored our decoys, load up, and head for our lease. We would then spend the rest of the afternoon and early evening putting out our decoys and cleaning the muskrats, etc. out of our sunken tank blinds. We would get to bed early and dream of the flocks of mallards that were about to descend upon our marsh the next morning.

It was also customary to take a Brittany or two along with us, and when there was a lull in the duck hunting we would move north near Alliance, Nebraska, to hunt pheasants and sharptails. This one particular trip about fifteen years ago, we followed the general procedure and went to the hunting area, where we turned our dogs loose to exercise and look around while we put out the decoys. My Brittany, Ginger, went out to canvas the territory. Just as the most beautiful sunset over Chimney Rock was taking place, Ginger came running up. She had a lot more than the usual orange spots on her and an odor you can't believe. She had encountered a skunk and was really in a pathetic condition.

Now, most sportsmen wouldn't give this much thought, but here we were with a brand-new station wagon that we couldn't put her in to take her to a motel three miles away that we couldn't put her in. So, I started out on foot to take her to a nearby farm to see if I could borrow their horse tank to give the dog a bath. I borrowed some detergent from Mrs. Schmidt, the farmer's wife, gave Ginger the best bath she had ever had in her life, and rubbed her off with some sacks. The newly acquired orange spots were gone, but the odor still remained. I gave her a second bath, but to really no avail. I borrowed a long section of corn-planter wire from Mr. Schmidt and staked the dog out for the night.

I drove to Bridgeport and started asking various people what they would do in an emergency like this and finally learned from the manager of a sporting goods store that tomato paste was the only answer. I went to the grocery store just before it closed, purchased two cans of tomato paste, and headed out to the farm. I completely covered Ginger with tomato paste until she looked like she had been peppered about ten times with 20-gauge number eights. This ended the first day of my hunting trip.

After the next morning's shoot, we went back to the farm, and, of course, the tomato paste had dried and was so stiff the dog could hardly move.

I bathed Ginger again in the horse tank and the skunk odor finally disappeared. Then it was possible to reestablish our friendship with the dog and we proceeded to have a successful duck and pheasant hunt.

I certainly hope you never have this experience, but if you do, I can highly recommend tomato paste.

A First at Walpole

EUGENE HARRIS

The call came from a good friend and Cleveland D.U. member. The question: Was I interested in a hunt? The place: Walpole Island, Ontario, Canada. The fowl to be harvested: black mallard. *Yes*! I immediately thought of a very close business friend. George, an avid upland-game and deer hunter, had never been up against waterfowl. This new and unique experience aroused a great deal of interest in my city friend. So, after much discussion and excited planning, we made our reservations for mid-October.

We departed on a crisp, golden October afternoon. Over four hundred miles and many hours later, we arrived at the Snye View Motel. The midnight hour and our travel-weary bones left us little time or energy for much activity, other than unloading the car and taking a welcome hot shower. We barely had time to warm the sheets, because the alarm jangled us awake at four o'clock, before the dawn. Dressed and well fed, we headed out to meet our Indian guide and his duck boat.

Our gear and the guide's black Lab stowed aboard, we sputtered off on a damp, predawn gray, thirty-minute cruise to the blinds. Riding along, the water lapping rhythmically at the hull, I told George he could have the first shot. This only served to increase his already growing excitement, initially stimulated by the mallards rising in raucous flight out of the misty marsh.

Arriving at the blind, we began the long, silent wait for daybreak. Mallards were scattering everywhere above our heads. George was like a little boy at his first circus. His voice almost cracking with anticipation, he whispered, "When can we shoot?"

"About ten minutes," replied the guide with experienced nonchalance.

George groaned, agonized. "They'll be gone by then!"

After a few minutes that must have seemed like hours to my companion, the guide instructed us to load up and get ready. George had three shells in his Ithaca pump before I could even reach for my shotgun. Following a few seconds of the best calling I had ever heard, the guide got results!

The first flock of black mallards to come overhead was greeted with a whispered "Shoot!" from the guide as well as the shouts, three of them, from George's Ithaca. Those three shells rapidly racked out, George yelled for assistance. "Give me some more shells!"

I was laughing so hard, struck useless by his comical enthusiasm, I was of no help to this new waterfowl hunter. After the first round was over, George asked me incredulously, "Didn't you shoot?"

"How could I?" I choked out, still roaring with laughter. George reached up, touched his head, and was surprised to find his cap missing. It was behind the blind, where it had landed after its owner blasted off a greeting when introduced to his first black mallard.

The hilarity over, we settled down to some serious shooting. Our limit harvested, we were in the boat and headed for our car by nine o'clock. The canoe unloaded, we were removing our boots and gear when I noticed another boat coming up the channel. Like ours, it was manned by a guide and two hunters with another black Lab in tow. Our dog noticed the boat, too, and was running wide open down the bank before the guide could call him back. The dog dove into the other boat and then Walpole Island gave a farewell performance: the darnedest, dampest dog fight we had ever seen! The last picture I carry in my mind of Walpole is two soaked hunters and one very disgusted guide slogging back to their righted canoe, the soggy, soon-to-be-reprimanded Lab alongside.

Packing to go home, George anxiously said, "Reservations for next year?" So, that's what we did.

Memories of a Son and Father

REX HANCOCK, D.D.S.

In looking back over the years, from my first exposure to the present, it is rather difficult to pick a hunt that was more enjoyable than another. I think that most hunters can recall a few hunts that have long lingered in the memory. My father carried me on his back for over four miles to expose me to the thrills of hunting. I was four years old. I can recall that my mother thought I was too young to go out in the rain on that day, but she finally consented and bundled me up. I got on my dad's back and we headed south to a slough back of George Ramey's.

As we approached the dam, Dad let me down and told me to be quiet, and he slipped up to the bank to take a look. I can recall him motioning for me to crawl to him, and then he whispered for me to look through the weeds. I saw my first wild ducks on the slough. Dad shot an L. C. Smith field grade 12-gauge single-trigger (which I still have). He put two extra shells in his mouth and then stood up. Just as the ducks sprang up from the water he shot twice, loaded his gun with the two shells he had hanging from his mouth, and fired twice again. I was in the weeds and couldn't see over the bank. I hollered at Dad, "Did you get any?" Dad told me to get up and come take a look. Four ducks were on the water. There was a slight skim of ice around the edge of the slough, and the ducks drifted and stopped at the edge of the ice.

The one thing I remember most clearly about this hunt was my dad taking off his clothes and wading and breaking the ice to get the ducks. He was shivering when he got back to the bank. I asked Dad if there were any more ducks to hunt but he told me that we would go again but he needed to go home and warm up. I got back on his back and we started home.

There was another pond just north of the Laddonia Cemetery, which was only about a quarter-mile out of the way, and Dad said to me, "Do you want to see if there are any ducks on Sipple's pond?" My answer was affirmative. As we approached the pond, Dad lowered me to the ground and told me to sneak up and take a look. This was a great thrill for a four-year-old—to be asked by your dad to do such an important errand as looking for ducks. I can recall crawling on my stomach and peeking over the bank. I saw a duck on the pond and motioned for Dad.

As he crawled up to me he asked, "How many are on the pond?"

I replied, "I saw one out there."

Dad rose up and hollered and the duck got up. He let it fly out a distance so I could see it in the air, and then shot it. The same routine followed—ice was around this pond also, and he took off his clothes again to wade for the retrieve. I was a cold, wet, but thrilled youngster. For the next three years I accompanied Dad on almost every duck hunt.

When I was eight years old my parents gave me a Lefever .410 hammerless single-barrel shotgun. My father spent hours with me teaching me safety and how to handle the gun. The first harvesting of game was a pigeon sitting on top of Sipple's barn. I then hunted squirrels with my .410 every week of the season.

In October of my eighth year I crawled up to Webber's Pond, north of Laddonia, Missouri, and shot my first mallards. I was taking no chances—I shot them on the water! I was disgusted because I only had one shot and told Dad I wanted a double-barrel like his. He told me that I was too small to handle a larger gun but when I grew older he would get me one. I hunted with the .410 through age ten.

Living on the edge of town offered many advantages to the youngster who liked to hunt. Dad thought I was old enough to hunt alone, and practically every Saturday and Sunday I hunted all day long. I would return home literally loaded down with rabbits, squirrel, quail, etc. At the age of ten I killed my limit of ten quail, all on the wing, and shot almost two boxes of shells.

On my eleventh birthday Ernest Grubb came by my home and told me that he wanted me to use his gun to hunt with. What a thrill: a Fox Sterlingworth 20-gauge. I hunted with this gun until I was twelve years old. On Christmas day that year my parents gave me a Lefever 20-gauge double, single-trigger. This gun cost thirty-seven-fifty and was purchased from Pete Erdel at Rush Hill, Missouri.

Several months later Dad told me that a very fine shot was going to stay at our home and he wanted me to go straight home from school, get my gun, and come by his office. That evening I witnessed one of the greatest shooting exhibitions I have ever seen. Dad, Ernest Grubb, and Ad Topperwein put on an exhibition of aerial target shooting with .22s. It was from Ad Topperwein that I learned much in trick shooting.

At the age of eight I would get up at four-thirty on Sunday mornings and go with Mr. O. K. Moore to run his trap line. He taught me how to make sets for muskrat, mink and coon. I ran my own trapline at the age of thirteen and continued this sport as a supplement to my wages as I worked in college.

After my graduation from the University of Missouri School of Dentistry I was faced with a great decision as to where I wanted to live and practice. I knew one thing—hunting and fishing was a must. I traveled through the Pacific Northwest and the central United States. I knew I could have gone back to my home town and had a good practice where my father was a dentist, but I had heard of the fabulous duck hunting around Stuttgart, Arkansas, and I thought I would drive to Stuttgart and look around. One of the first men I met in Stuttgart was "Chick" Major, the world-famous duck caller and craftsman of the Dixie Mallard Call. I was so impressed with Chick that I spent hours with him in his shop watching him turn out these calls. Chick gave me a call and tried to teach me how to "grunt" (take the air from the diaphragm and not blow)—up till then I had never attempted to call a duck. This was going to be a challenge, and my mind was made up. I was going to establish the practice of dentistry in the Rice and Duck Capital of the World.

I bought a lot, started construction on my clinic, and then moved to Huntsville, Arkansas, to practice for seven months while my office was under construction.

For the next few years I hardly missed a day of hunting. Probably one of the greatest rewards of an addiction to the great outdoors is the people you meet. I have been blessed with meeting some of the finest sportsmen in the country, from all walks of life, who have come to Stuttgart to enjoy the great heritage of duck hunting. I have kept a rough diary of people I have met, hunted with, and shared fond experiences with. A book could be written on just one year's experiences. Another lasting experience was hunting with one of the finest of all Labrador retrievers. A number of years ago I purchased a young black Lab from Roger Reopelle of Minneapolis, Minnesota. This dog undoubtedly was one of the finest, most intelligent dogs that ever retrieved a duck. This is saying a lot, but the first year this dog was hunted there were 1,229 ducks that were knocked from the air and Pepper retrieved 1,219. This convinced me that a fine dog is one of the greatest conservation measures that a sportsman can invest in.

I didn't do what my father did—take my son Jim on my back—but I did take him hunting with me at the age of four. We went to Crocketts Bluff, Arkansas, and hunted with Daniel Boone Bullock, who has one of the finest field shootings in this country. The following year Jim bagged his first duck, a mallard drake. I had purchased a single-barrel .410 and had to cut off the stock—it's only nine inches from the trigger to butt plate. His first duck was also shot on the water, but three years earlier in life than mine. Bryan, my second son, was also taken on his first duck hunt at the age of four, and I wanted him to harvest his first duck at the age of five. I took Bryan to Rogers Reservoir, south of Stuttgart, and put him in the front of the boat. I was paddling the boat through lots of buck brush and was scaring out lots of coot. Bryan shot several coot, and he hollered, "There's a brown one!" Just as he hollered it got up, a mallard hen, and he killed his first duck—and flying. He was so proud that he did not want to hunt any more, but wanted to go home and show the duck.

During the 1976–77 season I knew I had a problem: I had two young boys to take and I could not go unless I took them both. On the second day of the season, Bryan (now seven, and Jim eleven) went with me to Glenn Earlywine's, east of Stuttgart, to hunt in his rice field. Bryan was so short he could not see out of the pit, much less shoot unless it was straight up. Glenn got some boards and we fixed a platform in the pit that Bryan could stand on. Bryan and Jim both handle a duck call very well for their age, each having won second place in their division at the duck-calling contest held at the Stuttgart Youth Center. This contest was originated by the late Chick Major and his wife Sophie.

I got in the middle—had Jim on my left and Bryan on my right. A few small bunches of mallards were getting out of the Baker Reservoir. I put my call up and told my boys to call. About seven mallards broke from the sky and responded to their calling. They made one pass over the pit and the boys lost sight of them. I whispered to them to make the feed call—the mallards had turned and were making a second pass at the decoys. I told Jim to take those on the left and for Bryan to shoot at those on the right.

Four mallards hit the water. I could hardly believe it. What a thrill it was for me, their father, to be with them when they did such fine shooting.

We got back in the pit and they called another small bunch of ducks over. The ducks were a little spooky and the boys had not learned when to stop calling. The mallards were making circles, but just a little too far away. On about the third swing around I told them to shoot. Bryan shoots a 20-gauge over-and-under and Jim a 20-gauge auto. Jim knocked down two and Bryan one. Jim had his limit, and I told him to put his gun up and let Bryan get his last duck.

I told Bryan to do all the calling, and it was not long until four mallards passed over the field. The first call made them set their wings and come toward the decoys. Bryan got up on the platform, and it took two shots, but mallard number four hit the water.

I imagine that this hunt was my most memorable of any duck hunt. I have a trap in my back yard and my boys shoot clay targets several times a week. On this hunt the practice had paid dividends. I really can think of no greater thrill than to watch your young sons take their limit.

Greenwing

W. C. (BILLY) JEROME III (AGE TWELVE)

Ducks, ducks in the sky,
Flying low, and then so high,
Settling down, in the marsh,
Landing softly, not too harsh,
Swimming peacefully, some are puttering,
Taking off, all are fluttering,
Ducks, ducks in the air,
Ducks are beautiful everywhere.

Lesson in Timing

JOHN W. ROCKWOOD

Amemorable wildfowl-hunting experience happened to me many years ago. I was living on River Road, Willoughby Hills, Ohio, and had been invited to shoot ducks at Leroy Weir's Marsh at Middle Harbor, Ohio, on a Friday.

The shooting, according to all reports, had been excellent, everybody limiting out by ten A.M., so I made the mistake of advising my very pregnant wife that I would no doubt be home by four or five o'clock that day.

According to all the weather signs, it was the type of day that ducks should have decoyed in even if you were standing in the decoys. It was blowing from the northwest, spitting snow. However, the ducks seemed content to bask out on the lake, and by one o'clock, my partner and I had the sum total of three ducks. The whistle blew for us to return to the clubhouse, and that was the end of the shoot, but the beginning of another story.

When we arrived at the clubhouse, the weather was really beginning to close in, so I decided to call my wife and advise her I would be delayed, but much to my dismay, the phone company had gone on strike, and this was in the days when you could not dial direct, and the personnel, who were beyond a doubt not duck hunters, did not deem my call an emergency.

Arriving home finally about ten-thirty P.M. that night, I found my wife had decided I had either shot myself or drowned trying to retrieve a duck. She had called numerous people in the neighborhood, who decided I had undoubtedly had a good day and was enclosed in some bar, and the feathers were getting deeper as I bragged about the day's shoot.

She finally advised me, after some time, that Don Jones, a builder down the road, had said that when I finally did come home he wanted me to shoot with him, Sid Kingsland, and Art Clark on the Chagrin River in the morning.

At that particular moment, I was ready to say to hell with duck hunting; however, the blinds were mine, I was the only one who had decoys, and, after some persuasive talk by Don, I agreed to go. Arriving at the river blinds about half an hour before shooting time, I set out decoys in front of each blind and placed four goose decoys in some winter wheat in the back of the blinds. Sid and Don were in one blind and Art was with me.

Shooting time arrived and I looked down the river at the blind, where Sid and Don were, and I said to Art, "The damn fools are asleep. There are two ducks in their decoys," and with that they must have started talking. The ducks took off, and Art and I drowned them as they flew up the river in range.

As I waded out to pick up the ducks, I heard a bunch of Canadas telling the world to wake up. Retrieving the ducks, I beat it back to the blind. The geese spotted the decoys in the wheat field and came into range. Everyone opened up—twelve shots in all.

I started out of the blind and everyone shouted, "Where in the hell are you going?"

I said, "To pick up my goose."

No one had seen the goose fall except me, and they wouldn't believe it until I brought it back to the blind. This was the first Canada I ever bagged. I missed my other two shots by at least twenty feet, and all I can say is you can get "buck fever" goose shooting.

The moral of all of this is to never tell your wife when you go trout fishing or duck shooting what time you will be home, because I have yet to meet the crystal-ball gazer who can predict the time the hatch will occur or the ducks will fly.

Seventy-Three Years of It

FRITZ L. SCHWEITZER

That, if you please, is one hell of a lot of years, but all of them full of great memories of many hunts with many friends and with many wild experiences.

For me it all started out at age six with a single Stevens octagon-barrel .22 which my Dad taught me how to use and which now has been in the family for almost a century. That gun originally retailed at about two dollars and a half.

Next at about age ten came a Stevens single 12-gauge, a bonus for selling ten dollars worth of Larkins soap, and with that my first mallard, which I dropped across the Cuyahoga River just after the ice went out in March. That meant strip and swim and be your own retriever. I did both and I still shiver to recall it.

Let's leave out the high school and college years, for they were not too productive. Who, however, today would believe that in our high school days we rode our bikes to school usually with either a shotgun or rod strapped to the crossbar! Those days were mostly rabbit-hunting days with five good dogs and real good shooting through long seasons and just no "No Hunting" signs.

After that came some real good Canadian duck-hunting days with Jim Hendryx, an author from Lees Point, Michigan, and Jim Drewry from Cincinnati. We shot the marshes, lakes, and streams in the

Thessalon and Blind River areas. The Lake Huron area, out of Thessalon, was particularly good, but we got really put on one day canoeing down the Blind River, right on top of that big uranium discovery which came later. The bad part of that day came after Bucky Phillips of Thessalon and I put our canoe in and the Jims had brought our guns and shells from the car. Jim Drewry was shooting an L. C. Smith double 12. I was shooting an L. C. Smith double 16. They mistakenly put the bag of 12s in our canoe and drove off with my 16s to wait for us way downriver and take whatever shooting we jumped for them.

None of us knew that the area had been partially logged over and that the stream was plastered with downed trees and sandbars. All I can add to this is that we took the canoe out, carried it around, and put it back in. Thirty-eight times and a half-day later, with just one black, which we shot with Bucky's 10-gauge, we caught up with the Jims way down the river at the next bridge.

Anyway, the two Jims were great to have as friends and to hunt and fish with, and later I was on *This Is Your Life* with Jim Hendryx. I was one of the stooges and did want to relate some of the juicy things I knew about him, such as the time he and his partner had shot a man in a gambling brawl. They did have a couple of thousand in gold dust, but they lost that the first night out and the Mounties never did catch up. Anyway, the two Jims were great guys to hunt and fish and camp with and we did lots of all of it.

Shooting with them gave me a lot of experience in proper lead, such as one morning shooting from a blind in Boushars Bay in Lake Huron, eight mergansers came by low and in a well-spaced string. I gave the lead duck no lead at all and killed number seven, after which I began to get the idea.

The Canadian shooting came to an end in 1959, when Dr. Iolas M. Huffman of Ravenna, Ohio, bought six hundred acres of land in the Aurora-Streetsboro area, just four miles from my home in Aurora and twelve miles from Huffie's. We wanted a spot where we could always hunt, and I had personally surveyed the area many years before that to determine the possibilities if it ever became available. From then on we worked, and I mean hard. It meant thinning out 1,750,000 feet of lowland timber to start with, but with professional help. Then we built fifteen different dams, which gave us eight lakes and two really good marshes, which in total covered approximately 175 acres.

The lakes were fed by fifty-degree water from six artesian wells which we drove in by hand. These lakes we stocked with trout, bass, and other fish for the kids and the grown-up members, who not only helped us enjoy the place, but helped us with the work.

The kids really had a great time. They had their own private lake which Huffie kept loaded with bass from the other lakes. The kids learned to catch them and release them, knowing they would still be there to catch again. Those kids had fun, and lots of it, and that made it really worth the effort.

Food for the ducks was planted throughout both marshes and around all lakes. Each spring we released three hundred seven- or eight-week-old mallards, half-wild and half-tame club ducks, which promptly mingled in with the flight ducks, which had taken over approximately forty nests we built for mallards and woodies. We really raised lots of ducks, especially woodies.

This idea not only provided good shooting, but created a growing flight pattern which came through every year, to the point where we became more concerned and interested in the conservation results than in the shooting.

Things happened over the years too numerous to report on, but I can't not mention our dogs. We did have some characters, such as Huffie's Irishman, and Mickey, who one day tried to climb a rail fence only to have the top rail collapse and dump him on his tail. Perhaps we shouldn't have laughed at the sight, but we did, and he was insulted to the point where he retired to the middle of the next field and sat there and absolutely would not come over to us. So we kept right on ahead, in our field. Eventually, he swung way around and ahead of us, then let us catch up with him and the hunt was on. Then there was my English-man, who apparently had a sense of humor. One day after a few hours of field work and with no luck, we started back for the car. Timmy couldn't stand this no-game business, so he froze in the middle of a field which had almost no cover. I searched the area, then walked around him and finally asked Timmy what in the hell he was pointing. His eyes swung my way, his tail barely wiggled, then he froze again. I dropped down behind him and looked right down his nose and damned if he wasn't pointing a tiny field mouse crouching in the Y of a broken limb. I patted him on the rump, called him a name or two, and that dog simply ran circles around me, barking and jumping for joy. He simply had to show me he could find something to point. We both enjoyed it.

Then there was my Irishman, Barry. He loved to retrieve any game, and I let him hunt anything. One almost has to do that in Ohio, or at least our part of it.

One morning we dropped a mallard out in the marsh, a good forty yards out and in heavy, slushy ice. The Labrador we had along, not ours, simply refused that icy water. Not Barry, however; so without a command, he broke his way out and back—with the mallard. Later that day, he tried out the ice on one of our lakes and broke through about thirty feet out and couldn't break his way back, nor climb out of the lake, so I handed Frank Floyd my watch, gun, and coat and took out after him and made the retrieve. When we got in, I decided that the Labrador wasn't so damn dumb. Anyway, a real healthy snort back at the cabin cured me.

One spring when we were in Florida, Fritz Neubauer kept Barry for me and took him along on his daily trapping. Barry really caught on, for whenever a coon got caught and got out in the marsh with trap, drag, and the works, Barry would go out, in any weather, find the coon, finish it, and fetch the coon, trap, and drag back to Fritz. One night Fritz was in his sleeping bag in an old stable, sound asleep. Apparently Barry heard a nearby trap snap, so he investigated and sure enough, there was a drowned rat in the set. So Barry retrieved the works again, and believe it or not, took it in and dropped it all right on Fritz, knowing that he should be aware of it. Barry and Fritz got to be real pals.

Let's get back to the marsh, as we called it, and what was involved besides hunting and fishing. Actually, just owning the property and keeping it in good shape became quite a job. Keeping out poachers was another problem, which we solved to a large extent by joining the law as special deputy sheriffs. Vandals took their toll, so it wasn't all fun. The State Conservation Department for many years issued a monthly bulletin, so while we did jail a few, we mostly relieved them of a ten-dollar bill and in return gave them our check for that amount made out to the Conservation Department, and also their application for a ten-year subscription to the bulletin. For a while the state people wondered why so many were sending in ten-year subscriptions, and through no effort of theirs. They finally caught on by comparing the subscribers' names with the signatures on the checks. Anyway, just one year produced over one hundred years of subscriptions, plus a few yen for the village of Aurora when they got too tough.

An interesting situation almost always arose when I approached a poacher. I recall once when two East Cleveland police officers were going to hunt on the property come hell or high water. It took some strong persuasion to convince them that we, not they, owned the property, but they finally did get off and stay off.

One other persistent guy finally took a rap for assault. Several times

I had to relieve them of their guns and kept them until they became subscribers, etc. I don't recommend the practice too much when alone, for it could become slightly hazardous.

So, if you want to own a good lake or a bunch of them and a good place to hunt, give it a lot of prior thought, or perhaps let the years take their toll and decide that someone else could take over and do the work. That's what we had to do. A Cleveland corporation leased the property for a couple of years, and I'll never forget the first group of guests who were invited to shoot ducks. It turned out to be a beautiful, clear, windless day with very little in the way of ducks to shoot at in the morning. After lunch, still no action, except clouds of blackbirds going by between the marsh and the Cabin Lake. That turned out to be irresistible to the guests, so with a box of shells and a highball, they flattened out on the sloping side of the Cabin Lake Dam and had themselves a ball and forgot all about shooting ducks. Incidentally, that was the day that one of the guests, after Huffie and I had spotted them in various areas, was heard to say, "Do I have to hunt with that old bird?"—meaning Huffie. Huffie didn't hear the remark, but I did pass it on to him and suggested that he give the guest some instructions in jump shooting. So Huffie waded him diagonally, right through the marsh from one end to the middle on the far side, and that, if you please, cured him of all snide remarks re Huffie's age.

On that same day, another guest had brought his wife along, and she spoiled any chance he might have had by moving about. So after lunch, I took her fly fishing and regretfully had absolutely no luck, for after tiring of that, she spent almost two hours quoting the Bible. That lasted until the blackbird bombardment started, so we drifted over to watch that. Let it be known that she didn't convert me.

I haven't mentioned that our property turned out to be a really beautiful spot, great for parties, fishing, and shooting, and I'd like to add that no two men should be allowed to have as much enjoyment out of their efforts as Huffie and I. He was a great partner and friend and still is.

The state of Ohio eventually decided that it wanted the property for conservation and for recreation, so we ended up selling to the state, and ever since have watched it deteriorate. We're sorry we sold and do hope we can get the department to put it back in good shape for people to again enjoy.

I've told my story, I suppose, but as I said to start, seventy-three years is a long time. When you've engaged in an activity that involves dogs for such a period, you're bound to have had a good many odd experiences that stick in your mind, and I'd like to record a few.

One I will never forget happened in Ravenna one morning when I was riding my bike out East Main Street to meet up with Midge Alcorn. Just what we were up to that morning, I don't recall, but on the way out a dog came charging out at me with a hair-raising growl. I tried to boot him as I passed but missed. So, using a minimum of good sense, I went around the block and came back to give him a second chance, and this time I really dumped him but good. On that same day that same dog bit two men, one of them a good friend of our family, Bert Canfield, Midge's uncle. Both men died of rabies, and ever since then, I've counted my blessings. It just wasn't my turn.

Later, by many years, when we owned the marsh property, we had a new member who brought his wife and German shepherd down for a Sunday picnic. I hadn't met her, but saw her with her dog on the far side of one of our lakes, so I decided that a friendly way to meet her would be with a drink. I built two whisky-and-sodas and walked around to meet her, and all was well as we walked back to the cabin. I suggested that it might be well if we kept her dog on a leash and tied to a tree, inasmuch as we had other dogs and youngsters, all strangers to her dog. She agreed, so I reached down to pick up the chain, which was already fastened to the tree. That was a bad move on my part, for that was his chain, not mine, and with absolutely no warning, he went for my throat. I had no time to think as those big jaws opened right in my face, but I did react. I jammed that glass of whisky right into that opening, and this really brave and quick-acting gal dumped that dog over backward and straddled him, and that he didn't object to. Perhaps the whisky helped, but I'll always give her full credit for saving me from a very bad situation. Needless to say, we put the ban on that dog, and the owner agreed. The next day he gave the dog to the Army Dog Training section.

One more dog situation was quite interesting and it gave us great pleasure. Our big Barry, the Irishman, had a real good friend in a small hound belonging to Evie Petot. This dog, Bootsie, would come from two or three blocks away, visiting our Barry, and away they would go, hunting. Then Barry would always also go visiting Bootsie, and it was quite a sight to see these two good pals giving the birds or rabbits in Aurora a good working over. At schooltime, however, that was all over, for Barry had to take our youngsters to school, then pick them up again at noon, and this went on day after day. On Friday, however, our Englishman, who always joined in the trip to and from school, was invited in to put on his act for the first and second grades. It was a good show, with our kids having fun putting it on and the teacher and other kids all enjoying it.

My partner, Dr. Iolas Huffman, was nicknamed the Professor because he got so adept at trapping foxes. One day a stray dog got caught in a trap and believe it or not, for northern Ohio, along came a gang of wild strays and simply tore him to pieces and beyond identification.

The next day, driving down to the cabin, I saw this gang way ahead and had time to slam three shells in the magazine of my 16-gauge and keep on going until I got within perhaps thirty-five yards of them. They took a real quick going-over and just never showed up again.

V Formation

HARVEY O. MIERKE, JR.

Yank, our five-year-old golden retriever, thrust his nose over the bow to pick up the delicious smells of spring as the 1948-vintage wood-hulled forty-foot *Blue Beaver* headed out of Killarney along the northern shore of Georgian Bay. It was May 1975—the last of the ice had just blown offshore and our objective was to open the isolated Mahzenazing River Lodge for another seven-month fishing and hunting season. Plans had been made hurriedly as the season became unexpectedly and unseasonably warm, and with the attendant excitement the thorough planning that one might have wished for such an expedition was to a great extent lacking.

Tied alongside the diesel-powered *Blue Beaver* was a fifty-foot barge loaded with nine-hundred gallons of gasoline in three skid tanks, fifteen hundred-pound propane tanks, three barrels of diesel fuel, and one of kerosene, a twelve-kilowatt generator, and an elderly Allis Chalmers tractor.

"Sun's been hot for two days now—that rotten ice field should be gone in Collins Inlet by now," said Art as he eased the diesel's throttle open, popped a Labatt's Blue, and settled back in the helmsman seat for what would be a long slow trip—the first of hundreds the *Blue Beaver* and its sister ship, the *Blue Heron*, would make along this channel to bring guests and supplies to the Mahzenazing River Lodge and its sister camp, the Beaverstone Bay Lodge.

Leaving Art, I joined my wife, Lorna, and Mahzenazing's managers, the husband-and-wife team of Bert and Bev, on the open afterdeck as we entered the western end of the fifteen-mile-long Collins Inlet Channel.

"Look there!" said Bert as a flock of black ducks exploded into flight from a small bay just ahead.

"Duck soup," mused Bev, "is mighty good with nice plump spring ducks."

"I guess so," said Bert, shielding his eyes from the glare. "You bring my shotgun from the back porch?"

"Humph! I haven't got enough to do! Did you bring lard to fry smelts in case they're running in the river?" answered Bev.

"Not my job," said Bert.

"Well, I don't nursemaid your shotgun!"

I observed that I had seen some type of ancient hunting instrument in the forward compartment.

"Wal—dat's Art's old single-shot 20-gauge. Let's see if he got any shells."

"Hey, Bert," I called down into the cabin after him, "I don't remember there being a spring duck and goose hunting season."

Art grinned, peering over his sunglasses. "That's right, but sometimes they attack you. Fella's got to protect himself!"

Bert took a long drink of Coke from the can, refilled it with rye, and settled down with the old shotgun and a few mixed shells. "This thing's got the pattern of a blunderbuss—we'll have to have a flock of them land in the boat before they'll be in range."

I'd been down Collins Inlet every year since I was six, an area visited by yachtsmen from all over the Great Lakes for its natural beauty. Craggy cliffs of the Canadian Shield rose to red-tinted granitic gneiss with intrusions of white granite, white canoe birch clumps, silver poplars, and white pine against the ancient Cloche Mountains as a distant backdrop. We had seen the spectacular fall colors and spent weekends at Beaverstone Bay Lodge in January, traveling through otherwise inaccessible areas by snowmobile, but we'd never seen the north shore in the spring as the land emerged from the long winter. Hidden recesses where the distant spring sun hadn't penetrated held iridescent blue reservoirs of snow. Although it was too early for noticeable buds, there was an apple-green cast over the woods with rosy highlights as the twigs and branches took on a glow from the newly moving sap.

"What da madder wid you? Yur mudder don' lov you?" asked Bert as he saw Bev's crestfallen face emerge from the cabin.

"You stupid bastards didn't bring any food on this trip! Too busy with your dumb old tractor and a three-month supply of gas to go to the store on the dock and get a two-day supply of food!"

"Dumb old tractor going to move the new generator to the barn so you can run your dumb old washing machine," observed Bert.

"What you mean no food?" The full impact of her statement was beginning to register. "There's three boxes of canned foods left from last fall, and Kenny put two or three bags of stuff from the store in."

"Well," huffed Bev, "there's only baked beans, canned corn, and turnips left from last year, and when you ask a thirteen-year-old to do your grocery shopping, you get pop, candy bars, and junk food. There's nothing to eat here!"

As Lorna listened she was conjuring up a fresh-smelt and canned-turnip casserole and I was half tuned in as I lay on top of the cabin, my attention mainly on the great telescopic shots I was getting of the many blacks and mallards taking off and landing nearby.

"Goose for dinner!" shouted Art.

"Jesus Christ—I never seen anything like dat!" exploded Bert as he jumped over the canned goods to get to the shotgun he had put back in the cabin.

"What? Where?" asked Lorna.

"Twelve o'clock! A flock of geese headed right down the channel for us!" yelled back Art.

And there they were—eight, ten, at least fifteen big birds in V-formation about thirty yards ahead coming down the channel right toward us about fifteen feet off the water. As Bert loaded I quickly adjusted my lens, focused, and—

"Don't shoot, Bert!" I yelled as a flock of fifteen blue herons passed directly overhead.

"Son of a bitch! Sure looked like a bunch of geese to me. Never seen herons fly like that," said Art.

"Them heron fellas not much good to eat anyway," said Bert as he put the gun down.

"Ho! The great hunters! Can't tell a bunch of blue herons from a flock of Canada geese," laughed Bev, as she held her sides. "I think I'll have a drink on that one."

"Well," said Bert, "they're about the same size and were flying in V-formation." He paused. "You got any peanut butter in that box of leftovers?"

The Duck Streaker and the Coot Confessor

D. STEWART MORRISON

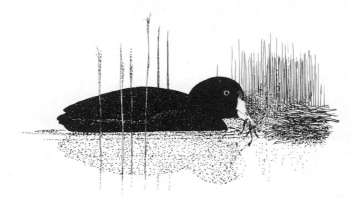

How was I to know that the furtive actions of a sixteen-year-old lad on his first duck-hunting trip would be copied by college students in the mid-seventies some twenty years later? But I'm getting ahead of myself.

I grew up in Nova Scotia in the Maritime Provinces of Canada, and through my dad, Dunc Morrison, who was an ammunition representative for the area, I developed a keen interest in shooting, hunting, and the outdoors in general. I began trap and skeet shooting at the age of fourteen. I begged to be taken duck hunting soon after, but I was never allowed to go until I was sixteen.

The day had finally arrived as we drove from Halifax to Wallace, a small village located on Wallace Bay off the Strait of Canso, a salt-water passage which separates Nova Scotia from Prince Edward Island.

I talked incessantly as we made the two-hour drive to our destination, asking my father all kinds of questions about ducks, range, lead, decoys, etc. Even our Labrador retriever, Crib, showed excitement, a character trait I had not suspected dwelled in the slow-moving form which always seemed to be lazing on the front lawn.

We were greeted at the motel which was to be our home for the night by friends and acquaintances of my father, including those who were to be in our party. The hunters came from all over Nova Scotia on this annual pilgrimage to Colchester County, which was the area where duck season traditionally opened fifteen days ahead of the rest of the province. All the dedicated duck hunters showed up in Colchester County for the October 1 opening.

After dinner, members of Dad's party and other friends gathered in our room to socialize, swap yarns, prognosticate on the next day's event, and generally enjoy themselves. I listened attentively, talking little, just absorbing the atmosphere of anticipation that prevailed. I have been on many hunting excursions since, but none has filled me with the same feeling of excitement as this first one.

Toward midnight the group broke up and headed for their separate rooms, to respond to their alarm clocks in four hours' time. I don't think I slept. I had visions of millions of flying ducks in my head.

Up at four, and we were off. The jovial camaraderie of the night before was now replaced by a more serious, yet still charged, atmosphere. Although the stars were out, it was a black night as we drove to our hunting locations, where the blinds had been built the weekend before. Dad and I let out our friends at their hunting spot and we headed for our blind, which was on a small freshwater pond separated from the saltwater bay by a beach ridge. While my father put out the decoys, I stood peering into the darkness, hearing the waking sounds of the marsh, coiled like a lion ready to spring into action.

The sun rose on a beautiful, still, Indian-summer day in one of Canada's most scenic locations. It was a great day for everything but duck hunting.

We took a few shots in the dim light of sunrise with nothing to show for our efforts. We heard a few early-morning blasts from hunters on floating blinds out in the bay, and then everything became quiet. The wary black duck had decided that his life that day would consist of rafting on the still waters of the bay with a little movement back and forth from one flock to another to keep up his social commitments. He was having very little to do with his wooden brethren who bobbed gently up and down in front of the floating bush-lined blinds, and even less with the rubber facsimile which floated serenely in front of us on our little pond. Duck hunting was over before it had begun.

My father and his friends soon concluded that a few hours' "sack time" before the evening shoot was the order of the day. They took Crib, the Lab, with them to retrieve a duck that our companions had lost in dense bullrush and then headed back to the motel. I declined to join them, as I was still too excited for sleep, and said I would meet them on the road when they returned at four P.M. It was then about eleven A.M.

I wandered along the shore of the bay, all the time watching the large flock of blacks that were congregating about one mile off in the middle. While I was poking along, a big black jumped from a small tidal pool in front of me and I experienced for the first time a duck's ability to fly away, and survive, when I thought I'd shot its heart out. I have observed this phenomenon many times over the intervening years, always with the same sense of wonder, but the surprise has been somewhat dampened by time.

I came to a point of land where Wallace Bay branched out into a smaller bay. The flock of blacks was sitting just off the entrance to the smaller bay and seemed to be having an enjoyable day. I walked about a mile down the shore of the smaller bay, where I came to a small point of land which jutted out a few yards into the water. It was there that I called a halt to my wanderings. I scraped up a pile of eelgrass into a little circular blind about three feet high, put my six rubber decoys in the water about thirty yards out, laid down my Model 31 Remington pump, lay myself back, and waited for action.

The action was so exciting, the sun so nice and warm, and my position so comfortable that I soon fell asleep, only to be awakened half an hour or so later by a splashing sound in among my decoys. I looked up and there right among my decoys was an oyster picker. He looked over at me, smiled and waved, enquired how the hunting was, and continued working his way up the shore, raking oysters as he went. Although I was relatively inexperienced, with some six hours of duck hunting behind me, I felt fairly certain that as long as he was out there, nothing would change, and it didn't! About half an hour later he was gone.

About the same time, around three P.M., it began to cloud up, the wind picked up, and the tide began to rise. The wind was offshore. I looked out at the raft of blacks. There seemed to be more activity, and they looked a bit closer to the lee side of the bay where I was. I decided to fire a shot to see what would happen.

Most of the ducks lifted, circled, and settled back down where they had been. A small flock broke away from the rest and headed for the shore and turned in toward my decoys. I crouched down behind my blind on my knees, shaking with anticipation—they were definitely coming in! I worked the safety on and off so much I almost wore it out.

They landed, five of the biggest black ducks I had ever seen, one hundred yards beyond the decoys.

I stayed down, back and knees getting stiffer by the minute, and they slowly swam into the decoys. It seemed to take a year. I stared at them, they stared at my rubber ducks, who appeared miniature in comparison, and all of us knew the situation was temporary. My first duck fell from a height of about one inch. A referee might have called it a low blow. I was so shocked I didn't even fire the remaining two shells in the gun.

I waded out, reached for my prize. That did it, what I have done on every duck-hunting trip since—I filled up my waders. The tide had risen.

I squished back to shore, laid my prize on the side of the eelgrass blind, flopped in, and tried the whole procedure again. Another group of blacks came in, a little closer, and three shots later they were gone; but so was my "dead" duck. While I was watching the ducks in the air, he had come to, if indeed he ever had been out, and decided to leave. I finally caught up to him about forty yards inland from the blind and brought him to bag with a flying tackle. This was not so easy to accomplish with my hip boots full of water.

The next hour was as exciting an hour as I have ever spent on the marsh. Two boxes of shells later, four black ducks lay sprawled among the decoys. I waited a while, but the activity ended. The ducks had left the bay. Then a terrible truth hit me—my ducks had drifted with the offshore wind into water over my head.

There was absolutely no way that those ducks were going to float away. I was prepared to go down with my ducks, so to speak. I slipped out of my clothes, glanced all around for oyster pickers, and "streaked" out to my prizes. On the way back I gathered up the decoys and dove into my blind. The whole effort had taken about 5 minutes, but it seemed like an hour. As I shivered and giggled my way into my clothes, happy and pleased with my accomplishments, a car horn sounded.

My father and his friends were waiting for me on the road about half a mile away. I gathered up my gun, decoys, and treasured ducks and headed for the car. I only wish someone had taken a picture as I approached the car: my smile was from ear to ear.

Although my dad has passed on, I had the pleasure of taking his namesake, my son Duncan, on his first duck-hunting trip just the other day—and that was another enjoyable experience.

So I enjoyed my boyhood in the Maritime Provinces of Canada, and did my share of waterfowling. But I heard story upon story of the wondrous world of ducks that existed in the west. We as lads dreamed of someday making our way west to partake of this bounty.

What we lacked in the east in terms of numbers was not necessarily made up by variety. Although we had a few sea ducks that were indigenous to our part of the country, and some puddle ducks such as blacks and teal, we lacked such outstanding game ducks as mallards, pintails, and canvasbacks in any meaningful numbers. We didn't even have many coots.

Some years later, the opportunity to move my family to Winnipeg, Manitoba, materialized and was eagerly grasped. Abundant waterfowling was a big, if unstated, part of the decision.

I soon became aware of some very major differences in the way Maritimers hunt ducks as opposed to the majority of their western counterparts. The differences, I believe, are caused by the abundance of ducks in the west, and by the variety of species, including the lowly coot.

I can recall, as a lad, hunting in Cole Harbour in Nova Scotia, making a blind out of sea-ice chunks, behind which we used to hide, as our decoys rode in front of us at anchor in the freezing seawater. We even wore white coveralls, and some went so far as to paint their guns white. The only black objects would be the trusty Lab, who was usually covered with a white sheet, or with frozen water, if he had just been on a retrieve. The old-timers carried a small "jar" of black rum which was needed to steel the body against snakebites. A can of Sterno kept the hands from becoming icebergs. We took every type of duck available, from sea ducks to the noble black duck, because there weren't many that came by. It's hard to be fussy under those circumstances.

When I first moved to Winnipeg, which was in the dead of winter, I waited all spring and summer with rising expectations for duck season. I made friends with a fellow worker who had grown up near the Libau Marshes north of Winnipeg. As the opening day grew closer I began to get restless.

"We should be building our blinds," I said.

"No need," I was told. "We can find some good hides in the marsh."

"Let's get our decoys ready."

He replied, "Shouldn't need them opening day—as a matter of fact, rather than go out opening Monday, let's go Saturday."

I soon learned that the western hunter is spoiled by a bountiful supply of ducks. He generally waits until the big northern greenheads are in, calls most other ducks "stomp ducks," and prefers stubble shooting to over-water shooting. Decoys and dogs are not used as often as in the Maritimes. Duck calls are almost unheard of. Most of all, a westerner is disdainful of anybody who would shoot a coot.

As I gained experience in western hunting methods, I adopted them, except I still carry a few decoys in the field, for old time's sake. I am especially glad the building of ice blinds has not caught on in western Canada. When it freezes here, the birds leave. I also learned my western companions' prejudices and disdain for anybody who would shoot a coot—a terrible sin worthy of the blackest punishment.

One misty fall morning finds me and two companions sitting on a flyway between two marshes, waiting for the action to begin. Out of the mist, two ducks come flying at me, slightly off my left shoulder, not very high—about a Station 8 skeet low house. My gun barked twice, quickly; the two birds were centered, and splashed to the water right at my companions' feet.

I waited for the congratulations, like "Good shooting, Stew," or "Got lucky, eh?"—but there was only silence. Have you ever heard loud silence? I walked over to the fallen birds, where the enormity of my sin descended upon me. I had killed two coots—stone dead. I heard some muffled conversation about "easterners"—another species held in low esteem in the west. My only retort, a weak one, was, "Well, they were good shots." Even I knew that I had committed a duck-hunting sin that was unforgivable.

It was at that point I decided the duck-hunting world needed a "coot confessor," some understanding "old coot" with a pointed beak, to whom duck hunters who had committed the unpardonable could go to be shrived. It would be worth money.

Live, Learn, and Lead

RICHARD W. PORTMANN

In the early 1930s at a very young and tender age, I was first introduced to duck hunting in the East Harbor marshes near Sandusky, Ohio. My father had taken my brother and me out with a small .410. My father was the finest shotgun "artist" that I have ever known, and he was wise enough to give us very simple instructions, which were to pull ahead and pull ahead some more.

I was in a blind alone across the pond from my father when four ducks buzzed by fairly close. I took careful aim at the lead duck, pulled the trigger, and the fourth duck in line fell dead.

I tried to explain that I shot at the last duck as it "seemed the closest" and my father smiled and did not say a thing.

After forty years of duck shooting, I was recently on the Eastern Shore of Maryland in a goose pit, shooting with a good friend, who was an experienced hunter. Ducks would occasionally buzz us at a high altitude, and finally we could stand the temptation no longer. Two blacks came by, quite high, several yards apart, we both fired, and the second duck fell.

For a few seconds we pretended we both had shot at the second duck, but finally I admitted I was aiming at the first one. Whereupon my hunting companion burst out laughing and admitted he had done exactly the same. Live, learn, and lead.

Season's End

CHARLES P. KEHRES

As I sat at the breakfast table at Memquisit Lodge looking over the placid waters of Lake Nipissing and seeing a pair of bull cans winging their way south, my mind reflected back to a glorious shoot I had with my dad on Sandusky Bay. It was in my senior year of high school and my dad, Edward Kehres, took me out of school for the last remaining days of hunting season.

Despite great reluctance from my mother, my dad and I drove from Cleveland to Nielsen's Marsh, located on the southwestern arm of Lake Erie. I was overjoyed to be playing hooky from school and looking forward to two wonderful days with my father, a great sportsman who enjoyed the outdoors, and with our black and white springer, Kip.

We left Cleveland at four in the morning and arrived at the marsh around five-thirty. As we pulled into the marsh, Chet, our punter, was sitting in his car. Chet helped get the gear into the boat. Our gear included our guns and a little picnic basket Dad always filled with sandwiches and a bottle of 100-proof Old Crow. Chet lifted up the lid of the basket, and I knew he had seen the bottle of Old Crow when a big grin came over his face. He had punted for my dad for many years, and they had a great camaraderie. He had told Dad years before that he had scored first in an Ohio state spelling contest. Well, as the years passed, Dad and Chet always had a little spelling contest during duck shooting, and whoever could outspell the other would get a turn at the Old Crow.

Chet was a big, powerful man; he could easily rock a boat back and forth to break the ice on the way to the blind. On that morning, so cold that the cattails were reflecting on the frozen surface of the marsh, it was tough going once again as Chet rocked the boat around in a circle, and pushed ice underneath the water and underneath the other ice, to make a hole for placing the decoys. It wasn't long before he had the blocks in place and we were ready for another cold winter shoot. We were no sooner seated than a single suzy came in, and we knocked it down. Glad to get a single so early in the morning, Dad got out his stainless-steel rods, about an eighth of an inch in diameter and four feet long, with a pointed tip. He stuck the pointed end underneath the neck of the duck and the other end in the marsh, so the duck became a super decoy. We called this duck our "pin-up" and set it away from the rest of the blocks.

As I think back, we had a good shoot and a lot of fun that day. We had almost our limit down. Kip brought them all back, except for a single which ended up over near the railroad track. With his shirt open and his pockmarked, weathered face bucking the cold north wind, Chet headed out to retrieve that one lost cripple. He must have been a good quarter of a mile away when Dad shot his last drake mallard. That duck hit the ice and slid a good fifty yards west of the blind, bouncing and skidding on the ice like a sack of potatoes. Kip marked the fall and took off over the ice for the downed bird. All of a sudden, much to his dismay and ours, he broke through the ice.

A day that had been so enjoyable turned suddenly into a nightmare. Dad and I tried to get to Kip, but to no avail. The ice was too thick for us to make it through with the boat, but not thick enough for us to walk on. We could do nothing but watch as the dog whined and struggled, trying to get out of the water. After ten or fifteen minutes, Kip's feet were barely hanging onto the edge of the ice. We saw we couldn't do anything and Dad said that rather than see the dog suffer, we had better shoot him. That set me back but good!

But then, much to my relief, we saw Chet in the distance going towards Kip. It took him nearly ten minutes to reach Kip, and it seemed like an endless journey. He was skidding the boat over the ice, then breaking through, and then poling a little farther and breaking through again. Finally he made it and picked up a nearly frozen dog. We were all greatly relieved, especially Kip!

We were supposed to go back home that day so I could return to school on Thursday. But one of the punters told Dad there were a great many canvasbacks out on the bay, and if we spent the next day shooting, he said it might turn out to be great. There were nearly two thousand cans rafting in the bay. What a thrill to think we might get a crack at them on the last day of the season!

It was another cold, beautiful fall day. The clearness of the day permitted a bevy of color that only the last day of the season could produce. We sat for a few hours looking at those ducks. Around four P.M., a breeze began to blow, and then, about four-thirty, a small flight of cans took off from the raft and headed toward the eastern part of the bay. As they gained altitude, they made a final run over the bay and spotted our oversized decoys at the edge of the water. As they came by, we knocked down a couple. It got quiet again and we were about ready to call it a day.

Suddenly we saw the remaining raft of cans rise off the water. As they began to gain altitude heading south, they made one last sweep over the bay as if to say farewell. Chet, desperate and wanting us to have a good shoot, gave a final pleading call. It was overwhelming to see that large flock of cans, over a thousand of them, turn and head back toward our blocks. They came in high formation over the decoys, and after one last call from Chet, they swung around and headed down over our decoys.

As he picked up his old Model 97 hammer gun, and I grabbed my new 870 "Wingmaster," Dad said, "Charley, just take the bulls." We shot for the next few minutes, which seemed, as the old hunting saying goes, just like being in heaven. It was a great shoot, the once-in-a-lifetime kind.

As the sun was setting, I could see the flames coming out of the end of my barrel, and with my final shot, I saw that the ring on my 870 had melted off the barrel.

Nolo Contendere

FERDINAND J. HRUBY, M.D.

It was in the morning of a crisp December day. We were standing in a waterblind on Maryland's Eastern Shore. The bright morning sun in a cloudless sky sent shimmering reflections bouncing off the tiny wavelets of the Miles River as we gazed across its half-mile width at the boxwoods on the far shore. The stillness of the bluebird day was interrupted only by the high-pitched calling of some distant swans. The sun glinting on their wings accentuated their whiteness with each downward thrust as they flew resolutely toward some hidden cove. Without question, this was one of the outstanding views on the entire Chesapeake Bay.

Not a goose to be seen, not a goose to be heard, but we were hoping that before long they would pick up from the fields where they had fed all night and come to water. On days like this, "hoping" is sometimes not enough, so we rationalized and philosophized as hunters under these conditions are wont to do.

Our reverie was suddenly interrupted by a loud hail from the shore behind us. This was not only startling, but downright sacrilegious on a day like this! Our startled heads popped up out of the blind. Wading cautiously toward us were three individuals who were immediately identifiable in spite of their farmerlike appearance as wardens.

As only the righteous and pure of heart can do, we watched with satisfaction as they made their uncertain way through the rising tidal water, cautiously holding their boot tops as high as they could. We basked in our purity—we were not only clean but we had not even fired a shot! Let 'em come! As they approached, I recognized the chief federal warden, with whom I had formed a passing acquaintance under similar conditions and who sprang from an illustrious and landed local background. In spite of his occupation he had somehow managed to survive, no mean feat in itself considering the attitudes of some of the more remote local gentry as well as those of a few of his own relatives.

At any rate, after curt introductions all around and after a cool rebuff to my friendly overtures, they proceeded with what they called "a routine check." This procedure has always damaged my pride. I figure that wardens should intuitively realize that I would never do anything outside the law, and therefore they would never waste their time in this fashion. As yet I have to meet a warden astute enough to recognize this.

At any rate, after a check of licenses and stamps the federal warden asked for our guns. Noting my companion's double guns, he waved them off with a desultory flip of his hand and reached for my old Model 11 Remington automatic. I must explain that this ancient grandpappy of the modern 1100 is my most cherished weapon; I purchased it for twelve-fifty while serving in the Armed Forces in the China-India-Burma theater in 1944. I watched with amusement as the warden extracted three 12-gauge shells from his pocket and proceeded to slip two in the magazine. As he pressed against resistance with the third shell, my amusement turned to horror as I watched it gradually slip under the carrier! Slowly he raised his bent head and gave me that "J. Edgar Hoover viewing the body of John Dillinger" look which is an integral part of every game warden's basic training.

I was not only speechless, I was numb! Seeing my state of near collapse, as I clutched the roof of the blind for support, he deliberately tilted the gun back and forth. A faint look of surprise flitted across his face as the sound of a sliding plug occurred with each inclination. Muttering something about a short plug being the same as no plug at all, he forthwith confiscated my old weapon, escorted me back to the shore, and ensconced me in the back seat of a nondescript and mud-covered sedan.

As he tooled happily along in the dilapidated Chevy, the federal warden glanced over his shoulder and cheerfully informed me that court was in session so I wouldn't have to make another trip all the way back from Ohio next month. I managed a feeble grin and thought how nice it would be if this guy ever had something wrong with his plumbing and walked in my office for treatment. As we flew along the narrow road, I couldn't help noticing the warden next to me whittling on a stick which he had picked up enroute to the car. Gradually it assumed the proportions of a 12-gauge plug. Wordlessly he handed it to me. A drink for a drowning man! Was this pure malevolence, or should I regard this as a ray of hope that someday I would be free and shoot my trusty old gun again? Inexplicably their attitude had changed. The game of hunter versus wardens was *over*! They had *won*! Suddenly we were all friends! But then I had known it all along—they were really nice guys!

After a drive that seemed like an hour but was only about twenty minutes, we arrived at the old and magnificent courthouse. As we sat on an antique bench awaiting my turn with justice, the state warden pried the cap off the magazine of my gun with a rusty nail. Out popped the spring and with it—to my everlasting disbelief—a 20-gauge mushroom plug. Not only was it a 20-gauge plug, but it was fairly new and nothing like the oily piece of sapling that belonged there. As the federal man rolled it back and forth lovingly in his fingers, a great comprehension began to dawn in my consciousness, and coincidentally the courtroom door opened. "You are up," said the bailiff.

There is something about these old Civil War courtrooms with their crossed flags, polished floors, and generous use of well-kept, lustrous woodwork that seems to raise the aura of justice above that familiar to us urban dwellers. Everything about the place was redolent of age and time and deliberate methodical adjudication. The only anachronism was the judge himself. True he was old, but he was also obviously in a hurry. As we awaited the charge he rose slightly from his seat high on the bench and glanced quickly out the window. Apparently unsatisfied, he did this twice more as the bailiff shuffled the papers.

"How do you plead?" the judge asked in a disinterested way after the charge was finally read. *"Nolo contendere,* your honor, but having full confidence in the court, I would like to plead my case."

"Well, make it short," he replied, and added to no one in particular, "there's a front moving in." And so I began.

"Your honor, last week I had the good fortune to be a guest at one of the most prestigious and productive duck clubs in the United States, let alone Sandusky Bay. Not only that, but my host was Mr. Ducks Unlimited himself—the longtime chairman of the board of this fine organization." I paused to see if this created an impression.

"Interesting," said his honor. "Ah am chairman of Ducks Unlimited down here." A brownie point for our side! "Hurry up!" said the judge.

"Well, your honor, it was one of those days. There was a low dark scudding sky, a cold wind blew off the bay, and it rained like Billy be damned without letup"—at this point I thought it best to use some local vernacular. "Nothing flew but teal, so—"

"Greenwing or blue?" interrupted the judge.

"Greenwing, sir, you see it was the last week in November and—"

"Get on with it," said his honor, and stole another surreptitious glance out the window.

"We were frozen and soaked right through," I continued, "and when we came in the fire felt great and bourbon never tasted better. It took at least an hour to get thawed out, inside and out, your honor, and by the time we had finished, the punter had cleaned and cased my gun and put it in my wagon. This is a first-class club, your honor, and—"

"Get on with it," said the judge, fidgeting on the bench. "What's the point?"

"The point, your honor, is that I never opened that gun case from that day until this and someone switched a 20-gauge plug for my old 12-gauge plug."

"Hmm," said the judge as this sank in. "Ah don't see why anyone would use any plug if they planned to break the law." With that he raised his bushy eyebrows in silent question as he turned to the federal man. He got a steady, cold, flinty look in return, and the meaning was obvious. Blood tells—especially south of the Delaware Memorial Bridge. After all, they were both Marylanders. Not only that, but they lived in the same county. I had had it!

A sudden gust of wind rattled the courtroom windows, and somewhere a door slammed shut. The judge sat bolt upright in his chair as if a time bomb had gone off. He took a quick look out the window, and what he saw galvanized him into instant action. "The court hereby admonishes the defendant that if he shot a two-barrel gun this would never have happened," he intoned, clipping his words short. "Guilty. The fine will be twenty-five dollars and costs—costs suspended."

With that he postponed the remaining cases on the docket and quickly adjourned the court. He rose from the bench, saying, "You still have time to go gunnin' this mawnin', doc, if you hustle." With that, he fairly ran across the room, his black felt boot-shoes making padding noises on the hardwood floor and his khaki hunting pants showing obviously below the hem of his black robe. Suddenly he spun around as he reached the door to his chamber.

"Good gunnin', son," he called, and with a wave of his hand he disappeared.

PART III

Discovery

K. C. R.

It was another one of those days. You know the kind: it's Indian summer—the duck hunter's anathema, which invariably occurs at some point during duck season. The local duck population present at the opening and for the following few days has almost all been moved south by a little cold front which moved through the area but was not severe enough to push any northern ducks down in front of it.

So there you are. You're in the blind which you scheduled weeks ago. The temperature is in the seventies. It's the warmest November in history (1975). Last year, at this same time, the thermometer read in the low forties and the shooting was great. So you signed up for the same dates again this year. But the sky is cloudless and windless and you would be more comfortable in swimming trunks and suntan lotion than hunting clothes and waders.

Well, you tell yourself in consolation, it's just nice to be out and it sure beats working. You even got a pretty good night's sleep last night, which all by itself is somewhat unusual. You feel good, but some ducks would make it better. So there you sit. You've been there since an hour before sunrise. Shooting time is half an hour before sunrise. You didn't put up any ducks on the way in. Bad sign. You still haven't seen or heard any since and it's now eight A.M. Prime time has come and gone. It's over now. So what to do. Give it more time? Hope for the unexpected? Maybe a minor miracle? Well, okay. Another half-hour. Fair enough.

Five minutes, ten minutes. Then in the distance, three—no, four ducks, but they go down several hundred yards away off to the east despite your best duck-calling effort. Looked like gadwall, but you can't be sure. Suddenly the light bulb goes on. You get smart. If the ducks won't come to you, you will go to them.

You stuff a few shells into your pocket. Up and out of the blind and taking Squid along, with four or five light plastic decoys, you head out across the mud flats to a dike overlooking the area where the gadwall settled in.

There are no birds there now. So you pick a spot on the water's edge in the midst of a clump of bushes. Enough for you and Squidance to blend in and mix with the geography. You sit tight and hope.

It's not long before a single appears where the four went in earlier. He's about to go down some distance away, well out of shooting range. You go to work on the call. You know you're not the best, but you like to call. It's a challenge. A game. A couple of hail calls keep him up and coming your way. Now a couple of chuckles. Don't overdo it. He's heading in for the dekes—but at the last minute, flares up and off to your right. Most important, in good gun range. You're still sitting on the dike and without changing position, the gun comes up, the lead looks right, you crook your finger, and 1¼ ounces of sixes are on the way. The hen gadwall, for so it proves to be, crumples and you have your first duck on this impossible day. Squid makes the relatively short retrieve and you're back at the waiting game.

So far, so good. You're batting a thousand. One shot, one bird, and at least you're not skunked. More time goes by. Nothing. The morning is almost gone and you have to pick up at noon. You're resigned to the one duck, which still is better than zip. On the table and pride-wise, too.

About thirty minutes left. What's that in the distance? Ducks? Yes, two. And heading your way. Again, they're about to go down much too far out. But at least today you're making duck music, and after almost dipping in, the two rise again, apparently spot your decoys, and prepare to join them.

As they make their close approach, wings cupped and feet down (a drake and a hen gadwall you can now identify), you fire from your same sitting position once again. Blam, blam! They both crumple, one in front on the water, the hen on the dike not fifteen feet away.

Squid makes the retrieves perfectly and the morning shoot is over. Three birds, three shots, three flawless retrieves. Even if neither the shots nor the retrieves were difficult, you feel good. Your change in location not only salvaged the day, but you called well and shot well and the dog performed well. After all, what more? Satisfied!

And as you wend your way back to your boat and head for home base, you reflect on what is perhaps a duck hunter's growth into maturity. You make a great discovery. Eureka! For the first time you realize that it isn't the size of the bag that determines a good shoot. A good day afield is composed of a great many things, variables which change from day to day. The sum total of all these pluses and minuses is what counts. And you start thinking of all of these and more as you head home and as you go to sleep that night. With a smile on your face!

There Is No Such Thing Any More As Good Cheap Duck Shooting!

K. C. R.

During a recent fit of the depression which generally seems to follow closely on the heels of the end of duck season, it occurred to me to total up the cost of my 1975 waterfowling. So I did. And I'm sorry I did. Very sorry. I'll never do it again. Hunt ducks, yes. Count dollars, no.

Anyone interested in what I came up with? Wives excluded, of course, and for educational and comparative purposes only. Remember you're sworn to secrecy and I won't tell your wife either.

No, I'm not going to report total pesos. For humanitarian reasons, that is top secret. But how about per duck bagged, or perhaps per pound? Well, we'll see. My amateur cost-accounting list includes the following:

Cost of skeet shooting to practice up for duck season, including shells, targets, shooting vest, ear plugs, gloves, shooting glasses, food during and drinks after, gas, oil, car depreciation, and just possibly a new skeet gun.

Cost of lunches, including cocktails for purpose of discussing the upcoming season's prospects. This is repeated after the season closes for purposes of review.

Cost of room, board, and training for one yellow Labrador retriever on a year-round basis.

Cost of one or more new duck guns, without which no season can really properly begin.

Cost of annual dues to duck club plus cost of room rental, food, special clothing for cold weather and warm weather, if any, and in-between innerwear, outerwear, etc., punter (guide service), duck pluck-ing, whiskey, tobacco, four boats (two large fully equipped ones for towing two small punt boats plus four outboard motors), new decoys to supplement or replace those already in use, new duck calls (there are always those new ones coming on the market which will enable you to call like a champion with no practice required), tips to all hands for good and special services rendered, several cases of shells, new waders and/or hip boots, new camera and/or lenses for shots you were unable to get last year, film, hunting licenses, duck stamp, etc.

Cost of speeding tickets received during trips to and from marsh.

Cost of long-distance telephone calls to check what's going on at marsh plus calls to report in to your duck-hunting widow while at marsh.

Cost of hunting car, station wagon, off-road vehicle or whatever, fully equipped with four-wheel drive and CB radio.

Cost of having especially good specimens of different species mounted.

Costs of all guests, which repeat many of above.

Cost of belonging to Ducks Unlimited and attending their annual fund-raising dinners, dinner tickets, raffles, auction, drinks, guests, etc.

Cost of—and here's the real zinger—baubles, bangles, and beads to keep your ever-lovin' off your back and reasonably happy during her annual temporary widowhood.

You will have quickly noted that no dollar amount was placed alongside any of the foregoing items, if for no reason other than sanity's sake.

However, I have privately short-circuited my pocket computer in order to come up with the dénouement promised earlier and one which the duck-hunting world awaits with baited (a *verboten* word in respect-able duck-hunting circles) breath.

The answer is, there is no such thing any more as good cheap duck shooting, and if that doesn't satisfy you, my suggestion is that you take up tatting instead. There are too many duck hunters around today any way.

New Gun

K. C. R.

It was the first day of the "split." We've had the split in Ohio now for several years. It all started because of Ohio's geography. The late duck season, or second half as it is sometimes called, is meant to accommodate southern-Ohio duck hunters. Ducks pushed farther south by advancing cold weather will tarry in the tributaries of the Ohio River and, of course, on the river itself. At this same time, northern-Ohio marshes are generally frozen. The ducks that do remain are mostly all rafting in the lake and seldom venture inland except to feed.

This latter had been the situation when Ken Horsburgh and I headed west out of Cleveland the night before. Several phone calls all elicited the same response: no ducks were moving. But we went anyway. I'd rather spend a duckless day in a marsh than sit at a desk chained to a telephone.

Shooting time started at noon on the split, just as it does on the first day of the regular season. It was nice to sleep in and enjoy a leisurely breakfast before donning our cold-weather gear and heading for the marsh in company with Paul Gonya, my regular punter at the duck club where I belong.

We had to go by car, rather than by boat down the river as we usually do. There was no other choice. The river was impassable, covered by four inches of ice. So we loaded the pickup with the usual decoys, including some geese, grass matting, guns, ammo, thermos, plus one unusual piece of equipment—a sled.

When we arrived at what we call the Lower Marsh, our first action was to ascend the outside stairs of the boathouse to an observation platform on the roof. From this vantage point, we could survey the entire marsh for miles in every direction. Ducks were quite noticeable by their absence. Those earlier bad-news reports were confirmed. The sky was clean!

After a brief conference, it was decided to transfer everything to a jeep owned by Leonard Glass, who manages the Lower Marsh, in order to drive out the dikes as far as possible. From that point, we would go on the ice to a blind known as Channel #1, dragging our gear with us on the sled, a distance of about a quarter of a mile.

We were no sooner on the ice than a couple of ducks were spotted on the move. Then a single appeared over a tree line. Well, what do you know? Things are looking up—maybe not much, but at least we were a little encouraged. At this point it didn't take much. About halfway out the familiar sound of geese came to us, floating over the frozen "wastes." The honking kept up and got louder. Then a black line lifted above the horizon to the south. The Canadas were coming. Another black line appeared under the first; then still another; then a fourth. Wow, would they keep coming our way? Soon it looked as though they would never stop. Unfortunately for us, however, while they were indeed heading in our general direction, it appeared that they would be either too high or too wide. And we were still a couple hundred yards from our blind; three of us with a sled piled high out on the ice in the middle of a half-mile-wide frozen channel, sticking out like three purple thumbs, and geese on the way.

Since the successive waves of Canadas were passing to the east and north of us, we continued on our way, trying to hurry on the slippery ice. Paul was in the lead with the sled. He started to lay out the dekes, putting three geese to the side nearest the passing waves of honkers. Ken was trying to take a picture or two, while I was still approaching the blind—burdened with gun, duffel, and shells. At this most inconvenient juncture, as seems to happen so many times, the honking took on a different tone. A small flight was indeed coming straight at us and at a definitely shootable altitude.

I yelled at Ken and Paul to freeze and managed, while dropping to my knees, to stuff a couple of number twos into my Winchester Super-X Model 1 12-gauge semi-auto gas scattergun. My *new* Winchester "One."

Back in early November, George Chandler—president of Winchester—had spent a couple of days with me duck shooting. One very successful day, in fact, we had shot from this same blind. He had brought two Super-X Model 1's with him. This shotgun had just been brought to market the first of the year as Winchester's answer to the fine Remington 1100. George asked me if I would like to try one, and because I had never shot one before, I readily accepted his offer. Well, to say I liked it would be an understatement. I loved it. The way it was made it just plain looked good. You know—quality. I liked its weight and feel; particularly and especially, I liked the way it came up to my shoulder and felt at home there. In any event, after George had returned home, taking both his guns with him, my first item of business was to obtain my own Winchester "One" just as soon as possible. Of course, all I really needed was another shotgun. But you know how it is. No matter how many you own, the lure of yet another can be irresistible, a handsome new model even more so. Besides, every shooter is very well aware that a new gun always shoots straighter.

This duck safari was my first opportunity to break in the "One." And what a debut it was. Those Canadas kept boring in toward us. Most of them perhaps a little too high and a little too wide, but then suddenly there were two at only about forty to forty-five yards. Still on my knees, I raised the "One" to my shoulder, swung past the lead goose of the two, and touched off. The big bird crumpled and fell. And so did the second one. Thump, thump on the ice and I had two of those great wildfowl, with the first shot from the new gun.

To put the frosting on the cake, the ducks started to move, and in quantity. While they didn't exactly decoy to us, they did give us a dip and a nod over the blind so that we limited out before the split season was an hour old. And while I didn't repeat my two-for-one feat, that new gun, that "One," seemed to just naturally point in the right direction. I can only say that I have never shot better and that I hope it lasts forever.

Maybe you're about ready for a new gun too. I can recommend it.

One of the Duck-Huntingest Gentlemen

K. C. R.

Henry Schmidt was basically a serious man. At least to my knowledge, no one ever called him Hank. It was either Henry or Mr. Schmidt. I think he ran his company that way. I know he hunted and fished that way. Never one to sit or stand still for long, Henry was a doer and a mover. I hunted ducks with him just once and fished with him only once, too, which of course hardly qualified me as an expert, but I'm glad to have had even those limited experiences. And I'll never forget them.

During his long tenure—1955 to 1975—as President of the Ottawa Shooting Club near Fremont, Ohio, whenever a new member joined the club, it was Henry's practice to invite the new member to join him for his first shoot at the club. To back up for a minute, the Schmidts had a lovely summer home located adjacent to the Ottawa Club marshes, and it was there that Margie and I were graciously invited for a weekend by Elisabeth and Henry to be introduced to the territory. I had just joined Ottawa and this was our first visit. The season wouldn't open for some weeks yet, but Henry, as always, looked after those marshes with a dedication almost impossible to equal. He knew them, every square yard of them, better than anyone, including the professionals who worked there.

So he introduced me to those beautiful marshes by boat, by jeep, and on foot. And the marshes to me. I will forever appreciate the time and interest he took in doing this for me. For him, I feel sure it was a labor of love and of pride. It also rubbed off on me, too, as the result of this experience with this man.

The next day we went trout fishing at the nearby Rockwell Trout Club. There I had a second view of Henry in action. He literally whipped that stream into a froth and limited out in half the time it took me.

A few weeks later, our early teal season opened, and Henry and I shared a blind for the first and last time and also only for a very short time. In the blind well before shooting time, along with Henry's regular punter, we mapped out our strategy for these little feathered missiles. Like so many well-laid plans, however, ours, while I thought we were doing okay, was not good enough for H. G. S., and so out of the blind he went to tramp the dikes.

You know the rest. Yes, he was back to the blind soon with his limit while I was still struggling.

This little tale could end right here, but it's not going to. There is something more to relate about Henry Schmidt. As I have said, he was always a man of action. He was National President of Ducks Unlimited in 1965–1966. When he assumed the office, D.U.'s headquarters offices were in New York City. Henry felt they should be located in the Middle West, nearer to the principal duck "factories" in Canada, in the heartland of America, with easier access from anywhere in the country. D.U.'s main offices were moved to Chicago, where they are located today.

More important was D.U. itself. The organization, while certainly viable, was on a plateau. The number of members and the amount of money being raised had flattened out for several years. Something needed to be done to regain that vital momentum. And Henry Schmidt did it. He brought in Dale Whitesell, formerly Chief of the Division of Wildlife for the State of Ohio, to act as the professional head of D.U. The rest is history.

Ducks Unlimited has been growing in members and dollars at approximately a 25 percent compounded annual rate ever since. Today D.U. is the premier conservation organization on the North American continent, and it is the Henry Schmidts—and there are many others like him in their devotion and contribution to Ducks Unlimited—who have made it so.

Every duck and goose in the sky is living testimony to the efforts of these men.

Squidance

K. C. R.

Of course, I think that he is something special. What else can you say about the second-best marsh dog in the world, particularly when he belongs to you?

His name is Squidance, which in Potawatamie Indian language means "fire" or "light." He is a yellow Labrador retriever who, when the sun is right, looks for all the world like a female lion.

Squid is all male, however: big and rough and tough. His single aim and greatest joy in life is retrieving birds to hand, preferably ducks. This passion is neither accidental nor the result of professional training. Squid was born into a litter owned by the chief of a Potawatamie tribe in the middle of some of the best duck country on the North American continent, an area of vast marshes surrounded by an even larger area of corn. This abundance of "mallard gold," or whatever you want to call it, and its proximity to plenty of shallow fresh water, creates a tremendous waterfowl "trap" which has attracted tens of thousands of ducks and geese for years and years and years. As Indian land, it has thus far been more or less protected from the ravages of "progress." The corn is raised under contract to one of the very large distilleries, which seems to be a happy arrangement for everybody, including the company, the Indians, the ducks, and the duck hunters who shoot the ducks and drink the whiskey.

Apart from corn-related activity, many of the local Indians make their living by hunting for the pot, trapping, fishing, and guiding duck hunters. As a result, Squidance was raised with a duck in his mouth, and by the time I acquired him at the age of approximately two and a half he had already retrieved approximately two thousand ducks in his short lifetime.

In all modesty, Squidance is one hell of a dog: one of those canines who are full of sound and fury, backed up by a pussycat personality, who would rather hunt than eat; who would rather hunt than anything. He may not be the best-trained Lab that ever hit the water, but he has the kind of marsh savvy which is the envy of a lot of field-champion owners.

When a shot is fired and Squid tackles the water like an all-pro in the NFL, he expects to bring back a duck. In fact, he will go to great lengths to bring back a duck. Recently, during a bluebird day when nary a cap had been snapped, my partner in the blind finally vented his frustration by downing a red-winged blackbird, thousands of which were present in this particular area.

This unfortunate "redwing teal" fell some distance away in the middle of a large, thick mass of tules. Squidance took off (and I mean "took off") to make what looked like a fairly easy retrieve. He disappeared into the tules, but instead of reappearing in a minute or two, he didn't show for twenty minutes. When Squid did show—what a surprise! Instead of the recently expired blackbird, in his mouth there was an equally dead and completely unexpected greenhead.

The surprises are actually infrequent. Most of the time, his performance is simply workmanlike and unspectacular. But then, good workmanship is not all that easy to be found these days. There is one thing about Squid in this respect. If two dogs go after the same downed duck and one of the two dogs is Squid, the result can invariably be predicted. Squid will bring home the webfoot, even if he has to take it away from his competitor. This trait, I will admit, sometimes upsets the competitor's owner.

Most dogs are lovers, as we all know, and Squid is no exception. Of course, most of us are dog lovers too. When we go for ducks, we stay only in motels or hotels which allow canines in their rooms. The trouble is that Squid either doesn't know he is a dog, and thus not supposed to use the furniture and other facilities, or else he thinks he's people and it's okay.

Whatever, Squid and I are partners and we share. We share the sofa. We share the bed. We share the food. His water is in the W.C. Ducks are a joint effort with us.

The nice thing about saying a few words about Squidance is that he is still alive and well and going strong. That's better than a brag about a dog who has passed on to that great duck marsh in the sky.

Now about this business of being second best. A yellow Labrador named Goldie, owned by an avid duck-hunter friend of mine, is absolutely and unequivocally the finest marsh dog I have ever hunted with or even seen. One thing more: Goldie is Squidance's father! Naturally, out of respect for his old man, I don't want to lay it on too thick about his son. Anyhow, I think I'll stop now and go have a little romp with Squid. We can hardly wait until next duck season.

Bag Limits

K. C. R.

My adopted country, Mexico, is well known for the tremendous number of waterfowl which winter there. It follows that the duck hunting is super. For some types, obviously nonmembers of Ducks Unlimited, it can be too super. That old debil Temptation can be very difficult indeed to resist, and for some duck hunters in this duck hunters' Shangri-la, it apparently can be impossible.

Actually, Mexican bag limits are uniformly generous, even including double limits on weekends, benefiting native and gringo alike. Nonetheless, in the way of slobs the world around, greed takes over on occasion, regulations are forgotten, and game bags are swollen to enormous proportions.

The tale is told of one such "citizen," filled full for years with these big-kill stories, who finally made the trip south of the border to see and do for himself. Meeting his guide on the morning of his first hunt, he casually (and cynically) inquired as to the daily bag limit then in effect. The reply was two. "Two?" he incredulously gasped. "You mean I've come all this way for only two?" "*Si*," agreed his guide. "Two gunny sacks full. That's all I can carry!"

Of course this happened many years ago. Now Ducks Unlimited de Mexico (DUMAC) is hard at work improving winter habitat for waterfowl and encouraging the observance of all game laws.

Super Shot

K. C. R.

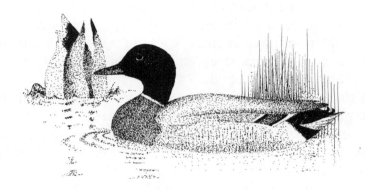

Singles are fun. Doubles are better. And triples are, well, uncommon. These terms in common waterfowling language indicate birds downed during one shooting sequence.

It happens now and then, of course, that two birds go down with one shot, whether accidentally or on purpose. But how about three for one? Once in a while, probably, but surely not very often. Have you ever done it, or seen it accomplished? I have asked that question of several dozen veteran duck hunters without a single affirmative answer. Obviously none were ex-market hunters.

Well, so what, you ask. So nothing, I answer. To me it's just another interesting waterfowling subject, like chokes and loads and dogs. And certainly it makes no difference whether the feat (and feat it is) resulted from good shooting or good fortune. What will be will be.

The fact is that I am pleased to report for the record that on Monday, November 8, 1976, yours truly was witness to such a happening in company with my shooting companion, who pulled off the trick, and my punter.

Russ Boston and I had driven to the Ottawa Shooting Club the afternoon before, where we wined and dined in lonely splendor, as for some reason there were no other members present. We were in bed early and up early, with our eyes on the "main chance," as they say.

It was decided to drive to the Lower Marsh that morning, which we did in my punter Paul's pickup. Low water levels indicated this course of action. We would also have the added advantage of increased mobility, since we could put my punt boat on the pickup and then cruise the dikes, going to wherever the action might be. We were going first to Channel #1 blind if we could get out to it, what with the low water.

In black dark, we arrived at the Lower Marsh boathouse, where Leonard, the man in charge, helped us load up the punt boat with decoys and other necessaries while we got into our waders and made ready. Then off we went in the pickup, driving on dikes made quite slippery by the recent wet weather. We soon came to the end of the line, dragged the punt down a steep embankment to the water, loaded up again, and headed for our blind.

On the way, we were encouraged by the substantial number of birds we put up, and many more could be heard as we disturbed their rest by our passage. It was still dark when we put out the dekes and settled in to wait for shooting time. That time came and went—no action. Then just at sunrise, as the sun was changing from a thin gold line to an orange half-circle, a flight of ducks appeared to the north-northeast, about one o'clock on the waterfowler's clock. We began to call. They continued to fly in our general direction. Closer. We continued to talk to them. Then it was here and now. The ducks, mallards, about eight or nine of them, made a straight pass at our blocks and then flared off a little to the left of the blind at perhaps thirty or thirty-five yards. I whispered to Russ, "Shoot, shoot." Which he did, and how! Talk about sights and sounds! Almost simultaneously, the sound of the left barrel of his Model 21 was followed by the sight of three birds falling. And what a sight. A sight to behold and always remember. Two huge red-legged northern greenheads belly up on the water and a suzy, not quite there but about to enter duck heaven, which she did without the necessity of a *coup de grace*.

A day made. A season made. A story to be told and retold, handed down, treasured.

Someday maybe it will happen to me.

A Hayen

K. C. R.

Stuttgart, Arkansas, bills itself as the Mallard Capital of America. Each year during the first weekend of duck season the World Championship Duck Calling Contest is held and a Queen Mallard is crowned. This is the heart of the Mississippi flyway duck country— the wintering area for the largest number of mallards anywhere in the world.

In 1974 a five-year-old boy, Bryan Hancock, youngest son of Stuttgart's nationally known conservationist Dr. Rex Hancock, using a .410 shotgun, downed his first duck.

He was asked later about this most important event in his young life. "What kind of a duck was it?"

His answer was pure Stuttgart and classic: "It was a hayen."

For as everybody knows, there are only two kinds of ducks in Arkansas: drakes and hayens. The fact that they are mallards is, of course, taken for granted.

Good going, Bryan!

Wade

K. C. R.

No, not "wade" as in water. Rather "wade" as in Wade Plantation: ten thousand acres of pine trees, soybeans, quail, pecans, ducks, peanuts, doves, corn, and lots of other good things. Located in east-central Georgia not far from Augusta near a small town by the name of Sylvania, the plantation dates back to 1827. That's antebellum!

Wade Plantation has been owned for the past ten years or so by H. T. "Tally" Mead, a waterfowl enthusiast and member of the Mead Paper family, among other things. The main house was built as a hunting lodge and would stand comparison with the best anywhere, including those in Europe. I felt immediately at home when I first stepped over the threshold. It's that kind of place. "That kind of place" also includes the owner's home with additional guest facilities, horse barns, garages for various vehicles, quarters for employees, ammunition and bird storage, kennels, plantation offices, et cetera. An obvious roughing-it situation. Or to put it another way: more than just a nice place to visit. Ah, but just to have the chance to visit. In that we were most fortunate, as you will see, and even so, I am only relating half of the story: the waterfowl-related part, which for me is always the best half. Anyway . . .

Squire Mead, as earlier indicated, likes ducks as a hunter and as a conservationist. A longtime National Trustee of Ducks Unlimited, Tally has managed Wade with ducks in mind, as well as quail and dove. Not that they come first at Wade, for the plantation is a working one and carries its own weight. Cash crops are the name of the game and wild game is their by-product.

It was the by-products that brought our group to Wade during mid-January 1977. Our principal purpose was to organize the first Ducks Unlimited Council for the State of Ohio. Present at the invitation of our host were a number of Ohio D.U. "activists," men who loved ducks and had proved it by helping to raise millions of dollars to conserve the resource by developing breeding and nesting habitat in Canada where three-quarters of our continental duck population is hatched.

We were at Wade to work for the ducks—first, that is. Second, however, we had other things in mind for the ducks. I was especially anticipating the opportunity of having a "look" at the ring-necked duck, sometimes known as a ringbill. This relatively small diving duck is a freshwater bird of the interior and in flight can be a real feathered missile, thereby providing super sport. "Ringy" is also super on the table as well, feeding as he does primarily (more than eighty percent) on vegetable matter. I was, therefore, naturally anxious to have a go at him both from a blind and from behind a knife and fork.

A go we indeed did have, and Ringy lived up to every expectation along with a couple of unexpected and pleasant surprises thrown in!

There are several small lakes of a few acres each at Wade, and it was to these we repaired on two early mornings and one late afternoon to visit the wintering grounds of a goodly number of ringnecks. Our first morning provided both surprises.

It was that blue-black time known as darkest before the dawn. You've already stumbled out of bed shedding the blanket of sleep, fumbled for clothing, downed some scalding black coffee, grabbed for your gun, and headed out the door. Now you're huddled in the blind trying to get organized and looking forward to what you always secretly hope every duck-hunting day of your life will be: one of those "chapters for the book"—one of those most memorable days when the ducks fly well but not too well and when you shoot better than you really know how; one of those perfect days when every bird and every shot is a picture forever.

Sometime I'm going to have a day like that. I've come close on occasion, and that's pretty good too. Still I always believe that someday it will happen to me. I hope I always will. Because that's duck hunting, or at least an essential part of it: that thrill of anticipation, not knowing, and at the same time knowing, what the day will bring.

Meanwhile, back to the blind, waiting. Suddenly I hear something.

It sounds like, on reflection, the noise made when a red-hot poker is plunged into cold water: a long-drawn-out Ssssst! What, I think, in the name of heaven was that? Then it comes again and, shortly, again: Ssssst! My poor early-morning and cold-benumbed brain refuses to come up with an answer. Then I hear it another time and still another. Sometimes a little closer, sometimes farther away, but always that strange Ssssst! The mystery deepens and the plot thickens. As this description-defying Ssssst continues to reach my ears, a trickle of first light seeps through and with it, finally, I see a little first light myself. That sound of fury, that sound of music, is Ringy coming in for a landing: wings close to the body, landing gear up, barreling in downwind at Mach I, and then at the last minute going into a tight turn into the wind, dropping his wheels and with flaps at full stop, skidding down onto the water's surface for a perfect three-pointer or however many points constitute perfect for a duck.

Talk about feathered missiles—I spent the time between dawn and sunrise just as an awed and impressed observer. What a spine-tingling thrill it was just to watch and to listen to that unfolding drama, which very definitely qualifies as one of my most memorable experiences of a lifetime. My gun was forgotten, but the scene will never be.

Eventually, I recovered, settled down to business, and collected my limit in fairly short order—all ringnecks—and they were particularly good that night for dinner. Mission accomplished. But for me the day was already special before it was even born. So went the first surprise of the day.

We all arrived back at the Lodge about nine or nine-thirty for breakfast and gathered to compare notes, as is the custom. At this juncture came the second surprise. We learned that for the first time in the 150-year history of Wade Plantation, a canvasback had been killed that morning on the property. Ohio State D.U. Chairman Fred DeCamp had won the honor with a fine bull drake, and the next day another drake was taken by Charley Kehres, a D.U. stalwart from Cleveland, while a can hen was also sighted. Certainly this was a landmark occasion for Tally Mead and Wade Plantation. I know it was for all of us who had the pleasure and good fortune to participate in the proceedings.

Oh yes, and not incidentally at all, the Ohio D.U. Council business was well attended to and is currently in thriving operation. Ain't it fun combining business (?) with pleasure (!). I can only say that our hearts are pure because our cause is just.

The Canvasback and The Canvasback Society

K. C. R.

"They can still be seen, the Chesapeake Canvasbacks, and to watch them as they slide, wings flaring, through a lead-gray sky is to know why they are and always have been the most majestic of ducks. But their day is gone. Hardly a breath ago, as late as the '40's, 100 'cans' might decoy at once on the Susquehanna Flats. Rafts of 50,000 would cover acre upon acre of water. Now the Flats are sterile as a salt lick, and on the great gunning rivers of Maryland's Eastern Shore—the Sassafras, the Chester and the Choptank—the noble canvasback is counted differently. 'Saw seven yesterday.' 'Must have been 20 of them, flew by high.' Which means a sport has vanished too. Paintings will have to serve. And memories."

—*Sports Illustrated*

"Alone in the iron-gray expanse of Chesapeake Bay, a small raft of canvasbacks rides the choppy water. An occasional duck suddenly arches its back and plunges into the depths in a fruitless search for food. It quickly bobs back to the surface and continues swimming into the wind with the slowly moving flock.

"Piercing the scudding clouds, a shaft of early winter sunlight bathes the ducks in a splash of light. The russet heads of the drakes glow, the white flanks and backs flash like strobe lights, the black breast and rump gleam like obsidian. Even the somber, dun-colored hens seem more colorful in the warm light. But the clouds, pushed by strong north-westerly winds, soon close ranks, cutting off the sun's bright rays, and the intense color of the drakes quickly fades.

"The gusting winds pick up strength. The cold water becomes rougher, making the ducks uncomfortable. They paddle faster until, tired of fighting wind and waves, they skitter across the water, take wing, and vanish into gray wintry skies.

"In days past, the sight of a small flock of 'cans' on Chesapeake Bay caused little comment. Huge flocks traded up and down the bay, frequenting the sheltered coves, open water flats and rivers. But the canvasback population has been decimated, and whether the 'can,' through man's criminal disregard for his environment, will follow the peregrine falcon into near extinction remains to be seen. Unless prompt and decisive action is taken, the canvasback, the most regal of water-fowl, will face even greater perils."

—National Wildlife Federation Magazine

The canvasback has long been regarded as "The King of Ducks," the gold standard to which all other ducks are compared. No species of waterfowl stirs the memories of sportsmen like the lordly can. Even the Indians prized the duck; the oldest decoys ever discovered in North America were canvasbacks. They were made from tules (large bul-rushes) by a vanished tribe of Nevada aborigines, the Tule Eaters, and are estimated to range in age from one thousand to two thousand years.

Early white settlers preferred the canvasback, an entirely New World species, because of its preference for vegetable food—no fishy taste spoiled the meat. (Its Latin name, in fact, *Aythya valisineria*, stems from its fondness for wild celery.)

Market hunters did their best to satisfy the demand for canvasback. On Chesapeake Bay, the cradle of American waterfowling, these hunters, believing the resource of waterfowl was inexhaustible, shot from sinkboxes or swept down on the big ducks in sail-driven boats, unleashing at the last moment tremendous volleys of shot.

According to old-time accounts, a market hunter could kill one hundred and fifty canvasbacks on a good day. Some took as many as seven thousand cans a season, especially on the Susquehanna Flats at the upper end of Chesapeake Bay, where the birds congregated by the tens of thousands to feed on the lush beds of wild celery. The dead birds were packed in barrels and shipped to markets in Baltimore, New York,

Washington, and Richmond, where they fetched top dollar. At the turn of the century, a pair of cans in the open-air markets of Baltimore would sell wholesale for from four to eight dollars depending on the season and abundance. A pair of redheads, by comparison, sold for one-half as much, scaup only one-fourth.

In recent years, it has been sportsmen who seek the fast-flying canvasback. No thrill in wildfowling can compare with the wild rush of canvasbacks coming in to the decoys during an autumn dawn.

And so it has happened that the canvasback has come to epitomize all that a duck should be. Just as a mystique exists with respect to waterfowl generally, there is a very special mystique surrounding the can. It has become symbolic of all ducks.

The wing beats of the can are strong and steady, and because it is the largest of all ducks, weighing over three pounds on occasion, its speed is deceptive. The canvasback is the fastest flier of all waterfowl, capable of seventy miles per hour on a good day. Riding in on a driving rainstorm, taking advantage of a strong tailwind, the canvasback's big body bores through the air at as much as a hundred miles per hour.

Another striking characteristic, in addition to its large size, is its coloration. The wide white band that circles the bird, particularly its wings and back, gives this duck its name. The head and the long neck of the male are a bright russet red. The breast and the tail, and both the upper and undertail coverts, are black. The female's back and wings are a more sooty white and she is brown, where the male is red or black. A large male can is over twenty-one inches in total length and has a wing-span of thirty-three inches. Unlike the females of most of the other ducks, the female canvasback is almost as large and as heavy as the male.

The one physical characteristic, however, which sets the canvasback apart from all the others and which has become its trademark is its large wedge-shaped head. This head silhouette is always a giveaway, a means of positive identification, even when conditions prevent the use of any other.

Now all of this is not news, nor is the fact that the canvasback is in trouble. The canvasback is not yet officially an endangered species, although the National Wildlife Federation has petitioned the Department of Interior to have it placed on the threatened-species list. But what is extinct, as the daily bag limit on the canvasback has fallen from fifteen to ten to four to two to one to none, is a sporting way of life. The can is nostalgia on the wing, doomed by the times, as Canadian farmers drained his breeding grounds, as his rivers turned to sludge and his flyways to smokestacks. Unlike the mallard and the Canada goose, the canvasback does not take kindly to the notion of living in the back yard of man. His imperiousness may be the death of him.

The good news is that people have finally become concerned. People, whose actions are responsible for his plight, are beginning to do something about it. A special government study has been conducted in an attempt to pinpoint the causes of the decline. A Canvasback Workshop sponsored recently by the Wildlife Society attracted twice as many participants as had been anticipated. The biologists are hard at work.

Thus far, however, this concern has been evidenced almost entirely by governmental-agency people and other professionals. The "King" deserves more than that. Sport hunting of the canvasback is, or rather was, the equivalent of fly-fishing for Atlantic salmon. Federal and state policy should be aimed at returning the canvasback population to levels five or ten times what they are today. It is time for civilians to get into the act. And they are.

For the first time ever, a national conservation organization has been formed to benefit a single species of sporting waterfowl: The Canvasback Society, whose motto is: "That the can will not only survive, but thrive."

The Canvasback Society recognizes that better understanding of the canvasback and its needs is the key to the solution of its problems. Therefore, the cornerstone of the organization is the Technical Committee, composed of the best-qualified waterfowl biologists available who have special experience and interest in working with the canvasback. Under the guidance of this scientific body the Society will strive:

1. To conserve, restore, and promote the increase of the Canvasback species of duck on the North American Continent.
2. To encourage, support and sponsor biological research which deals specifically with the Canvasback.
3. To establish and maintain a reference library containing all known scientific knowledge relating to the Canvasback and to make such information available without charge to the ornithological community and to all other interested persons.
4. To cooperate with other conservation organizations in those programs which relate to the Canvasback.
5. To educate the general public in furtherance of the general welfare of the Canvasback.

The accomplishment of these objectives will, of course, depend on adequate financial support. All contributions to the Society are deductible for federal-income-tax purposes. All those people throughout the United States and Canada who especially admire the canvasback are invited to become "Canvasbackers" by demonstrating their concern accordingly.

Write The Canvasback Society, P.O. Box 101, Gates Mills, Ohio 44040.

Long live the King!

Sportsmanship

K. C. R.

To me a sportsman is simply a gentleman out of doors. Subconsciously or otherwise he follows an established code of behavior, a code considerate of both his fellow man and the game he hunts. Unfortunately not all hunters are sportsmen and therefore they are not gentlemen either. Also unfortunately, it is the bad actors who get the publicity and give our favorite sport a bad name.

It's late but I hope not too late to do something about this deplorable state of affairs. To this end I should like to submit for consideration the following:

A WATERFOWLER'S ETHIC

Inasmuch as I have been blessed more than most by being permitted to experience the joys of waterfowling and in respect of my desire to perpetuate this opportunity for generations to come, I therefore will adhere to all game laws, will identify species, and determine the bird is within shootable distance before pulling the trigger and will otherwise conduct myself as a gentleman sportsman, treating other waterfowlers as I would have them treat me.

Epilogue

K. C. R.

Myth has it that we hunters will all meet one day in another world, there to enjoy forever the pleasures of our kingly sport. What a happy thought that is—that of the Happy Hunting Ground. I hope it is true, for what wonderful people will be there, surely including all my duck-hunter friends who responded so well to my request to record their most memorable waterfowling experience. I thank them all again. And I would be proud to share a duck blind with any of them, any time, anywhere, here or in the hereafter.

The Reckoning

It's fine to have a blow-out in a fancy restaurant,
With terrapin and canvas-back and all the wine you want;
To enjoy the flowers and music, watch the pretty women pass,
Smoke a choice cigar, and sip the wealthy water in your glass.
It's bully in a high-toned joint to eat and drink your fill,
But it's quite another matter when you

Pay the bill.

It's great to go out every night on fun or pleasure bent;
To wear your glad rags always and to never save a cent;
To drift along regardless, have a good time every trip;
To hit the high spots sometimes, and to let your chances slip;
To know you're acting foolish, yet to go on fooling still,
Till Nature calls a show-down, and you

Pay the bill.

Time has got a little bill—get wise while yet you may,
For the debit side's increasing in a most alarming way;
The things you had no right to do, the things you should have done,
They're all put down; it's up to you to pay for every one.
So eat, drink and be merry, have a good time if you will,
But God help you when the time comes, and you

Foot the bill.

—Robert Service

Reprinted by permission of Dodd, Mead & Company, Inc. from *The Collected Poems of Robert Service.*

"On the other hand,
we have all shot a lot of birds!"